AGENCY OF FEAR

Books by Edward Jay Epstein

AGENCY OF FEAR

OPIATES AND POLITICAL POWER

IN AMERICA

★

Edward Jay Epstein

G. P. PUTNAM'S SONS, NEW YORK

SBN: 399-11656-7

Library of Congress Cataloging in Publication Data

Epstein, Edward Jay, 1935–
  Agency of fear.
  Bibliography.
  Includes index.
  1. Narcotics, Control of—United States.
2. Narcotic laws—United States. I. Title.
HV5825.E55 1976   363.4′5′0973   76-14443

PRINTED IN THE UNITED STATES OF AMERICA

For Sansi Duncan

PREFACE

This book is based on the view that the American president under ordinary circumstances reigns rather than rules over the government of the United States. To be sure, the president is nominally in command of the executive branch of the government, and he has the authority to fire the officials that in fact control such critical agencies as the Federal Bureau of Investigation, the Central Intelligence Agency, the Internal Revenue Service, the Joint Chiefs of Staff, the criminal division of the Department of Justice, etc. (though he does not in many cases have the authority unilaterally to appoint a replacement). In practice, however, this presidential power is severely mitigated, if not entirely counterbalanced, by the ability of officials in these key agencies to disclose secrets and private evaluations to the public that could severely damage the image of the president. For example, in theory, six presidents, from Franklin Roosevelt to Richard Nixon, had the power to fire J. Edgar Hoover as head of the FBI, but in each case he had the power to retaliate by revealing illicit activities that occurred during their administrations (as well as information about the private lives of the presidents). This potential for retribution by government officials is compounded by the fact that in the vast complexity of the executive branch a president cannot be sure where embarrassing secrets exist, and he must assume that most officials have developed subterranean channels to journalists, who will both conceal their sources and give wide circulation to the "leak." A president could seize control over the various parts of the government only if he first nullified the threat of disclosures by severing the conduits through which dissidents might leak scandalous information to the press. This prerequisite for power is in fact exactly what President Nixon attempted when he set up a series of special units which, it was hoped, would conduct clandestine surveillance of both government officials and newsmen during his first administration. If he had succeeded in establishing such an investigative force, he would have so radically changed the balance of power within the government that it would have been tantamount to an American coup d'etat.

A coup d'etat is not the same as a revolution, where power is seized by those outside the government, or even necessarily a military putsch, whereby the military government takes over from the civilian government; it is, as Edward Luttwak points out in his book *Coup d'Etat,* "a seizure of power within the present system." The technique of the coup involves the use of one part of the government to disrupt communications between other parts of the government, confounding and paralyzing noncooperating agencies while displacing the dissident cliques from power. If successful, the organizers of the coup can gain control over all the levers of real power in the government, then legitimize the new configuration under the name of eliminating some great evil in society. Though it is hard to conceive of the technique of the coup being applied to American politics, Nixon, realizing that he securely controlled only the office of the president, methodically moved to destroy the informal system of leaks and independent fiefdoms. Under the aegis of a "war on heroin," a series of new offices were set up, by executive order, such as the Office of Drug Abuse Law Enforcement and the Office of National Narcotics Intelligence, which, it was hoped, would provide the president with investigative agencies having the potential and the wherewithal and personnel to assume the functions of "the Plumbers" on a far grander scale. According to the White House scenario, these new investigative functions would be legitimized by the need to eradicate the evil of drug addiction.

In describing the inner workings of the "war on heroin" I have relied heavily on the files supplied to me by Egil Krogh, Jr., who was the president's deputy for law enforcement before he was imprisoned for his role in the Plumbers' operations. This archive includes verbatim transcripts of conversations the president had with leading advisors; handwritten notes describing meetings between John Ehrlichman, John Mitchell, H. R. Haldeman, and other principals in the administration's "crusade"; option papers drafted for the Domestic Council; scenarios designed for the media; internal analyses of political problems; drafts of presidential speeches; private reports on the drug problem; briefings for the press; and outlines of conversations Krogh had with the president. Krogh, after he was released from prison, spent more than three weeks assisting me in analyzing the material, and I then went over many of the documents with Jeffrey Donfeld, who was Krogh's assistant on the Domestic Council. The archive is by no means complete—the White House retained a large portion of Krogh's files—and it presents information only from the perspective of the White House. I therefore filled in the archive by interviewing officials in the various agencies that were to be affected by the White House plans for a "reorganization." These interviews took over three years, and reflect personal animosities as well as bureaucratic perspectives. Because the circumstances surrounding each interview bear directly on the credibility of the interview—why, for example, did Krogh provide me with such embarrassing documents?—I have decided to reveal all the sources for this book and comment on the motives, problems, contradictions, and gaps that I found in the interviews and documents. Unless otherwise specified, whenever references are made to persons explaining, commenting, observing or otherwise divulging information, they were made to me for the purposes of this book, and a fuller explanation of when, where, and why is provided in the final section of the book. Books and documents are listed in the Bibliography.

The research for this book was financed in large part by the Drug Abuse Council, Inc., a privately financed foundation which was established to provide another perspective on problems of drug abuse. Assistance was also provided by National Affairs, Inc., the Smith-Richardson Foundation, and the Police Foundation. *Esquire* helped subsidize my reportage of poppy-growing in Turkey, and *The Public Interest* magazine supported my investigation of methadone clinics and helped me obtain the Krogh file. Research on various parts of the book was done for me by Hillary Mayer, Suzanna Duncan, Elizabeth Guthrie, and Deborah Gieringer, to all of whom I am grateful.

I am also indebted, for their insights into the political process, to Edward Banfield, Daniel Bell, Allan Bloom, Edward Chase, Nathan

Glazer, Erving Goffman, Andrew Hacker, William Haddad, Paul Halpern, Bruce Kovner, Irving Kristol, Edward Luttwak, Jerry Mandel, Daniel Patrick Moynihan, Victor Navasky, Bruce Page, Norman Podhoretz, Mark Platner, John Rubenstein, William Shawn, Jonathan Shell, Leslie Steinau, Edward Thompson, Lionel Tiger, Paul Weaver, William Whitworth, and James Q. Wilson. The conclusions that I draw from their insights are, of course, entirely my own.

E. J. E.
New York City, 1976

CONTENTS

A coup consists of the infiltration of a small but critical segment of the state apparatus, which is then used to displace the government from its control of the remainder.

—EDWARD LUTTWAK, *Coup d'Etat*

PROLOGUE

The Secret Police ★

"Sometimes there's a thin line between the hunted and the hunter...."
—An anonymous federal narcotics agent interviewed by the New York *Times* on June 25, 1973.

On the night of April 23, 1973, Herbert Joseph Giglotto, a hardworking boilermaker, and his wife, Louise, were sleeping soundly in their suburban house in Collinsville, Illinois. Suddenly, and without warning, armed men broke into their house and rushed up the stairs to the Giglottos' bedroom. Giglotto later recalled, "I got out of bed; I took about three steps, looked down the hall and I [saw] men running up the hall dressed like hippies with pistols, yelling and screeching. I turned to my wife. 'God, honey, we're dead.' " The night intruders threw Giglotto down on his bed and tied his hands behind his back. Holding a loaded gun at his head, one of the men pointed to his wife and asked, "Who is that bitch lying there?" Giglotto begged the raiders, "Before you shoot her, before you do anything, check my identification, because I know you're in the wrong place." The men refused to allow the terrified couple to move from the bed or put on any clothes while they proceeded to search the residence. As books were swept from shelves and clothes were ripped from hangers, one man said, "You're going to die unless you tell us where the stuff is." Then the intrusion ended as suddenly as it began when the leader of the raiders concluded, "We made a mistake."

The night raiders who terrorized the Giglottos that April night were members of a new federal organization called the Office of Drug Abuse Law Enforcement (ODALE). On the same evening in Collinsville, another group of raiders from ODALE kicked in the door of the home of Donald and Virginia Askew, on the north side of town. Virginia Askew, who was then crippled from a back injury, fainted as the men rushed into the frame house. While she lay on the floor, agents kept her husband, Donald, an operator of a local gas station, from going to her aid. Another agent kept their sixteen-year-old son, Michael, from telephoning for help by pointing a rifle at him. After the house was searched, the agents admitted they had made another mistake and disappeared. (Virginia Askew the next day was rushed to a mental hospital for emergency psychiatric therapy.)

In another demonstration, that Easter week, of their extraordinary powers, a dozen agents of the Office of Drug Abuse Law Enforcement broke into a farmhouse on Cemetery Road in Edwardsville, Illinois, and imprisoned one of the occupants of the house, John Meiners, a salesman for the General Electric Company, for seventy-seven hours. "I was asleep about three A.M.," Meiners said, "when the agents rushed in and pushed me against the wall." A pistol was held to his head, and, in Meiners' words, "they began to ransack the house." Walls were smashed and windows were broken, and stereo equipment, a shotgun, golf clubs, and a camera were confiscated by the agents. Meiners was then forcibly taken to police headquarters and questioned for more than three days without being told of the crime he was alleged to have committed or being allowed to telephone a lawyer or anyone else. Finally, the General Electric salesman was released without a charge ever being filed against him.

None of the ODALE agents who broke into these homes carried the required search warrants, nor did they legally have any authority to enter forceably any of these homes to effect an arrest. The Fourth Amendment of the Constitution of the United States guarantees "The right of the people to be secure in their persons, houses, papers, and effects, against unreasonable searches and seizures" and that "no Warrants shall issue, but upon probable cause, supported by Oath or affirmation, and particularly describing the place to be searched and the persons or things to be seized." The warrantless raids by the ODALE agents were subsequently characterized as "extra-legal" by Myles J. Ambrose, director of that office, and the agents were suspended. In an interview in *U.S. News & World Report* in 1972, prior to the Collinsville raids, Ambrose explained that extraordinary procedures, to the limit of the law, were necessary because the nation was engaged in an all-out war against drugs and that the very survival of the American people was at stake. One purpose of the Office of Drug Abuse Law Enforcement was to facilitate the arrests of pushers on the street, Ambrose said further. In effect, this meant that local Justice Department lawyers assigned to ODALE could obtain warrants to authorize agents to break into homes in order to effect an arrest. The office further had the power to go before special "grand juries" to seek indictments of the arrested individuals.

These particular incidents were reported in the press because they involved "mistaken identities" (agents had broken into the wrong homes). These agents were immediately suspended and a full-scale investigation was launched, although they were finally acquitted after being tried on criminal charges. However, at the time, little attention was paid to the unique powers of the Office of Drug Abuse Law Enforcement. Indeed, most commentators on these particular cases, though outraged that innocent people had been terrorized, did not question the legitimacy of ODALE itself, or question the need for deploying strike forces with extraordinary powers against narcotics dealers, who were presumed to be an equally extraordinary enemy.

Despite the matter-of-fact acceptance of the Office of Drug Abuse Law Enforcement by the press and the public, there was little precedent in the annals of American law enforcement (or government) for such an investigative agency. It had been established on January 27, 1972, by an executive order of President Nixon, without approval or consideration by Congress. The office operated out of the Department of Justice, but, interestingly, its director, Myles Ambrose, also had an office in the Executive Office of the president. ODALE was empowered by presidential order to requisition agents from other federal agencies, including the Bureau of Narcotics and Dangerous Drugs, the Bureau of Customs, the Internal Revenue Service, and the Bureau of Alcohol, Tobacco and Firearms, and to redeploy these agents into strike forces. These forces could use court-authorized wiretaps and no-knock warrants, as well as "search incidental to arrest" procedures. This unique office could also feed the names of suspects to a target-selection committee in the Internal Revenue Service, which would then initiate its own audits and investigations. The office received most of its funds not from congressional appropriations but from the Law Enforcement Assistance Administration (LEAA), an appendage of the Justice Department created by Congress in 1968 for the purpose of financially assisting state and local law-enforcement units (not presidential units). Most of its operations were financed by funneling grants from the LEAA to local police departments that participated with ODALE in its raids against narcotics suspects. This method was necessary because LEAA was never authorized by Congress to disburse its funds to federal agencies.

As long as President Nixon could focus the attention of Congress and the press on the "menace" of heroin addiction destroying America, the hope was that this new office could execute his orders free of any normal restraints from the "bureaucracy," from congressional subcommittees, and from the press, which normally reported only the stories presenting the government's statistics in the war against drugs. The power of this new instrument thus depended directly on the continued organization of fear by the White House.

PART ONE

The Vampire Comes to America ★

The coup is a political weapon, *and its planners have only political resources.*

—EDWARD LUTTWAK, *Coup d'Etat*

1

Legend of the Living Dead

Richmond Pearson Hobson, even as a young man, had the romantic vision necessary to heroes. On June 3, 1898, as a newly graduated lieutenant of the naval academy at Annapolis, he guided the USS *Merrimac* into the narrow mouth of Santiago Harbor in Cuba. Though the Navy described his ship as an antiquated tub, Hobson saw it as a magnificent fighting ship and saw himself that night as "Homeric manhood, erect and masterful on the perilous bridge of the *Merrimac.*" The Spanish-American War had just broken out, and the Navy planned for Hobson to trap the Spanish fleet in Santiago Harbor by scuttling his ship in the main channel. To this end, Hobson heroically had tied a string of homemade torpedoes to the hull of the *Merrimac,* but owing to a failure in the ship's steering mechanism, he was unable to get the tub into the blockading position before the charges exploded. The *Merrimac* rapidly and ineffectually sank without interfering with any of the Spanish shipping lanes, and Hobson himself was rescued by the Spanish and imprisoned in Morro Castle, outside Havana. After Spain surrendered, Hobson was repatriated. The United States Navy, faced with the difficult choice of either court-martialing Hobson or decorating him for valor, chose the latter alternative and made Captain Hobson the first celebrated hero of the short-lived Spanish-American War. Hobson thus experienced what he later described hyperbolically as "the ecstasy of martyrdom." President McKinley personally decorated Hobson, and the Navy arranged a national speaking tour for its new hero. As crowds swarmed about the man reputed to have blocked the entire Spanish Armada, his popularity grew, and he became known as "the most-kissed man in America" (Hobson's Kisses, a caramel candy, was even named after him). By 1906, the celebrated hero of Santiago Harbor had been elected to Congress.

Captain Hobson was at the turn of the century a hero in search of a grand cause. He first attempted to exploit his reputation as a military genius by calling for America to build a navy larger than all the other navies of the world combined, in order to protect the world against the "yellow peril" in the immediate form of Japanese military strength, which he saw increasing in Asia. He argued at every public gathering he could find that American naval supremacy was the "will of God." When his first crusade failed to excite continued interest in the nation's newspapers, and his speaking engagements dwindled, he switched his moral drumfire to a far more pervasive enemy—alcohol, which he termed "the great destroyer."

Captain Hobson's crusade against alcohol, like his crusade against the yellow peril, attempted to mobilize public opinion into an apocalyptic battle between the forces of good and evil, the outcome of which would determine the fate of Western civilization. Describing this ravaging battle, he gave statistics in various speeches for all occasions—"Alcohol is killing our people at the rate of nearly two thousand men a day, every day of the year"; "one out of five children of alcohol consumers are hopelessly insane"; "ninety-five percent of all acts and crimes of violence are committed by drunkards"; "nearly one half of the deaths that occur are due to alcohol"; "a hundred and twenty-five million white men today are wounded by alcohol." In adding up the economic cost of alcohol, he asserted that the "total loss" was more than "sixteen billion dollars," or one quarter of the gross national product of the United States. He posited a medical theory whereby alcohol attacked "the top of the brain . . . since the upper brain is the physical basis of thought, feeling, judgment, self-control, and it is the physical organ of the will, of the consciousness of God, of the sense of right and wrong, of ideas of justice, duty, love, mercy, self-sacrifice and all that makes character," and from that he reasoned that "the evolution of human life, the destiny of man and the will of God" were at stake in the struggle against alcohol. (When alcohol reached the "top of the brain" of "negroes," according to Hobson's theory, "they degenerate . . . to the level of the cannibal." Similarly, "peaceable redmen" became "the savage" when they drank alcohol.)

Proposing in Congress that alcohol be totally prohibited, he forged a dramatic nexus between alcohol and crime. Innocent men were converted to violent criminals in almost all cases, he argued, because alcohol had degenerated the "gray matter" in their brains. Not only did alcohol destroy self-control in 95 percent of criminal cases, but it created an economic need for those afflicted with the disease of alcoholism to steal in order to pay for their chronic habit. In multiplying the number of alcoholics by the daily cost of the habit, Hobson arrived at his $16 billion estimate of the cost of crime engendered by alcohol.

By 1915 Captain Hobson had become the highest-paid speaker on the lecture circuit in America. He helped organize (with financial support from John D. Rockefeller, Jr.) the Women's Christian Temperance Union (WCTU), which helped galvanize national support for Prohibition. Congress ordered his speech to the House of Representatives in 1912, entitled "The Great Destroyer," to be republished in 50 million copies by the Government Printing Office. (The order was never carried out by the GPO.) Defeated in his attempt to win the Senate seat for Alabama, Hobson organized the American Alcohol Education Association, which attempted to marshal American youth behind his crusading banner.

The dramatic mythology that Hobson had popularized, if not created, which put alcohol at the root of all of society's evils, was undermined ironically by the passage of National Prohibition legislation in 1921. Neither crime rate nor death rate was diminished by the banning of alcohol; indeed, each rose during Prohibition. Human nature did not markedly change for the better. Hobson no longer had a demon on which to unleash his virtually unlimited moral indignation. In the 1920s, thus, Captain Hobson was again in quest of a great cause.

For almost a year Captain Hobson retired from public life—or at least from public speaking engagements—and sought an issue around which another moral campaign could be organized. He soon found a new "greatest evil," which not only could be held accountable for all crime and vice but had the added advantage over alcohol of being a foreign import, thus coinciding with the xenophobia of the times. This new devil was a drug called heroin.

Heroin (from the German *heroisch*—"large, powerful") was first developed by the A. G. Bayer Company, of Germany, in 1898 as a "nonaddictive" pain-killer. This white powdery substance (known scientifically as diacetylmorphine) was refined from morphine, a natural alkaloid of opium, which for thousands of years had been derived from the dried juice of the unripe capsule of the opium poppy. When morphine was first isolated from opium in 1803, it was thought to be a universal panacea, called by physicians "God's own medicine," and was recommended for fifty-four diseases, which included everything from insanity to nymphomania. As late as 1889, morphine was recommended in medical journals as a drug for treating those addicted to alcohol on the grounds that it "calms in place of exciting the base of passions, and hence is less productive of acts of violence and crime." However, by 1898, morphine addiction was considered a serious national problem. And heroin (even though three times as powerful a pain-killer as morphine) was now recommended in medical journals as a new means of treating morphine addiction. The attempt to cure drug addiction by substituting one drug for another again proved to be a failure, and in the early 1900s, confronted by a growing number of heroin addicts, the American Medical Association defined heroin as a dangerous and highly addictive drug not suitable for medical treatment. At the same time, the United States State Department, under increasing pressure from American missionaries working in Asia who were concerned with the morality of opium trade, supported the idea of international laws to regulate narcotics. In December, 1914, Congress passed the Harrison Narcotics Act, which attempted to control narcotics in the United States through licensing and taxation.

Federal laws did not, however, diminish public concern over heroin. A spate of newspaper stories during the final days of World War I suggested that Germany was attempting to addict the entire American population through heroin by mixing the powder with cosmetics. And in New York City, public officials increasingly attributed bank robberies and anarchist bombings to heroin-crazed fiends. Though the postwar scare stories in the press tended to be inconsistent and fragmented, they provided Captain Hobson with fertile grounds for a new crusade. Unlike alcohol, heroin was a foreign and mysterious drug; its powers were not known to the general public. Hobson quickly foresaw the potential of reorganizing the available bits of information and assertions about this new drug into the specter of the vampire. In a frenzy of public appearances, lectures, and writings, he termed narcotics addicts "the living dead." In explaining the operations of this "demonic" drug, he used the same convenient pseudomedical jargon that he had previously used in denouncing alcohol. For example, explaining in the September 20, 1924, issue of *The Saturday Evening Post* that addiction is essentially a "brain disease" responsible for most crime, he gave the following quasimedical explanation:

> The entire brain is immediately affected when narcotics are taken into the system. The upper cerebral regions, whose more delicate tissues, apparently the most recently developed and containing the shrine of the spirit, all those attributes of the man which raise him above the level of the beast, are at first tremendously stimulated and then—quite soon—destroyed. . . .
>   At the same time the tissues of the lower brain, where reside all the selfish instincts and impulses, receive the same powerful stimulation. With the restraining forces of the higher nature gone, the addict feels no compunction whatever in committing any act that will contribute to a perverted supposition of his own comfort or welfare.

According to the "scientific" explanation that Hobson popularized, the degeneracy of the "upper cerebral regions" turned the addict into a "beast" or "monster," spreading his disease like a medieval vampire. Hobson explained thus: "The addict has an insane desire to make addicts of others." As evidence of this vampire phenomenon of the "living dead," Hobson gave examples of how a mother-addict had injected her eight-year-old son with heroin; how teenage addicts infected other teenagers by secreting heroin in ice-cream cones; and how lovers seduced their partners with heroin. He suggested the calculus (which President Nixon adopted a half-century later) that "one addict will recruit seven others in his lifetime." He also fully played up the xenophobic appeal of heroin's coming from foreign lands, stating, "Like the invasions and plagues of history, the scourge of narcotic drug addiction came out of Asia. . . ." Also, like the irreversible bite of the mythical vampire, Hobson asserted, "So hopeless is the victim, and so pitiless the master," that the heroin addicts are termed "the living dead."

After having established the dreaded imagery of the vampire-addict, Hobson went on to organize his crusade. In a short time he had mobilized such groups as the Women's Christian Temperance Union, the Moose, the Kiwanis, the Knights of Columbus, the Masonic orders, and various other lodges in his battle against heroin. (The cause of temperance having been mitigated by the Prohibition law, the heroin crusade provided a new sense of purpose for many of these organizations.) He created the World Narcotic Association and the Narcotic Defense Foundation, whose goal was to raise $10 million in ten years for "the defense of society from the peril and menace of narcotic addiction." He also published his own journal of "narcotic education."

By 1927 Hobson claimed to have recruited "21,000 major clubs and organizations" into his various "narcotic education programs." The development of the radio networks after the First World War gave him a new national pulpit, and time was provided for his uninterrupted lectures on four hundred stations for "Narcotics Education Week," which he inspired the government to promulgate. He thus spoke to an audience of unprecedented size, and warned in 1928 that virtually all crime in America was a symptom of the new wave of heroin addiction. On the NBC network, for example, he told a nationwide audience:

> Most of the daylight robberies, daring holdups, cruel murders, and similar crimes of violence are now known to be committed chiefly by drug addicts who constitute the primary cause of our alarming crime wave. . . .
> Drug addiction is more communicable and less curable than leprosy. Drug addicts are the principal carriers of vice disease, and with their lowered resistance are incubators and carriers of the strepti coccus, pneumo coccus, the germ of flu, of tuberculosis and other diseases.
> New forces of narcotic drug exploitation devised from the progress of modern chemical science, added to the old form of the opium traffic, now endanger the very future of the human race. . . . The whole human race, though largely ignorant on this subject, is now in the midst of a life and death struggle with the deadliest foe that has ever menaced its future. Upon the issue hangs the perpetuation of civilization, the destiny of the world and the future of the human race.

In 1929, Hobson journeyed to Los Angeles and, again using radio, warned his West Coast audience that "drug addicts are the cause of our crime wave with its daring holdups, cruel and unnatural murders, and the chief factor in the disappearance of girls who fall to the underworld in ever increasing numbers, now estimated at seventy-five thousand per year." He argued that the "suffering of slaves" was "easy and light" compared to the "living death of drug addicts." He now asserted that addicts were responsible for crime's placing "a burden exceeding ten billions of dollars yearly on the American people." At one point he placed the number of heroin addicts as high as four million, and stressed that this "army of addicts" would contaminate all other Americans in a few short years. Up until his death, in 1937, Captain Hobson continued to broadcast to millions of Americans on the perils of narcotics, and distribute through his many organizations tens of millions of pages of educational material to schools and media. Since there were few (if any) systematic studies of heroin during this period, Captain Hobson's energetic crusade created for a large segment of the American public the stereotype of an addict as a vampirelike creature with an insatiable appetite for crime and destruction and a need to infect with his disease all who came in contact with him.

Hobson's legend of the living dead lived after him. The apocalyptic battle he depicted between the forces of good and the army of addicts provided countless politicians, police officials, and medical bureaucrats with a conceptual framework from which they could advance their particular interests. The Hobsonian notion that heroin transformed innocents into uncontrollable "desperadoes" became a persistent part of police rhetoric. For example, in explaining a "crime wave" to the newspapers in the late 1930s, New York City police commissioner Richard E. Enright said that addicts, "when inflamed with drugs ... are capable of committing any crime"; and his successor, Commissioner John O'Ryan, went further in attributing "wanton brutality and reversion to the life of the beast" to narcotics, which, he explained (apparently on Hobson's authority), "penetrate the upper brain and inflict swift and deep injury upon the gray matter ... so a transformation of the individual follows quickly. . . ."

Although such "scientific" explanations of crime provided a convenient rationale for an expanded police department, they were based on little more than the rhetoric that Hobson himself borrowed verbatim from his earlier crusade against alcohol. In fact, in more than fifty years of analysis, scientific studies have not substantiated the image of the crazed heroin fiend or "the living dead." On the contrary, virtually all of the medical and pharmacological investigations have found that heroin is a powerful analgesic that depresses the central nervous system and produces behavior characterized by apathy, lessened physical activity, and diminished visual acuity. Instead of inducing "wanton brutality," this medical evidence suggests that heroin—and other opiates—decreases violent response to provocations (as well as hunger and sex drives in individuals). For example, in studying the relation between drugs and violence, the National Commission on Marijuana and Drug Abuse concluded, in 1973, "Assaultive offenses are significantly less likely to be committed by . . . opiate users." To be sure, doctors have consistently found that heroin is a habit-forming and dangerous drug, but it does not necessarily produce violent behavior. Nor, of course, has any evidence been found suggesting that it suppresses moral instincts, as Hobson claimed, or reverses the evolutionary process.

Hobson's theory that heroin was the root cause of most crime in America also appealed to a number of liberal doctors and medical bureaucrats. After the Harrison Narcotics Act was passed, some doctors established clinics in which they legally dispensed narcotics to addicts to prevent them from suffering from what was known as withdrawal symptoms. In a number of notorious cases these clinics simply became wholesale narcotics distributors, selling heroin and morphine to all comers. The federal government held that such clinics were in violation of the Harrison Narcotics Act, which originally attempted to regulate the nonmedical sale of drugs. Medical authorities argued that the applicability of the act depended on the medical purpose for which the drug was being used. However, in 1922, in *U.S.* v. *Behrman,* the Supreme Court held that regardless of medical intent, such treatment could be construed as illegal under the act, and agents moved to close down the narcotics clinics and arrest thousands of doctors dispensing heroin and morphine.

Many doctors interested in treating narcotics addicts assumed that these actions by the federal government impinged on the legitimate domain of medical expertise. Their protest that addicts should be treated by doctors, not police, had little popular appeal, since there was little concern for the individual addict on the part of the public. However, when Captain Hobson connected in the public imagination the addict and the crime problem, he also provided the doctors and liberal reformers with a publicly acceptable rationale for medical treatment. Accepting Hobson's assertion that addicts committed billions of dollars' worth of crimes (which was based on no evidence whatsoever), these reformers argued that the addict was driven to crime because he was "enslaved" by his insatiable need for heroin. They argued that because the drug was illegal and expensive, addicts were forced to steal to obtain the money for it. On the other hand, if doctors were allowed freely to dispense, at low cost, heroin and other narcotics to addicts, they would have no need to commit thefts, and the American public would be spared billions of dollars' worth of crime and violence. In other words, these doctors proposed that the crime problem was essentially a medical problem, and given the freedom and resources to open narcotics-maintenance clinics, they could solve the problem.

This "enslavement theory" gained added currency in the 1960s with politicians and reformers who sought a palatable explanation for the increase in crimes in the city. Since heroin was imported from abroad, local police commissioners and mayors could claim that their urban crime rate could be controlled only if the federal government and foreign governments curtailed opium production at its source. For example, in 1972, New York City police commissioner Patrick V. Murphy testified:

> Local police agencies cannot . . . effectively stem the flow of narcotics into our cities, much less into the needle-ridden veins of hundreds of thousands of young people. Only the Federal government is capable of making effective strides, through the massive infusion of funds to damming or diverting the ever-rising, devastating flood-tide from the poppy fields of the Middle East, South America, and Indo-China into the bodies of pathetic victims in the United States.

In suggesting most crime was not the work of hardened criminals but of innocent individuals afflicted with an unquenchable addiction, the enslavement theory had great appeal to those objecting to stricter police measures as a solution to the crime problem. Despite its advantages, however, the empirical evidence gathered about drug addiction in the twentieth century runs counter to the main tenet of the theory. Reviews of criminal records of addicts have shown, without exception, that most addicts had long histories of criminal behavior that predated their addiction, or even their use of drugs.* In

* See, for example, J. Tinkleberg, "Drugs and Crimes," appendix, National Commission on Marijuana and Drug Abuse, 1973; C. J. Friedman and A. S. Friedman, "Drug Abuse and Delinquency," National Commission on Marijuana and Drug Abuse, 1973; J. C. Jacobi, N. A. Weiner, and M. E. Wolfgang, "Drug Use and Criminality in a Natural Cohort," National Commission on Marijuana and Drug Abuse, 1973.

other words, according to all existing studies, heroin does not necessarily convert innocent persons into criminals: generally, criminal-addicts are first criminals, then addicts. Though heroin undoubtedly is used by a large number of individuals engaged in crime and other risk-taking behavior, there is little persuasive evidence suggesting that it is the *cause* rather than an effect in most cases.

Hobson's formulation of heroin as a chemical that would, after ingestion, render one a slave for life also provided medical practitioners with a rationale for maintenance treatment. In ruling on the Harrison Narcotics Act the courts had in effect subscribed to the theory that addiction was a dangerous condition defined by the continuous use of heroin. Thus, if the agent—heroin—were completely withdrawn from an addicted person, the "disease" would no longer exist. On the other hand, Hobson's notion that heroin induced an irreversible change in the victim whereby he was "normal" only when taking heroin, and abnormal without it, justified the dispensing of heroin by doctors as a form of medical treatment. (Methadone maintenance is merely a modern-day extension of this logic.) However, the contention that heroin irreversibly enslaves the user has not been confirmed by any large-scale study of drug use. In Vietnam, for example, the U.S. Army found by testing urine specimens that more than 250,000 American soldiers had used heroin, and that of these, some 80,000 could be classified as addicts (in that they used it every day for long periods and suffered withdrawal symptoms). Yet, more than 90 percent of these users and addicts were able voluntarily to withdraw from the use of heroin without any medical assistance or without any permanent aftereffects. Follow-up studies showed that less than 1 percent of the total number—and less than 6 percent of the addicts—used heroin again in a two-year period after they were discharged from the Army. Doctors and scientists studying this massive data were compelled to conclude that heroin use did not necessarily lead to addiction, and that addiction was not necessarily irreversible. Indeed, the Vietnam data suggested that in large part addiction resulted from problems in adjusting to an unfriendly environment (i.e., the war in Vietnam) rather than from the chemical effects of the drug itself. Though Vietnam may be a special case in many respects, it has also been found in studies of prisoners that after they have been withdrawn from heroin, they perform normally for the balance of their terms in prison.

Hobson's definition of narcotics addiction as a threat to the very existence of civilization subsequently became the official justification for the federal government's mounting a massive law-enforcement program against drug smugglers, dealers, and even addicts. Hobson argued in his book *Drug Addiction—A Malignant Racial Cancer* that, as suggested by the cancer metaphor, addiction knew no racial boundaries, and it would spread from the yellow and black to the white race by "contaminating" the vulnerable youth. The suggestions he gave in his educational material—that white girls were seduced by narcotics into a life of prostitution by men of other races—were subsumed by public officials, one of whom was Harry J. Anslinger, the director of the federal Bureau of Narcotics from 1930 to 1962. In explaining the purpose of his law-enforcement bureau, Anslinger gave the public lurid descriptions of how Orientals used drugs to entice "women from good families" into brothels. (The persistence of this cancer theory can be found not only in contemporary stories about heroin spreading out of the ghetto but also in the newspaper reports that Patricia Hearst was "drugged" into joining an interracial group of urban guerrillas.) Anslinger soon found that the Hobsonian rhetoric could be applied to marijuana as well as to heroin, and in the mid-1930s, in asking for funds to expand his bureau, he sounded the alarm of an epidemic of marijuana addiction, asserting that this "dope addiction" had brought about "an epidemic of crimes committed by young people." After publishing an article on this subject in 1937, entitled "Marijuana: Assassin of Youth," he succeeded in having Congress pass the Marijuana Tax Act in 1937. Anslinger's campaign to depict marijuana as a crime-breeding drug was debunked to such an extent by later critics that the prewar film *Reefer Madness,* which supposedly depicted how marijuana converts innocents into criminals, is today enjoyed on college campuses as a parody.

During World War II, Anslinger waged a press campaign to convince the American public that Japan was systematically attempting to addict its enemies, including the American people, to opium, in order to destroy their civilization. Although there was no other evidence of the putative "Japanese Opium Offensive," Coast Guard ships and Internal Revenue Service investigative units were directed to work with Anslinger's bureau. In 1950, during the Korean War, Anslinger again used the Hobsonian theme, leaking a report to the press that "subversion through drug addiction is an established aim of Communist China," and that the Chinese were smuggling massive amounts of heroin into the United States to "weaken American resistance." The New York *Times,* after reporting the assertion as fact, explained in an editorial, "Communists . . . are eager to get as many addicts as possible in the territory of those to whom they are opposed." Again, despite the yellow-peril hysteria of the time, no evidence was ever found that China was sending heroin into the United States.

For a host of reasons, then, Hobson's vampirelike visions of addiction were kept alive by politicians, police officials, doctors, and enterprising bureaucrats. The drama of the "living dead" subverting our civilization was reported with great enthusiasm by the press rather than questioned. The themes were not woven together into any coherent pattern until the early 1960s, when the governor of New York, Nelson Rockefeller, ingeniously transformed Hobson's vampire-addict notion into a political design.

2

Nelson Rockefeller

The hysterical image of the vampire-addict that Captain Hobson propagated in the 1930s was brilliantly refined into a national political issue in the 1960s by Nelson Rockefeller, who, in projecting this nationwide "reign of terror," had at his disposal an unprecedented family fortune. The Rockefeller fortune was begun by Nelson's great-grandfather William Avery Rockefeller, a nineteenth-century dealer in drugs who, like modern narcotics dealers, dressed in extravagant silk costumes, used aliases, and never carried less than a thousand dollars in cash on his person. "Big Bill," as he was commonly called, hawked "herbal remedies" and other bottled medicines which, if they were like other patent medicines being sold in those days, contained opium as an active ingredient. Long before opium—the juice from the poppy—became the base of patent medicine in America, it was used in Asia as a remedy for dysentery and as a general pain-killer. Because it was a powerful analgesic, hucksters on the American frontier made quick fortunes selling their various "miracle" preparations.

In any case, Big Bill, who advertised himself as a "Cancer Specialist," was sufficiently successful in selling drugs to stake his son John Davison Rockefeller to the initial capital he needed to go into the oil business in Cleveland. Young Rockefeller found that oil was far more profitable than herbal medicine. He foresaw that concentration and combination rather than competition were the order of the future. Moreover, he realized that the leverage for gaining control over the burgeoning oil industry lay in the hands of the railroads. Since oil was more or less a uniform product, costing the same at the wellhead and fetching the same price at the market, any refiner who could ship his oil to market for even a few cents less a barrel than his competitors could eventually drive them out of business. With this insight Rockefeller played the railroads in Cleveland against each other until he was given a surreptitious discount, or "rebate," by the railroads, which provided him a decisive advantage over his competitors. By the turn of the century Rockefeller's company, Standard Oil Company, refined more than 90 percent of the oil in the United States and two-thirds of the oil in the world. Rockefeller's personal fortune was equal to some 2 percent of the GNP of the entire United States.

Rockefeller's only son, John Davison Rockefeller, Jr., used the fortune to launch a number of crusades of his own, including financing a large part of the movement to prohibit alcohol in the United States (an effort in which Captain Hobson was then playing a leading role). Although his crusade against alcohol ultimately failed, he was not discouraged from public enterprises. He built Rockefeller Center at the height of the Depression as a monument to the family's enterprise, and encouraged his second-eldest son, Nelson, to enter public life.

Nelson first learned the techniques of propagating and controlling information when he was appointed coordinator of inter-American affairs at the age of thirty-two by President Franklin Delano Roosevelt, and given the responsibility of running a $150-million propaganda agency in Latin America. To gain complete control over the media of Latin America, Rockefeller engineered a ruling from the United States Treasury which exempted from taxation the cost of advertisements placed by American corporations that were "cooperating" with Rockefeller in Latin America. This tax-exempt advertising eventually constituted more than 40 percent of all radio and television revenues in Latin America. By selectively directing this advertising toward newspapers and radio stations that accepted "guidance" from his office, he was effectively able to control the images that the newspapers and radio stations of Latin America projected about America during World War II. By 1945 more than 75 percent of the news of the world that reached Latin America originated from

Washington, where it was tightly controlled and shaped by Rockefeller's office. In developing this mode of psychological warfare, Rockefeller learned not only the vulnerabilities of the press but the techniques of manipulating news. By supplying a daily diet of some 30,000 words of "news"—including editorials, articles, news photographs, and "exclusive features"—to the media of Latin America, Rockefeller came to appreciate the reality that journalists acted mainly as messengers of dramatic and titillating stories, rather than as any sort of independent investigators. As long as Latin Americans were spoon-fed manufactured anecdotes and dramatic happenings that fell within the generally accepted definition of "news," they would not question the interest or politics that lay behind the disclosure of this information to them. This education in the management and manipulation of news was to prove invaluable to Nelson Rockefeller in his political career after World War II.

After serving briefly in the Truman and Eisenhower administrations, Nelson Rockefeller decided in 1958 to run for elective office as governor of New York State. As the former coordinator of information in Latin America he had little difficulty in mobilizing support for himself in the media, and he succeeded in projecting an image of himself as a liberal, or, at least, as an enlightened Republican. Appealing to both the liberal constituency in New York City and the Republican constituency in the upstate areas, Rockefeller was easily elected governor. His more expansive ambition of being elected president, however, presented a much more difficult problem in image management. The highly sophisticated polls of public opinion that Rockefeller commissioned in the early 1960s (and George Gallup, of the Gallup Poll, had worked for him in Latin America) indicated that a Republican candidate could not win in a national election without attracting large numbers of the more liberal-leaning independent voters—and this would require maintaining a liberal-Republican image. Yet, Rockefeller was also aware that to win the Republican nomination and the support of the more conservative stalwarts of the Republican party required a hard-line and even anti-liberal image. As a result, the more Rockefeller tried to amass support in the media, and among independent voters, by projecting a liberal image, the more he lost support among more conservative Republicans. Unable to resolve this dilemma of conflicting images, Rockefeller was decisively rejected by delegates at the 1964 Republican convention, who instead enthusiastically endorsed Senator Barry Goldwater, who went on to lose the general election by a disastrous proportion of the vote.

After his 1964 defeat, Rockefeller ingeniously developed an issue which seemed to resolve the political dilemma by appealing to both the hard-line element in the Republican party and the liberal-to-moderate element among the independent voters—the drug issue. By proposing measures for oppressing drug users that were more draconian than anything ever proposed by Senator Goldwater or by his most hard-line followers, Rockefeller hoped to placate the law-and-order Republicans by toughening his image. At the same time, analysis of public opinion showed that the more liberal independents and modern Republican voters would not object to measures that enhanced their personal safety. As Rockefeller subsequently pointed out, in 1973, in a speech to the New York State legislature, "Every poll of public concern documents that the number one growing concern of the American people is crime and drugs—coupled with an all-pervasive fear for the safety of their person and property." To exploit this well-researched "all-pervasive fear" and turn it into a national political issue, Rockefeller worked to establish in the popular imagination a connection between violent crimes and drugs. He argued that even if drugs did not in themselves induce violent behavior, the user, physiologically dependent on the drug, felt compelled to steal in order to pay for his habit. Rockefeller correctly foresaw that this more sophisticated "dependency theory" * could be used to inspire another wave of fear in the public (as well as among intellectuals) that heroin addicts were jeopardizing the lives and property of citizens, and therefore drastic action was necessary.

Masterfully employing the tactics of psychological warfare that he and his staff developed in Latin America during World War II, Rockefeller first began expanding the drug issue during his gubernatorial reelection campaign in 1966. Depicting heroin as an infectious disease that, like the common flu, could be spread to unwilling victims in both the ghetto and the suburbs, Rockefeller boldly declared that the epidemic of addiction in New York State had reached the proportions of a plague and was threatening the lives of innocent middle-class children. Demanding "an all-out war on drugs

* Of course, one could apply a similar "dependency theory" to other disabled groups—alcoholics, cripples, blind people, or even divorced women with two children—arguing that since their disability prevents them from easily obtaining employment, they need money to compensate for their disability, and they will be compelled to steal.

and addiction," he rushed a law through the legislature providing for the involuntary confinement of drug addicts for up to five years for "treatment," even if they were not convicted of any crime. Although the courts had consistently ruled that addiction itself is not a crime, this new procedure, known euphemistically as "civil commitment," permitted officials to lock up addicts in "rehabilitation centers," even if they were not convicted of a crime.

While the phrases "treatment" and "rehabilitation center" were shrewdly designed to imply a medical model dealing with drug addiction, and thus appealed to Rockefeller's liberal constituency, there was in 1966 no program of medical treatment for addiction in New York State. There was not even a concept or an operational definition of what addiction was or how it could be treated. If, for example, addiction were defined as being the physical dependence on a drug, then coffee and tobacco would fall in the same category as heroin under the "civil commitment" law. On the other hand, if addiction were defined as being a permanent metabolic change in the nervous system—one that was irreversible—then the various programs of detoxification, or gradual withdrawal from heroin, being used in "rehabilitation centers" would not treat the disease any more than withdrawing patients from insulin would treat diabetes. Indeed, at the time of the passage of the 1966 law, doctors could not even agree whether addiction was produced by the chemical agent heroin or by the environmental depravity in which the addict lived. Rockefeller shrewdly perceived, however, that he did not have to concern himself with these medical problems and confusions. Demanding the imprisonment of some 25,000 addicts in New York (the number he was giving in those days) without time-consuming trials, Rockefeller realized that he could bait his liberal opponents in the election—Frank D. O'Connor, the Democratic candidate and a former prosecutor, and Franklin Delano Roosevelt, Jr., the Liberal party candidate—into opposing this new and hastily conceived law. When in the heat of the campaign O'Connor did in fact criticize Rockefeller's rehabilitation program as "an election-year stunt" and "medically unsound," Rockefeller was finally in a position fully to exploit the drug issue. In speech after speech he asserted, as he did in a rally in Brooklyn on November 1, 1966:

Frank O'Connor's election would mean narcotic addicts would continue to be free to roam the street—to mug, snatch purses, to steal, even to murder, or to spread the deadly infection that afflicts them possibly to your own son or daughter. Half the crime in New York City is committed by narcotic addicts. My program—the program that Frank O'Connor pledges to scrap—will get addicts off the street for up to three years of treatment, aftercare, and rehabilitation. . . .

(Rockefeller never gave a source for his assertion that half the crime in New York was caused by drug addicts; nor did he give sources for most of the other statistics he used.)

Fully resurrecting the vampire imagery of an earlier time, Rockefeller brilliantly exploited the fear that New York citizens would lose their lives and children to murderous addicts. Since Rockefeller lost few votes among the addicts he was threatening to quarantine in prison, he easily won reelection. As a Democratic leader explained on CBS television, O'Connor underestimated the fear of people about rampant crime: "Parents are scared that their kids might get hooked and turn into addicts themselves; people want the addicts off the streets, they don't care how you get them off."

Through the instrument of this generalized fear, Rockefeller was able not only to harden his law-and-order image to meet the political requisites of his own party (and to win elections) but also to project a new nationwide menace which he alone among the nation's politicians had the "experience" to solve. His newly created Narcotics Addiction Control Commission (NACC), which supposedly supervised the involuntary rehabilitation of addicts under the 1966 law, had on its staff many more public-relations specialists than medical specialists. Turning to the modus operandi that Rockefeller developed in Latin America, the commission published its own nationally circulated newspaper, *Attack,* as well as newsletters, pamphlets, and background briefings for journalists interested in writing on the new "reign of terror." This new agency was thus able systematically to coordinate and cultivate a highly dramatic image of the heroin addict as a drug slave who ineluctably is compelled to steal and ravage by his heroin habit—a disease which can be "treated" only by quarantining the addict. If Rockefeller had not succeeded in establishing a quasimedical vocabulary for heroin addiction, this proposal might have been recognized as a repressive form of pretrial detention for suspected criminals.

The size of the addict population in New York proved to be conveniently flexible over the years 1966–1973. When it was necessary to demonstrate the need for greater police measures or more judges,* Rockefeller and his staff expanded the number of putative addicts from 25,000 in 1966 to 150,000 in 1972 to 200,000 in 1973. For other audiences, and especially when Rockefeller wanted to show the efficacy of his program, the army of addicts was conveniently contracted in public speeches to under 100,000. (If the addict population had really increased from 25,000 to 200,000 between 1966 and 1973, as can be inferred from Rockefeller's various claims, this 800-percent increase would hardly demonstrate success in his extraordinary war against addicts.) Rockefeller suggested in one of his tracts against heroin that "addiction appears to spread exponentially." The image of an uncontrollable epidemic of heroin addiction being responsible for most crime in America appealed not only to police officials around the country, who could use this fear to justify the need for more men and money, but also to doctors and hospital administrators who were eager to expand their treatment facilities and rehabilitation staffs. Thus, little resistance was offered to the dubious medical claims put forth by Rockefeller's public-relations men. By December, 1971, the alleged army of addicts in New York had been hyped to such proportions that Rockefeller could seriously write in the *New York Law Journal:*

> How can we defeat drug abuse before it destroys America? I believe the answer lies in summoning the total commitment America has always demonstrated in times of national crisis. . . . Drug addiction represents a threat akin to war in its capacity to kill, enslave and imperil the nation's future: akin to cancer in spreading a deadly disease among us and equal to any other challenge we face in deserving all the brain power, man power, and resources necessary to overcome it.

Continuing, he rhetorically asked, "Are the sons and daughters of a generation that survived a great depression and rebuilt a prosperous nation, that defeated Nazism and Fascism and preserved the free world, to be vanquished by a powder, needles, and pills?"

In the next few years Rockefeller used statistical legerdemain with

---

* One by-product of this putative "reign of terror" was that Rockefeller was able to gain authority in 1973 to appoint one hundred "narcotic judges" in New York State, and since judgeships are one of the most prized rewards of New York State politics, Rockefeller also gained a measure of influence for himself.

unprecedented skill to convert heroin into a multibillion-dollar issue. Since the police generally assumed that many addicts were criminals who had shoplifted, burglarized abandoned buildings, "boosted" merchandise from parked trucks, forged welfare checks, and committed other forms of petty larceny, Rockefeller and his staff decided that by simply multiplying the total number of estimated addicts by what they assumed each addict's habit cost him to maintain, they could ascertain, as one of his advisors put it, an impressive "billion-dollar figure." For example, if they assumed, as they did in 1970, that there were 100,000 addicts in New York and that each addict had a habit of $30 a day, they could calculate that the "army of addicts" was compelled to steal $1,095,000,000 worth of goods to pay for their combined habit. The estimated numbers were quite elastic, if not totally arbitrary, for political purposes. By playing with the estimate they could arrive at any figure they believed was necessary to impress the populace with the danger of addicts.

There was, however, a stumbling block to the billion-dollar estimates. The total amount of reported theft that was not recovered in New York City in the Rockefeller years was never more than $100 million a year, and only a fraction of this could be considered stolen by addicts (since the largest segment, automobiles, was stolen by teenage joy-riders, and eventually recovered). Governor Rockefeller thus commissioned the Hudson Institute, a "think tank" with close connections to the Rockefeller family and institutions, to reanalyze the amount of theft which possibly could be attributed to addicts. After studying the problem, Hudson Institute reported back to Rockefeller in 1970: "No matter how we generate estimates of total value of property stolen in New York City, we cannot find any way of getting these estimates above five hundred million dollars a year—and only a part of this could be conceivably attributed to addicts." The governor, schooled in the art of controlling information, found it unnecessary to accept such a statistical defeat. He simply persisted in multiplying the maximum possible amount of theft in New York City by ten and arrived at a figure of $5 billion, which he attributed entirely to heroin addicts. Rockefeller's long experience in psychological warfare had taught him that large, authoritative-sounding numbers—like $5 billion a year—could be effectively employed in political rhetoric. Thus, in testifying before the United States Senate in 1975 that addict crime was costing the citizens of New York State "up to five billion dollars," Rockefeller could be fully confident that no senator would bother to chip away at his hyperbole.

In May, 1970, Rockefeller's staff, apparently excited by the wave of national publicity their heroin imagery was gaining for the governor, presented plans to declare a "drug emergency" and asked President Nixon and Mayor John Lindsay to set up "emergency camps" to quarantine all of New York City's addicts. In commenting on the plan, Rayburne Hesse, a member of Rockefeller's NACC, wrote in a private memorandum, "The press would love the action, the editorialists would denounce the vigilante tactics . . . civil libertarians would be aghast . . ." and for these reasons went on to recommend the plan. The point, however, was not to round up addicts but simply to fuel the national concern. Thus, although the plan was disseminated to the press and aroused much publicity, it was never put into effect.

Rockefeller's crusade against addicts reached its zenith in 1973, when the governor declared that a reign of terror existed with "whole neighborhoods . . . as effectively destroyed by addicts as by an invading army." The elements of fear in his heroin story had already been articulated and established by the various publications and briefings of his narcotics commission. Again in the century, addicts had taken the place of medieval vampires—infecting innocent children with their disease, murdering citizens at large, causing all crime and disorder. Rockefeller thus had little difficulty in 1973 in pressing through the legislature laws which totally bypassed the discretion of both the court and the prosecutors, and made it mandatory that anyone convicted of selling or possessing more than a fraction of an ounce of heroin (or even amphetamines or LSD) would be imprisoned for life. This new "Attila the Hun Law," as it was called in the state legislature, extended the mandatory life sentence to sixteen-year-old children, who heretofore had been protected by the youthful-offender law. For information leading to the arrest of drug possessors or sellers, thousand-dollar bounties would be paid. And in another legal innovation the bill provided a mandatory-life-imprisonment sentence for the novel crime of ingesting a "hard" drug before committing any number of prescribed crimes including criminal mischief, sodomy, burglary, assault, and arson. Under this new law a person would be presumed to be guilty of ingestion if he took any of these drugs within twenty-four hours of committing any of these crimes. Since addicts by definition continually took these drugs, they could be rounded up and mandatorily sentenced to concentration camps for life for committing any of a number of petty crimes, for which judges previously would have hesitated before putting them in prison at all. As Rockefeller shrewdly anticipated, the passage of such extraordinary laws (which were only slightly modified by the state legislature) created an instant furor in the nation's press. Rockefeller thus strengthened his reputation among the hard-line element of the Republican party without losing much support elsewhere, since few people in America were concerned with the fate of drug addicts. Rockefeller later justified the law by explaining in his Senate testimony that "about 135,000 addicts were robbing, mugging, murdering, day in and day out for their money to fix their habit. . . ." Though this depiction of a huge army of addicts carrying out daily mayhem against the citizens of New York no doubt further excited popular fears, it hardly fit the police statistics at Rockefeller's disposal. If 135,000 addicts maintained their "day-in, day-out" schedule, they would have had to commit something on the order of 49,275,000 robberies, muggings, and murders a year, which would mean that the average resident of New York would be robbed, mugged, and murdered approximately seven times a year. In fact, there were only about 110,000 such crimes reported in New York City in 1973, or only 1/445th the number of crimes that Rockefeller claimed were being committed solely by addicts. Even here, as Rockefeller was well aware, virtually all analyses showed that the addicts were responsible for only a minute fraction of the violent crimes he attributed to them in his constant rhetoric. Most murders and manslaughters were the result of intrafamily disputes, not addiction. Most muggings were the work of juveniles, not hardened addicts. Indeed, the Hudson Institute concluded, in the aforementioned study commissioned by Rockefeller, that less than 2 percent of addicts in New York financed their habit by either robbery or muggings (and they also concluded that there was only a fraction of the number of hardened addicts that Rockefeller claimed there were). Moreover, in 1972, another analysis by the New York City police department concluded, "Both the volume and seriousness of addict crime are exaggerated." Only 4.4 percent of those arrested in the city for felonies against person—which include murders, muggings, and robberies—were confirmed drug users (and only a small percentage of these could possibly be classified as addicts). Addicts generally refrain from such crimes against persons, according to most views of addict behavior, because it involves too high a risk of being caught, imprisoned, and withdrawn from their drug. Petty crimes against property, however, such as burglarizing abandoned houses, involve much fewer risks and potentially much higher profits. The proposals for putting addicts in concentration camps for life, thus, if actually carried out, would have an infinitesimal effect on decreasing violent crimes against persons. The "Attila the Hun Law" was never enforced with any great enthusiasm against addicts—or even against pushers. The purpose was to provide Rockefeller with a law-and-order image that would satisfy even the most retrograde member of the Republican party. And Rockefeller played the politics of fear so adroitly in the national media that President Nixon borrowed from him many rhetorical images and the statistical hyperbole linking heroin and crime in the public's mind. In his brilliant coordination of information and misinformation about addicts, Rockefeller succeeded in making the heroin vampire a national issue and himself vice-president, even if in the next two years the laws themselves proved unworkable.

3

G. Gordon Liddy:
The Will to Power

Until the late 1960s, the "drug menace," despite the apocalyptic metaphors associated with it, served mainly as a rhetorical theme in New York State politics. The addicts arrested in occasional police sweeps were almost always booked, for the statistical record, then released in what became known as "revolving door" arrests. G. Gordon Liddy, however, foresaw a more durable purpose in the drug menace: the public's fear of an uncontrollable army of addicts, if properly organized, could be forged into a new instrument for social control.

George Gordon Battle Liddy, named after a New York political leader, was born on November 30, 1929, in Brooklyn, New York. Brought up a staunch Catholic, Liddy was educated at St. Benedict's Preparatory School in Newark, New Jersey, and at Fordham University, where he made a reputation for himself as a fervent anti-Communist. Upon graduation in 1952, Liddy immediately enlisted in the Army, with the aim of becoming a paratrooper. An appendicitis attack, however, disqualified him from airborne training, and instead he fought a more prosaic war in Korea as a lieutenant in the artillery. Discharged in 1954, he returned to Fordham Law School, where he distinguished himself on *Fordham Law Review* and graduated in 1957.

For the next five years Liddy realized a childhood ambition by serving in the FBI under J. Edgar Hoover. After the gunpoint capture of one of the ten most wanted fugitives in 1959, Liddy became the youngest supervisor in the entire FBI and was attached to J. Edgar Hoover's personal staff at FBI national headquarters, in Washington. Combining a skill with words and a zeal for anticommunism, Liddy served as Hoover's personal ghostwriter, writing law-and-order articles for various magazines and preparing speeches for the director to give at public functions. He quickly became well versed in the use of dramatic metaphors and symbolic code words in the rhetoric of law and order. From his vantage point on the director's personal staff he also became familiar with the extralegal operations of the FBI, such as break-ins and wiretaps. Despite his admiration for Hoover, he realized during these years of service that the FBI was an inefficient and bureaucratic agency, and was somewhat less than an effective national police force. In a memorandum to President Nixon ten years later he analyzed the deficiencies of the FBI and concluded that because it conformed too closely to rules and to congressional measures of performance, it could not be counted on as a potent instrument of the presidency. Disappointed in the FBI, Liddy resigned from Hoover's staff in 1962 and went into private law practice with his father, Sylvester L. Liddy, in New York City. (The exact nature of his private practice during these years has never been ascertained.)

Since his wife, Frances Purcell Liddy, came from a lawyer's family in Poughkeepsie, New York, he decided to move there in 1966 and apply for a job as an assistant district attorney in Dutchess County. Raymond Baratta, then district attorney of Dutchess County, interviewed Liddy and found him "militant but soft-spoken." Liddy carried with him sealed recommendations from the FBI, and Baratta, impressed with his energy, decided to give him the position he sought. Liddy quickly became famous, if not notorious, in Poughkeepsie as a gun-toting prosecutor. During one criminal trial he even fired off a gun in the courtroom to dramatize a minor point in the case. He also proved himself a local crusader against drugs. Joining forces with the chief of police in Wappingers Falls, he traveled from high school to high school in the county, lecturing on the dangers of narcotics and employing the rich rhetoric of Captain Hobson. The police chief, Robert Berberich, recalled in 1975 that Liddy carried with him samples of "everything but heroin" for his lectures. In speeches before church groups and fraternal orders in 1966, Liddy also warned, in a variation of Hobson's yellow-peril theme, that the addicts of New York City would eventually make their way up the Hudson Valley and contaminate Poughkeepsie with their vice and crime. As the "legal advisor" in 1966 to the Poughkeepsie police department he also went along on every marijuana and narcotics raid that he could find or inspire, and his colleagues in the district attorney's office found him brilliant in presenting what otherwise would be routine arrests to the local newspapers. Despite his constant efforts to alarm the citizens of Dutchess County, Liddy found that "the menace . . . was still thought of as principally a threat to others."

On a cold midnight in March, 1966, Liddy finally found a way to shatter the illusions of Dutchess County and gain national publicity for himself. The coup began with a raid on the home of Timothy Leary, a former psychologist at Harvard who had gained some prominence (and notoriety) from his experiments with the hallucinogenic drug LSD. After being dismissed from Harvard for distributing LSD to students, he made the mistake of renting a large mansion in Liddy's bailiwick at Millbrook, New York. LSD was neither an addictive drug nor one associated with crime, but Leary's presence in Dutchess County provided Liddy with a golden opportunity. "For some time, the major media had been covering the activities of Dr. Timothy Leary," Liddy subsequently explained in *True* magazine. "Leary's ability to influence the young made him feared by parents everywhere. His message ran directly contrary to everything they believed in and sought to teach their children: 'tune in' (to my values; reject those of your parents), 'turn on' (drug yourself); 'drop out' (deal with your problems and those of society by running away from them)." In other words, Liddy realized that Leary could be portrayed as a Pied Piper, using mysterious drugs to turn the young against their parents. He also noted, "Local boys and girls have been seen entering and leaving the estate . . . fleeting glimpses were reported of persons strolling the grounds in the nude." He thus suggested that drugs were eroding the morality (and virginity) of Dutchess County youths, or, as he put it, "to fears of drug induced dementia were added pot induced pregnancy." He even foresaw that if citizens' fears about drugs were properly stimulated, "there would be reenacted at Millbrook the classic motion picture scene in which enraged Transylvanian town folks storm Dr. Frankenstein's castle." Even though Liddy was mixing his myths up a bit (Transylvania was the haunting place of the vampire Dracula, not of Frankenstein's monster), he correctly perceived the connection in the public imagination between the drug addict and the medieval legend of the living dead. And it was this connection of fears that Liddy set out to exploit with his midnight raid.

In planning the night operation, Liddy explained, "We hoped to find not only a central supply of LSD belonging to Leary, but also his guests' personal supplies of marijuana and hashish ... it was necessary to strike quickly, with benefit of surprise, if the inhabitants were to be caught in their rooms and any contraband found in the rooms established as possessed by the tenants." To avoid the necessity of having to depend on testimony of witnesses, Liddy planned to wait until Leary and his friends were all asleep in their rooms, then, to catch them red-handed, "We would perform a classic 'no knock' entry--that is, kick in the front door." After that, Liddy himself was to lead "a quick charge upstairs by the bulk of the force of deputies, who were then to fan out and hold the inhabitants in their rooms pending a systematic search."

All, however, did not go as Liddy planned. Instead of retiring at about eleven P.M., as Liddy presumed, the residents of the estate gathered at about that time in the living room and began showing a film. Liddy recounted in *True* magazine in 1974: "The deputies assumed that the movies were pornographic, and there was some competition for the assignment to move into binocular range to obtain further information ... [but] presently the lucky man returned to report in a tone of complete disgust, 'It ain't no dirty movie; you'll never guess what them hippies are watching. A waterfall.' "

The film did not finish until nearly one A.M., by which time most of the deputies were extremely cold and exhausted. Finally, the raiding party moved in on the sleeping foe. Liddy introduced himself to Dr. Leary, who meekly surrendered. And some incriminating marijuana and LSD were indeed found on the premises. However, because Liddy had not fully advised Leary of his rights, as they were defined by the United States Supreme Court in the *Miranda* decision that year, the judge dismissed the charges against Leary and his followers. Though Liddy viewed the Supreme Court as an "unelected elite" that had usurped power in the United States, he acquiesced in the decision. After all, he had successfully "exposed" Leary in the newspapers of Dutchess County (and Leary subsequently left the county), and he had established his own reputation as a drug fighter.

By successfully waging his crusade against drugs (albeit in a county which had few, if any, criminal addicts), Liddy established a formidable reputation for himself in the county. The next logical step was gaining power. Liddy saw life itself as a contest for power. He said, on a national television broadcast some years later, "Power exists to be used . . . the first obligation of . . . someone seeking power is to get himself elected. . . ." In this contest for power Liddy posited that the man with the strongest will for power would win. He wrote his wife, philosophically, "If any one component of man ought to be exercised, cultivated, and strengthened above all others, it is the will; and that will must have but one objective—to win." In June, 1968, Liddy first attempted to win the race for office by running against the incumbent, Albert Rosenblatt, for the Republican nomination for district attorney of Dutchess County. He had little support from Republican politicians and was defeated in a party caucus by a vote of 25 to 4.

Liddy next turned the focus of his attention to the Republican nomination for Congress from the Poughkeepsie district. Openly challenging Hamilton Fish, Jr., who held the Republican seat, he mounted a bitter primary campaign in the summer of 1968, which the Democratic opponent, John S. Dyson, described as "hyperadrenaloid and bitterly anti-communist." He traveled from fraternal lodge to fraternal lodge in Dutchess County, relentlessly pursuing the theme of vampire-addicts jeopardizing the life and safety of Dutchess County citizens. Law and order became his battle cry; his campaign advertisements contained such slogans as "Gordon Liddy doesn't bail them out—he puts them in" and "He knows the answer is law and order, not weak-kneed sociology." Despite the vigor of his campaign, he was defeated in the primary by the incumbent, Hamilton Fish, by only a few thousand votes.

Liddy had lost a few battles in 1968, but not the war. Victory, he realized, proceeded from a superior mind-set, and not from any temporary configuration of voters: "The master who instructed me in the deadliest of the Oriental martial arts taught me that the outcome of a battle is decided in the minds of the opponents before the first blow is struck." Liddy, in a letter to his wife published in *Harper's* magazine in October, 1974, credited the "mind-set of the . . . SS division Leibenstandarte" for the Nazi victories, and contrasted this with "the ill-disciplined, often drugged dropouts that make up a significant portion of the nation's armed forces today." He entered the congressional fray again in 1968, this time as a candidate for the nomination of the New York State Conservative party. And as the strongest law-and-order candidate of Dutchess County, he easily won this nomination.

Liddy now presented Hamilton Fish with a serious problem in his bid for reelection to Congress. The public-opinion polls showed in September, 1968, that it was going to be an exceedingly close race between Fish and Dyson. As the Conservative candidate and the locally celebrated prosecutor who had "captured Timothy Leary," Liddy threatened to win enough votes among conservative Republicans to ensure Fish's defeat and a Democratic victory. Though Liddy himself could not win the election, he had cleverly maneuvered himself into a position to make a deal. Gerald Ford, then the Republican leader in the House of Representatives and a friend of Hamilton Fish's, went that fall to Poughkeepsie and personally arranged for Liddy to endorse the candidacy of Hamilton Fish. In return for abandoning his Conservative campaign Liddy was promised a high position in the Nixon administration, if Nixon was elected. Liddy also agreed to head Nixon's campaign effort in Dutchess County.

After Nixon's victory in 1968 Hamilton Fish returned to Congress, and Gordon Liddy also went to Washington. In 1969 Liddy was appointed special assistant to the secretary of the treasury. He served directly under Eugene T. Rossides, who had direct responsibility for all the law-enforcement activities of the Treasury Department, including the Customs Bureau, the Alcohol, Tobacco and Firearms unit, the Internal Revenue Service enforcement division, and the Secret Service. Rossides, a shrewd and enterprising Greek American who had been an all-American football player at Columbia University and had managed a number of Governor Rockefeller's campaigns in New York City, now planned to expand the role of the Treasury Department in law enforcement. He found that Gordon Liddy's high energy level and determination were just what he needed in the impending struggle for power within the administration. Liddy thus became Rossides's "spear carrier." One of his first assignments was to work on Task Force Number One, a joint task force being set up by the Justice Department and the Treasury Department to combat narcotics smugglers. Rossides was concerned that John Mitchell would use this task force to expand his own Justice Department domain to the detriment of the Treasury Department's customs bureau, and Liddy was given the task of protecting and promoting Treasury interests on the task force. Though most of the energy of the presidential task force was consumed in bureaucratic wrangles, Liddy foresaw the 'full potential of the drug issue as an instrument for reorganizing agencies of the government. It contained an undisputed moral vantage point—since no one in the Nixon administration could be expected to sympathize with addicts, or even with drug users—and could therefore be used to support extraordinarily hard-line positions. Moreover, since the drug problem implied a new and mysterious threat (no one in the Nixon administration had very much knowledge about the effects or the epidemiology of narcotics), one could argue that existing agencies and methods were inadequate to meet this new menace. Because they were dealing with an unprecedented "epidemic," any innovative measure, no matter how unorthodox, could be considered and discussed. Liddy's experience in the FBI had taught him that government agencies tend to expend their potential power on routine activities in their established areas of competency, and that a new area of competency, such as the drug menace, could lead to a new potential for power.

Rossides also assigned Liddy to work as his representative on the working group of the ad hoc committee established by the president to deal with international narcotics traffic. Rossides was especially interested in suppressing the opium grown in Turkey. On the working group Liddy met with executives from the CIA and other intelligence agencies. Although the CIA was prohibited by its charter from domestic activities, drug traffic was international in scope; therefore, Liddy realized, it provided a unique liaison between the intelligence community and the government.

In drafting various pieces of legislation for the Treasury Department (including sections of the Organized Crime Control Act of 1970 and the Explosives Control Act of 1970) Liddy also had considerable contact with congressional subcommittees. Here again he found the drug issue a great potential for power: though few individual congressmen fully understood the medical issues involved in drug abuse, most understood the potential political consequences for failing to support measures directed against drug abuse. More important, congressmen tended to see drug abuse as an issue that didn't fall within the traditional lines of authority of any single agency, and were therefore more willing to consider "reorganization" measures to deal with it.

Liddy's expertise in drug abuse brought him into direct contact with the inner circle of the White House. He especially impressed Egil Krogh with his knowledge of the Leary case and his subsequent plans for legally or illegally extradicting Leary from Afghanistan, where he was then a fugitive. By 1971, when Liddy was enforcement legislative counsel of the Treasury Department, the White House had become progressively interested in ways of bypassing the bureaucrats in the various investigative agencies of the government, such as the FBI, Customs Bureau, and CIA. G. Gordon Liddy had developed a plan for using the war against heroin as a cover for reorganizing various agencies of the government, or at least for making them more effective. Thus, with his "will to power," Liddy began drawing up memoranda for the White House staff for the creation of a unique special police unit attached, in all but name, to the White House, with uncommon powers to deal with drug abuse.

A coup consists of the infiltration of a small but critical segment of the state apparatus, which is then used to displace the government from its control of the remainder.

—EDWARD LUTTWAK, *Coup d'Etat*

PART TWO

The Politics of
Law and Order

★

Of course the fragmentation of the police in the United States has largely resulted from the deliberate intention of denying the federal government a possible instrument of tyranny.

—EDWARD LUTTWAK, *Coup d'Etat*

4

The Barker of Slippery Gulch

Richard Milhous Nixon did not follow any of the charted channels of American politics in his extraordinary passage to the presidency. Whereas other American presidents could point to their "humble origins" with some sort of romantic pride (or even describe their family summer home as a "log cabin"), Nixon really suffered during his childhood from poverty. His father, Frank Nixon, moved to California at the turn of the century after having been frostbitten working in an open streetcar in Columbus, Ohio. After working as a farmhand and oil roustabout, he attempted to cultivate lemons outside Los Angeles. After Richard was born, on January 9, 1913, Nixon abandoned the "lemon ranch," and the family moved to the Quaker community of Whittier, California. They were so impoverished that Nixon's mother was forced to work as a scrubwoman in a sanatorium in Arizona in order to pay for the treatment of Richard's brother Harold, who suffered from tuberculosis. At the age of ten Richard Nixon was sent to work as a farm laborer to help out his family. He fully understood the degrading nature of poverty; at the age of fourteen he was forced to work as a barker for a fortune wheel for the Slippery Gulch Rodeo, a cover for illegal gambling rooms in back of the "rodeo."

Young Nixon also exercised his oratory skills on the Whittier High School debating team and won prizes for the best oration on the Constitution. He graduated from high school in the depths of the Depression, and worked his way through a small Quaker college in Whittier while living at home and supporting his family. Then, winning a scholarship, he attended law school at Duke University. Although he distinguished himself and graduated third in his class, all the prestigious New York law firms where he applied for a job turned down his application, apparently because he did not have the right contacts or connections. He continued to eke out a living as a clerk in a local law office in Whittier for the first few years after law school; then, when World War II broke out, he joined the Navy as a junior officer. He was eventually sent to Middle River, Maryland, to assist the Navy in liquidating contracts for a flying-boat project (in which Howard Hughes also took an active interest).

Late in 1945, a few months after he completed the settlement for the Navy on the boat project, Nixon was invited by a group of local businessmen, in his hometown of Whittier, to seek the Republican nomination for the congressional seat then held by Jerry Voorhis, a liberal Democrat. But until that time, Nixon had had no grounding in local California politics—indeed, he attended his first political rally in 1945—and therefore, in lieu of local issues, he played upon a more generalized fear: the fear of communism. In likening communism to an invisible virus that infects the body politic, he was able to arouse fears among the public that even avowed non-Communists might serve as carriers of this dread disease. Thus, even though his opponent Voorhis was outspoken in his criticism of communism, Nixon labeled him in the public's mind as a tool of communism. The politics of fear worked for Nixon, and he was elected to Congress in 1946 and reelected in 1948. In 1950 he defeated Helen Gahagan Douglas for her seat in the United States Senate, having defamed his opponent as the "pink lady" and a "dupe" of communism. In the Senate, he so adroitly managed the putative menace of international communism that General Dwight D. Eisenhower chose him as his vice-presidential candidate. In 1952, seven years after he entered politics as a Navy veteran, the former barker from Slippery Gulch was elected vice-president of the United States.

During the next eight years, as vice-president, Nixon traveled widely to the various power centers of the world, including the Soviet Union, and served as one of President Eisenhower's main liaisons with the National Security Council. In a sense, then, even as vice-president, Nixon had relatively little experience with domestic issues in America.

In 1960, however, Nixon found that times had changed in American politics: the fears of communism which he had so successfully exploited in the late forties and early fifties had subsided, and Americans were becoming increasingly concerned with domestic problems rather than international ones. In a close election in 1960 he was defeated for the presidency by John F. Kennedy; and two years later he was defeated by Pat Brown for the governorship of California. Rather than a national hero of the Republican party, he was now a defeated man without a future in politics. In 1963 former vice-president Nixon moved to New York City and joined, as a senior partner, the law firm of Mudge, Stern, Baldwin and Todd.

Though he had not entirely abandoned his dreams and schemes of being president, Nixon realized that the menace of communism on which he built his early reputation no longer was an effective focus for organizing the fears of the American public. Since the Cold War had waned as a national concern, domestic issues received increasingly more attention in the national press. The former vice-president had no claim to any special knowledge or competence in these domestic fields; he was rarely called upon for public comment. Indeed, after his 1962 defeat in the California gubernatorial election, ABC News presented Nixon's "political obituary." If he was again to become a center of political attention, Nixon foresaw that he would have to identify himself with the control of a new menace. Thus he turned to the growing unease that was being reported out of the major cities in America—riots had erupted in Los Angeles, New York, and other major cities in the mid-1960s (and though not a new phenomenon in themselves, they were for the first time nationally televised); crime rates, as reported by the FBI, had practically doubled between 1960 and 1967; and polls were indicating that personal safety from crimes was rapidly becoming the dominant concern of the electorate. Until then, the law-and-order battle cry had been used mainly by local politicians for local problems and as a shibboleth for the race problem and crime control; Nixon found he could now use it to organize fears on a wider scale. In 1967 Nixon, using much the same rhetoric as that employed against the threat of international communism, attempted in an article in *Reader's Digest*—entitled "What Has Happened to America?"—to elevate local crime to the status of a national menace jeopardizing the very survival of the nation. Successfully capturing law and order as a political issue, he argued that "in a few short years ... America has become among the most lawless and violent [nations] in the history of free people" because liberal decisions in the courts were "weakening the peace forces against the criminal forces." As in his earlier war, against the Communist menace, Nixon suggested that government officials and judges were soft on crime and were subverting the efforts of police to prevent criminals from preying on an innocent society.

After he received the Republican nomination for president in 1968, he immediately ordered his chief speech writers to develop law and order into a major theme of his campaign. Nixon, of course, did not invent the issue of law and order. Until 1968, however, the law-and-order issue in American politics was confined mainly to the state and local levels, as noted in the case of Nelson Rockefeller, and scant, if any, mention of this motif can be found in prior presidential campaigns. To be sure, politicians had earlier urged "wars" or "crusades" against alleged criminal conspiracies—notably, the Mafia—as a means of achieving a national reputation. (Estes Kefauver and Robert F. Kennedy had both waged highly publicized wars against conspiracies of organized crime and had gained national prominence for their efforts, though there were few indictments.*) For the most part, however, these earlier efforts were intended only to produce the sort of publicity which would allay the fears of the public by exposing a few symbolic "chiefs" of the underworld (who usually turned out to be bookies). Nixon played on the law-and-order theme in a very different way: the target he directed his audience's attention to was unorganized crime that directly threatened the life and safety of all— muggings, murder, robbery, rape, and burglary. The threat to the public safety that he depicted was not a handful of Mafia chiefs but the subversion of the legal system by those who were more sympathetic to the rights of criminals than to the protection of the innocent. Nixon shrewdly perceived that law and order could be effectively transposed into an issue of the Democrats' undermining of public

---

* Victor S. Navasky has given an excellent account in *Kennedy Justice* of how Attorney General Kennedy presented Joseph Valachi, who claimed to be a member of the criminal conspiracy while in prison, to the national media in order to mobilize support for legislation expanding wiretap and other authorities being proposed by the Kennedy administration—clearly an adumbration of the future.

authority. Even at this early stage, Nixon realized that unless he could preempt the crime issue for himself by generalizing it, Governor George Wallace, who was making an independent bid for the presidency in 1968, could be expected to exploit it to attract votes among Nixon's natural constituency.

Though Nixon successfully developed law and order into a principal issue of the 1968 campaign, he intentionally avoided defining the problem in anything more than a vague way. Patrick J. Buchanan, a thirty-one-year-old journalist from St. Louis who was then working as Nixon's chief speech writer on the law-and-order issue, recalls the polls' suggesting that the public believed that lawlessness could be dealt with by a more determined effort of the federal government. However, at that stage, Nixon's speech writers had little specific knowledge about the characteristics or causes of crime and disorder. Although Governor Nelson Rockefeller had brilliantly pioneered the heroin menace in New York State, and Nixon himself realized the political potential of a drug-abuse menace, the candidate's strategists were not yet fully conversant with the vocabulary of dread that was used by Rockefeller to exploit the drug issue. As late as September 12, 1968, Buchanan teletyped Martin Pollner, a member of Nixon's law firm and campaign staff who had been a former prosecutor in New York City, that it was "vital that we get some background on the narcotics problem in this country." Pollner immediately consulted with John W. Dean, III, another lawyer working in the Nixon campaign, and then wrote a four-page memorandum to Buchanan—"Potential Materials and Recommendations for R.N.'s Position on Narcotics and Drug Abuse." Then, with the help of Peter Velde, another lawyer on the campaign staff, Pollner sent another memorandum on the "narcotics problem in southern California." These analyses detailing the problems of law enforcement and rehabilitation, however, were far too specific for Nixon. The speech he gave on the subject of narcotics in September, 1968, in Anaheim, California, for which Buchanan requested this research, began with Nixon's describing a letter that he had supposedly received from a nineteen-year-old drug addict. Then, using the Hobsonian imagery of heroin's corrupting innocents, he asserted, "Narcotics are a modern curse of American youth. . . . I will take the executive steps necessary to make our borders more secure against the pestilence of narcotics." But narcotics remained only a subsidiary issue in the 1968 campaign. The strategists instead played upon the more general fear of personal violence, saturating television across the nation with commercials that showed an obviously nervous middle-aged woman walking down the street on a dark, wet night while an announcer stated, "Crimes of violence in the United States have almost doubled in recent years . . . today a violent crime is committed every sixty seconds . . . a robbery every two and a half minutes . . . a mugging every six minutes . . . a murder every forty-three minutes . . . and it will get worse unless we take the offensive. . . ." The commercials ended with the message, "This time vote like your whole world depended on it." After winning the election by a narrow margin, Nixon was expected to deal effectively with the menace to law and order that he himself had helped to popularize. But for him it was an opportunity, not a problem.

5

The Bête-noire Strategy

It proved far easier to find the rhetoric to excite public fears over lawlessness than the controls for reducing crime and disorder. During the 1968 campaign Nixon had persistently attacked the "permissiveness" of the Democratic attorney general, Ramsey Clark, and pledged that the first step in his war on crime would be to replace him with a more determined and tougher chief law officer. "Ramsey Clark had been symbolic of the laissez-faire liberal approach to crime control," Egil Krogh, then deputy assistant to the president for law enforcement recalled. "The promise of a new attorney general was all part of the same idea that crime had gotten so much out of control that he was going to take stringent measures." Nixon chose as a replacement for Ramsey Clark his law partner and campaign manager, John Newton Mitchell. Like Nixon, Mitchell was indeed a determined man: he worked his way through college and played semipro ice hockey, one of the more violent sports available. In World War II he sought the most dangerous service available in the Navy, and was a commander of the PT boat squadron in which John F. Kennedy served as a lieutenant. As one of the leading municipal-bond lawyers in New York City, he dealt constantly with local politicians across the country interested in gaining a favorable opinion for a tax-free bond issue. He joined Nixon's law firm as a senior partner in 1967 and made an immediate impression on Nixon. Little more than a year later, he agreed to be the campaign manager for Nixon's presidential effort, and seemed to many in the campaign to be the only person to whom Nixon deferred. Mitchell, a self-made man who enjoyed his wealth, wanted to return to his law practice, but reluctantly agreed to serve his new friend as attorney general.

In January, 1969, only a few days after he had assumed office, President Nixon convened a meeting in the White House on possible law-and-order initiatives. The small inner circle of advisors who attended that meeting included John Mitchell, who in those early days acted as a "prime minister" to the president; John Ehrlichman, a Seattle land-use lawyer who had served as tour director in the 1968 campaign and was now counsel to the president; Egil Krogh, the young deputy to Ehrlichman; Daniel Patrick Moynihan, a former advisor to Presidents Kennedy and Johnson who was then the counsel for domestic affairs; and Donald Santarelli, a twenty-nine-year-old lawyer who had drafted many of the position papers on crime for the 1968 Nixon campaign, and who was in the process of joining the Justice Department as a strategist for the crime-control program.

The meeting began with President Nixon's defining law and order as his "principal domestic issue." In the extensive interviews that Egil Krogh had with me over a two-month period in 1974 he recalled that in that January meeting the president used general terminology such as "we are a tough, law-and-order administration, and we are going to crack down on crime." Since the rhetoric used during the campaign in 1968 was basically "get tough," Krogh explained, "there was a clear motivation to be able to deliver to the electorate in 1972 a record of improvement in crime control." Nixon stated that the two categories of crime that would be most useful to diminish were armed robbery and burglary, since they "instill the greatest fear" in the electorate. As Nixon continued to describe his objectives for crime control, John Mitchell began slowly shaking his head in a negative manner, and pulling on his pipe as if it were some sort of semaphore signal. Asked whether he thought there was any problem, Mitchell leaned back and explained that most of the crimes that the president was interested in controlling did not fall under the jurisdiction or powers of the federal government. Except for Washington, D.C., where the federal government did have direct jurisdiction, crimes such as homicide, assault, mugging, robbery, and burglary were not violations of federal law but of state or local law, and even if the federal government found an indirect way of intervening in the problem, the local government would get the credit for diminishing those classes of crimes. Moreover, John Ehrlichman pointed out, the established agencies of the federal government, such as the FBI, the IRS, the Bureau of Narcotics and Dangerous Drugs (BNDD), and the Treasury Department, had traditionally been reluctant to involve themselves in any sort of offensive against such local crimes. In all, there were only a few thousand federal agents (not including the CIA or the Department of Defense) and they could not realistically be expected to have much effect on street crimes in the urban centers of America. Such crimes were committed, according to the best police estimates, by teenage youth acting on spur-of-the-moment inspirations or on targets of opportunity. Nixon quickly comprehended, Krogh said, that "the reach of the federal government's power in law enforcement did not penetrate to the state or local level . . . where most of the street crime people were afraid of existed." Donald Santarelli was called upon to sum up the situation. He later recounted, in an interview with me:

> In the light of many promises made in the 1968 campaign, and the unerring belief that the Nixon administration had to do something dramatic in the area of law enforcement, it was necessary for me to put the actual ability of the federal government in perspective for the president and top advisors. . . .
>
> I told them that the federal government simply did not have the machinery or authority to deal with crime in America outside the District of Columbia. . . . The only thing we could do was to exercise vigorous symbolic leadership. . . . With the president and attorney general as spokesmen, we could elevate the issue of crime to the level of the president.

The new strategy thus emerged. Ehrlichman suggested to Krogh that since "there were clear limits on what the federal government could do," the alternative was to "jawbone . . . to stimulate action at the state and local level simply by making the issue [verbally]." Though the administration lacked the "tools" actually to reduce crime, it could wage a symbolic war on crime. In 1974 Krogh explained to me that during the first year of Nixon's administration, a whole range of "symbolic strategies" were discussed. Harsh-sounding legislation could be proposed to Congress which would have little effect on law enforcement but would greatly enhance the administration's public reputation for toughness (and if Congress failed to enact these laws, it could be blamed for "softness" toward crime). Repressive-sounding words such as "preventive detention" could be bandied about by administration officials, thus provoking an outcry in the "liberal press" which would add to the appearance of the relentless war on crime by the administration. A presidential spokesman could also directly attack judges in the courts for being sympathetic to criminals in order to make the administration seem, by contrast, hard-line. The Nixon strategists thus decided early on that though they could not directly reduce street crime in America, they could gain enormous publicity for their crime offensive by calling attention to their repressive-sounding plans and ideas for law enforcement, and thereby create a bête noire for the liberal press to focus on.

Since President Nixon was by 1969 cultivating a new image for himself as a reasonable and moderate man (and allowing Vice-President Agnew to make the more provocative speeches), John Mitchell was chosen for the role of Mr. Law and Order. Krogh later explained, "The president felt that Mitchell would represent the law-and-order image that had been developed" by the "speech-writing staff" and would effectively use their "language of crime control" to stir public reactions. Mitchell's public role was to identify himself with a remorseless, hard-line attitude toward crime and criminals. In both public appearances and private briefings for the press he was to stress the urgent need for isolating criminals from the rest of society through strict application of the laws and long prison sentences. When, for example, H. R. Haldeman, the president's chief of staff, was planning a presidential briefing on drugs for television writers in April, 1970, he decided on a strategy whereby the president would "tie in the attorney general in such a way as to position him in the minds of TV writers and producers as the spearhead of the anti-drug movement within the administration," according to a White House memorandum. John Mitchell's criticism of the supposed laxity of criminal judges was also "part of the speech rhetoric [and] part of the political needs at the time," according to Krogh's later explanation to me of the 1969 strategy. As for the "political law-and-order bills" that Mitchell exhorted Congress to pass, Krogh then explained, "It was my view that while these bills would suggest a tough law-and-order demeanor by the administration, the legislation itself did not provide an enhanced ability to the police department or to the courts to reduce crime as such. The no-knock legislation struck me, and also Mr.

Ehrlichman, as almost inherently repressive in tone." Indeed, Jerry Wilson, then police chief of Washington, D.C., specifically told Ehrlichman and Krogh that the no-knock legislation was unnecessary since the police had "adequate authority to enter a dwelling" where there was a probable cause, and the police chief viewed the no-knock bill as "law-and-order window dressing rather than as initiatives that would strike at the core of the problem." Such technical advice was disregarded, however, since the act of proposing draconian-sounding law-and-order bills was intended to serve "a political purpose," as Krogh put it, "rather than really being directed at curbing the real problem." Thus, tough-sounding law-and-order bills were proposed. An internal memorandum in the files of President Nixon's Domestic Council (circa July, 1970), entitled "Crime Control and Law Enforcement, Current Status—Political Position for the 1970 Election," commented, "The administration's position in the crime field depends on our ability to shift blame for crime bill inaction to Congress." To their surprise, however, the Democratic-controlled Congress rapidly passed even the most repressive-sounding crime bills by lopsided margins (since not even Democratic congressmen wanted to appear to their constituents as voting against a law-and-order bill).

To be sure, the private views and unpublicized actions of the attorney general did not always fit the public image being projected— Mr. Law and Order. For example, during one cabinet meeting that Krogh recalled, Mitchell strongly objected to President Nixon's demand for mandatory rather than flexible sentences for drug offenders. Even though the President replied, "That's my position, and I cannot have it look as if I am weak or receding from a hard-line position," Mitchell argued that the mandatory sentences would be "irrational" and "counterproductive." Ultimately, the president adopted Mitchell's more moderate view (although Mitchell's position was not made public). Although Mitchell asked the more sophisticated public to watch "the deeds, not the words" of the administration, the bête-noire strategy frightened and provoked the more liberal audience. Numerous political commentators in the press interpreted Mitchell's bombast quite literally as a call for a national police crackdown. Such negative publicity was intentionally not repudiated by the White House or the attorney general, since there existed in fact a curious coincidence of interests between the Nixon strategists, who wanted to depict a *hard-line* attorney general, and their political opponents, who wanted to depict a *repressive* attorney general.

Journalistic attacks, such as Richard Harris's book *Justice,* which emphasized the dramatic differences between Attorneys General Ramsey Clark and John Mitchell in their administration of justice, played willy-nilly into the bête-noire strategy by heightening the repressive image of the new attorney general.

This convergence of political imagery strongly reinforced the notion that the country was entering a period of political repression—much to the chagrin of some members of the Nixon administration. For example, Krogh's young staff assistant Jeffrey Donfeld complained to Attorney General Mitchell in 1970 that some of his statements were being misinterpreted by the public as calls for political repression, and suggested that the administration's rhetoric on law enforcement could be toned down so as to avoid any confusion. By the time that Donfeld walked back from the Department of Justice to the White House, word had reached his superior, Egil Krogh, who summoned him to his office and explained good-naturedly, "Fool . . . don't you think those guys know what they're saying! Don't you think it is all calculated for a specific purpose?" At that moment Donfeld realized that "they weren't trying to correct the charge of repression . . . it was all a matter of perspective and from their perspective, a tough image was exactly what they wanted." Daniel Patrick Moynihan, a Democrat with a liberal constituency, was unwilling to be part of a bête-noire strategy and fought for nearly six months to have the Justice Department respond to the charges being made in the press that the administration was committing genocide or otherwise attempting to murder the leaders of the Black Panther party in the United States. Though the charges were demonstrably false in a number of cases—most of the alleged shooting incidents occurred before Nixon assumed office (and while John Mitchell was still a bond lawyer)—the image-makers in the Department of Justice were not completely adverse to publicity that identified the attorney general as someone who was battling black militants, and Moynihan's protests fell on deaf ears.

Though the bête-noire campaign achieved success in some quarters—notably, the media—in identifying John Mitchell and the Nixon administration with the image of a hard-line, law-and-order offensive, it failed to impress the public at large. The Domestic Council crime-control memorandum quoted earlier began by noting, "According to the polls, the public is not yet persuaded that the administration has succeeded with the anti-crime drive." Moreover, crime statistics, which the memorandum termed "the major indicator for success or failure," showed a large increase in all the categories of street crime against which Nixon had pledged an offensive, and newspapers, especially the Washington *Post,* were now citing this failure with great concern, and sometimes with hidden glee. The administration's record of prosecutions and convictions also turned out, upon evaluation, to be much less drastic than its rhetoric—prosecution of federal drug cases actually dropped by almost 10 percent between fiscal 1969 and 1970. Even in the District of Columbia, where the administration had direct influence over the policies of the police department, crime had increased markedly. As the 1970 mid-term election approached, the Nixon strategists realized that new and more dramatic efforts would be necessary. They thus suggested, in another crime-control memorandum, that the attorney general develop "certain highly visible efforts in the crime area" such as "organized crime crackdowns . . . to clearly demonstrate—in the public mind—totality of the administration commitment." The Domestic Council memorandum noted that although "organized crime is being attacked through eleven strike forces soon to be increased to twenty-one strike forces . . . this program needs more publicity." And to that end it asked that Mitchell specifically consider the "apprehension of top-level hoodlums involved in organized crime on a regular basis." The law-enforcement planners in the White House believed that the continuous arrests of suspects with Italian-American or "racketeer" names would be reported by the press as a major crackdown on the Mafia (even if the suspects were released immediately), according to Krogh's interpretation of the memorandum. He explained to me that the White House was concerned with "visibility," which was understood by the Nixon White House to mean simply getting the president's efforts in the headlines, and the most direct means of achieving such coverage of the crime issue was simply for the attorney general to make a series of spectacular arrests.

Mitchell, of course, was aware that previous administrations had established their reputations by making a few highly publicized arrests of men suspected of belonging to the Mafia or other organized-crime groups. In 1962, for example, Attorney General Robert F. Kennedy dispatched one hundred FBI agents (and a large number of sympathetic journalists) to Reading, Pennsylvania, to raid an otherwise quiet dice game. As Victor Navasky pointed out in his account of the Justice Department under Kennedy, this proved to be "a brilliant publicity coup—since it advertised the new Kennedy anti-crime legislation. . . ." In such raids Attorney General Kennedy pioneered the development of strike forces, or groups of federal agents detached from their normal duties and chains of command. These strike forces quite commonly made illegal break-ins (or "surreptitious entries," as they called them) in order to plant concealed microphones in the homes of suspected gamblers or racketeers. Even though such illegally obtained information could not be used to prosecute criminals, the disclosures were leaked to magazines and newspapers to keep the campaign in the headlines. Until 1967, this was the traditional way of waging war against the Mafia. However, when J. Edgar Hoover became embroiled in a damaging controversy after it was revealed in court cases that the FBI had illegally broken into residences on behalf of the strike forces, and the new attorney general, Ramsey Clark, refused to give authorizations for such activities, the situation changed radically. Even though Mitchell may well have been willing to authorize the renewal of such activity, J. Edgar Hoover was understandably reluctant to again endanger the reputation of his agency. (Attorney General Kennedy, although he had also authorized such activity, later publicly denied it, leaving Hoover out on a precarious limb.) Moreover, in 1970, Mitchell himself was under a drumfire of attack in the press and in the courts about the authorization of wiretaps, and this made disclosure of electronic surveillance for national-security purposes much riskier—at least as far as the FBI was concerned. Although Mitchell could increase the number of strike forces, as the memorandum recommended, they were far less effective instruments for generating publicity without the potential for disclosing embarrassing information from wiretaps and electronic surveillance.

Suggestion in 1970 of rounding up Italian-American gamblers and racketeers also presented a political problem for Mitchell. An Italian antidefamation league, with such notable sponsors as Frank Sinatra, was claiming with some justification that the use of terms like "Mafia," "Mafiosa," and "Cosa Nostra" was creating the false impression that Italian-American citizens were behind all organized crime in America. Since Italian Americans were a group that the Nixon strategists hoped to appeal to in the 1972 election, Mitchell acceded to these protests by prohibiting the Department of Justice from using such epithets to describe organized crime. Under these conditions there seemed little profit in image-making to be gained from the traditional Mafia hunt.

As became increasingly clear from privately commissioned public-opinion polls, the attempts of the Nixon strategists at image manipulation had by and large failed. Although John Mitchell had been successfully projected as a repressive attorney general and bête noire by the liberal community, the more conservative constituency on which Nixon depended for reelection was not made fully aware of the war on crime. Nixon's speech writers blamed the media for suddenly changing the issue from repression of criminals to "repression of dissent," as Patrick Buchanan explained to me. In any case, the Nixon strategists demanded, in their "Prognosis for the 1972 Election," that the Nixon administration be in a position by 1972 to claim that it "has mounted the most massive effort to control crime in the nation's history." Apparently they still hoped that "statistical results [would] come from the District of Columbia, where the administration has direct control over the number of police and the comprehensiveness of the drug fight." Nixon himself demanded "substantive" results, which meant to Ehrlichman and Krogh that they would have to produce statistics and numbers on arrests and convictions. Mr. Law and Order reminded Ehrlichman and Krogh that there was only one area in which the federal police could produce such results on demand—and that was narcotics. The program for narcotics control, which Krogh himself had quietly developed, now turned out to be the only alternative for realizing the law-and-order results which Nixon demanded.

6

The Education of Egil Krogh

Egil Krogh, Jr., was born in Chicago in 1939, the son of a Norwegian immigrant. After majoring in English at a small Christian Science college in southern Illinois, dropping out of business school at the University of Chicago, serving three years as a naval communications officer in the Pacific, and selling hats in a department store in Seattle, he finally graduated from the University of Washington Law School in June, 1968. Upon graduation, Krogh was offered an apprenticeship in the Seattle offices of John Ehrlichman, a long-time friend of Krogh's family; but he never had the opportunity to practice land-use law, as he had planned. In a few short months "Bud" Krogh followed Ehrlichman to Washington, where he was given the impressive-sounding title deputy counsel to the president, although in reality he was still Ehrlichman's personal assistant. Although Krogh had little experience in either government or politics (he had not even actively supported Nixon's quest for the presidency), Ehrlichman asked him to oversee the sensitive areas of federal law-enforcement and internal-security matters. Before he had even turned thirty, Krogh thus found himself willy-nilly presiding over an unprecedented presidential law-and-order campaign. It was all a learning period, and he readily acknowledged his naïveté to me in 1975, during a series of interviews.

He recalled:

> I had been given the District of Columbia liaison responsibility in February, 1969, and I remember in a meeting with the president he said, "All right, Bud, I'd like you to stop crime in the District of Columbia," and I said, "Yes," I would do that. So I called the mayor, Walter Washington, and asked him to stop crime, and he paused for a moment and said, "Okay," and that was about it.

As the first year of the Nixon administration progressed, Krogh soon found that "there wasn't much feel for the kinds of programs that would work in the area of law enforcement and crime control" and, like the president, he found to his dismay that the federal government lacked the wherewithal to diminish street crime in any substantial way. Now he quickly realized that his telephone order to Mayor Washington to "stop crime" revealed a picture of naïveté in the extreme. He also found as he became more aware of the machinery of government that most of the other remedies for crime available to the federal government were equally ineffectual. In his political education Krogh found that he "didn't have the luxury . . . to conclude that because the problem was so complex and seemingly intransigent nothing should be done." After discussing the problem with Ehrlichman, Krogh learned the prime requisite of "intelligent politics." Since "the president had campaigned on his desire to reduce crime nationally," Krogh found out that Nixon could not now state, "I've discovered that the federal government has little jurisdiction over street crime in the cities, towns, and counties; and therefore it is a matter for the states to handle. Good luck!" Krogh did what he could to reduce crime—he pressed for better streetlights in Washington, D.C., more police patrols, and other such measures, but they failed. Krogh was thus faced with his first crisis in the Nixon administration; as he explained it to me:

> During the period from January to December, 1969, the crime rate measured by the FBI reports indicated that crimes per day continued to climb dramatically . . . and during November hit an all-time high. . . . When the president learned the news, he became extremely upset and concerned. He called Mr. Ehrlichman and told him this must stop and that very immediate measures had to be undertaken to reduce the crime rate [in D.C.] by those in the District government, or else he would get a new team.

Ehrlichman immediately called a meeting of his new organ, the Domestic Council, at Camp David to redress the situation. It was the first—and, as it turned out, the only—full meeting of the Domestic Council. This new White House group, originally conceived of as a sort of domestic counterpart of the National Security Council, was quickly converted by Ehrlichman to a personal instrument of power. He assembled a staff of young men in their twenties and early thirties with little or no previous experience in government, such as Krogh, and had them reduce the flood of ideas and suggestions from competing sources to a series of option and decision papers on given issues. By carefully structuring the pros and cons of the various options, and assessing the political as well as substantive ramifications of possible decisions, Ehrlichman eventually established a direct channel of information to the president which became impervious to the qualifications and caveats of scholars, bureaucrats, and even cabinet officials who had previously contributed to policy. In this initial meeting, in December, 1969, however, Ehrlichman simply went around the table and asked various staff assistants what measures had been taken in the area of crime control. Some of the staff assistants pointed to the "scare legislation" that had been proposed by John Mitchell, and other bits of symbolic politics. Finally, Ehrlichman turned to Krogh and asked him what actions were pending that might affect the crime rate. Krogh answered with brutal candor, "None." The entire council fell silent. Then, with an air of desperation, Ehrlichman reiterated the president's orders: "The crime rate must somehow be brought down."

As soon as he returned to Washington, Krogh called Graham Watt, the deputy mayor of the District, and Police Chief Jerry Wilson, and ordered them to prepare immediately a report on what could be done in the District in terms of improving the police force and reducing crime, at least statistically. Even at that point, however, Krogh realized that though pouring resources into the District of Columbia on an emergency basis (and changing statistics-reporting methods) could bring about an appreciable improvement in at least the crime statistics in the capital, these measures could not be reasonably expected to ameliorate crime in the rest of the nation. Despite the presidential injunction, and the threat to deploy a new team, there was still no concept of what could be done to implement a national law-and-order program. By 1970 all the Domestic Council was able to suggest, in a crime-control memorandum, was the shifting of the "burden for responsibility in controlling crime to the state and local government which have jurisdiction over local law enforcement."

Such a strategy had the obvious advantage of providing a "solution" to the dilemma of rising street-crime statistics. Since there were ten times as many local police as federal police, and the local authorities had immediate jurisdiction over their local streets, they could more plausibly be assigned the responsibility for the success or failure of crime control. The rationale of devolving responsibility also fit neatly with the conservative view that the federal government had usurped legitimate functions of local governments (which presumably ought to be returned), and it could be supported by such other programs of the Nixon administration as revenue sharing and block grants to the states. If this strategy was adopted, the Law Enforcement Assistance Administration could be used as an instrument for aiding local police departments—and gaining credit for the Nixon administration. Elliot Richardson, then secretary of Health, Education and Welfare, advocated such an approach. For example, in the spring of 1971 his general counsel at HEW, Will Hastings, suggested in a draft that he drew up for a presidential message on narcotics addiction, "The federal role . . . must be one of leadership, of capacity building: By providing support . . . the federal government can assist state and local agencies in dealing with the problem. The local authorities must assume primary responsibility." The response of the White House strategists, however, was not favorable to this conservative strategy of devolving responsibility. An analysis of the HEW draft by the Domestic Council's staff asked critically, "Is the President ready politically to abdicate responsibility . . . by implicitly placing the burden on state and local government?" Ehrlichman answered that such an abdication would not be politically acceptable to the president. He explained to Krogh that although "most of the activities in the field are local . . . conceptually we should not stress that the federal government was shifting responsibility back to the states because the administration was clearly identified with handling the problem. . . . The President was out in front on the issue, and . . . as a matter of policy he should stay there." Krogh then realized, as he later told me, "To publicly disavow responsibility at the federal level and extend it to the states would have been perceived as a cop-out—and something that was directly inconsistent with what [the president] had campaigned on."

The suggestion of lawfully using the LEAA in the war against crime also presented a political problem. According to the legislative formulas then existing, the vast preponderance of LEAA funds had to be given in block grants to the states, which then allocated the money, without any. control from Washington, to local agencies. The Nixon administration thus would have little control over which police departments received funds—and for what purposes they were used— and most of the money could be expected to be filtered down to the cities controlled by the Democrats (if only because, at that time, most city governments were Democratic). In evaluating the uses of LEAA, Domestic Council analysts noted that "there was profound GOP opposition [to] the theory of block grants" and that, moreover, it "makes more difficult the coercing of the states into reordering their priorities to emphasize street crime." With the twin objectives of reducing street crime and "maintaining the image of a massive administration assault on crime," the Nixon strategists recommended a change in "LEAA formulas to remit more funds invested in high crime areas," and thus to focus publicity on administration efforts. The memorandum concluded pessimistically that expanded LEAA grants would tend to induce "a bad reaction from GOP," and give credit for "more highly visible deterrents at local levels" to local politicians.

In any case, the issue of shifting the burden was decisively settled by Nixon himself in May, 1971, after an earlier meeting among Ehrlichman, Richardson, Krogh, and others. According to Krogh's notes of that meeting:

> Secretary Richardson recommends that the thrust of new initiatives be experimental, thereby shifting the burden of responsibility to the states. Expectations are [thus] not raised that the federal government is undertaking a multi-year responsibility. Can the President afford politically to abdicate responsibility on this issue?

Ehrlichman then recommended to the president that "our posture not be worded in a tone which suggests, 'it's the problem of state and local government.'" President Nixon endorsed the option recommended by Ehrlichman, thereby ending any further consideration of the alternative of portraying the states as responsible in maintaining law and order.

Confronted with the seemingly impossible task of bringing about highly visible reductions in the reported muggings, burglaries, and robberies across the nation, and having found that all conventional levers of government could not easily be brought to bear on this problem, Krogh was compelled to seek out new and unorthodox tactics for prosecuting the war on crime. As Ehrlichman's emissary for the District of Columbia he had met Robert DuPont, a young and articulate psychiatrist who had been operating with missionary zeal a drug-treatment center in the District. Early in 1970, DuPont suggested to Krogh and his staff a "magic-bullet" scheme for quickly reducing crime statistics across the nation: since narcotics addicts committed much of the street crime in America in order to obtain money to pay for their drug habit, DuPont argued, the federal government could immediately reduce crime by breaking the dependence of addicts on illicit suppliers. The young psychiatrist impressed Krogh with "a statistical analysis which demonstrated that his client had reduced crime in the District" (even though it turned out, as a 1972 study by the National Commission on Marijuana and Drug Abuse found, that the correlation he presented was based on a statistical artifact). The proposition put forth by Captain Hobson in the 1920s—that crime was itself a disease caused by narcotics and cured by breaking the addictive habit—was thus rediscovered in 1970 by Krogh. G. Gordon Liddy, who was then developing law-enforcement programs for the Treasury Department, also impressed Krogh with the potential for a massive federal offensive against narcotics as a means of dealing with the law-and-order problem. Liddy dramatically described how Rockefeller had masterfully identified narcotics with the crime problem in New York State, and periodically stirred the popular imagination with his highly publicized crackdowns on addicts. He argued persuasively that the Nixon administration could achieve the same effect. Most important, the president himself had shown a keen interest in the possibilities of a war on drugs. Daniel Patrick Moynihan, concerned about the reports of heroin abuse in the ghettos, had persuaded the president that the State Department should do everything diplomatically possible to curtail opium production in foreign countries such as Turkey, and that the president should elevate the suppression of narcotics to an issue of national security policy. The State Department, however, concerned about diplomatic complications, did little to implement this presidential directive. Moynihan later recalled, in a telegram to Kissinger:

> In August 1969 I made a trip abroad with this matter primarily in mind
> ... in Paris I met with the American minister ... [and] told him of the
> Washington decision to make the international drug traffic a matter of

highest priority in foreign affairs, and this elicited ... genuine puzzlement. The minister knew almost nothing of the subject and certainly had no inkling that his government back home was concerned about it.

Krogh himself had some doubts about the immediate consequences of such a full-scale attack on narcotics production and distribution. He wrote in a memorandum to the Domestic Council on July 23, 1970, "If the supply of opiate and other addicting drugs is curtailed, the price of these drugs would likely rise, and the demand will continue, for the buyer is addicted; crime could go up in order to acquire more money for the more expensive drugs." In other words, if addicts were really stealing to pay for their habit, government efforts to reduce the supply of heroin could result in more, not less, crime. Krogh, however, was persuaded by his staff that the "crackdown" would drive most addicts into "treatment programs," where they would be effectively taken off the streets. He thus proposed a double-pronged attack on narcotics: while the State Department and National Security Council attempted to diminish the supply of heroin in the world available to the American market, and the Bureau of Narcotics and the Customs Bureau attempted to arrest as many of the smugglers and distributors of heroin as possible, the White House would also work to expand the treatment programs so that they could absorb a large number of addicts. Although John Ehrlichman also had doubts about the complexities involved in a war on drugs, especially since it was not an area that was yet researched by the White House, he was persuaded by Krogh that it was the only real alternative the White House had to reduce crime statistics by the 1972 election. The war on narcotics thus received White House sanction.

PART THREE

The Nixon
Crusades

★

Both sides of the bargain recognize ... the supply of sophisticated weaponry is allied usually with general trade and ideological and political links. At what point is the degree of dependence sufficient to affect the feasibility of the coup?

—EDWARD LUTTWAK, *Coup d'Etat*

7

Operation Intercept

Though there was little the Nixon administration could do to bring the law and order it promised to the streets of America, it soon found opportunities abroad to battle dramatically foreign drug smugglers. It will be recalled that Captain Hobson had already prepared the public for the theme of foreign devils contaminating Americans with drugs, and that enemy countries were traditionally identified as the major source of the narcotics traffic in the United States. Thus "Japanese militarists" were blamed as narcotics traffickers in World War II; Iranian nationalists were singled out in 1951 after they nationalized the oil concessions in Iran; revolutionary Cuba was cited as a supplier of American marijuana after Castro seized power in 1957; Communist China was accused of "a continuing twenty-year plan to spread addiction among free people"; the Soviet Union and its satellites were named in the New York *Times* at the height of the Cold War as major smugglers of heroin; and, in 1962, North Vietnam was added to the list of narcotics offenders by unnamed administration sources. The charges were based more on the needs for propaganda against hostile enemies than on firm evidence of narcotics traffic.

The Nixon administration, however, decided to extend the war on drugs to friendly nations, which made easier opponents. Thus Mexico was chosen as the first target in the new heroin crusade. Task Force One, which was created by President Nixon in 1969, attempted to combine the talents of the Bureau of Narcotics and Dangerous Drugs and the Customs Bureau for a joint operation against Mexican smugglers. The operation was under the dual command of Richard Kleindienst, the deputy attorney general, and Eugene Rossides, the assistant secretary of the treasury for enforcement and operations. Kleindienst, a former campaign director for Barry Goldwater, reluctantly agreed to the task force to demonstrate that law-enforcement agencies in rival departments could jointly solve a problem. Eugene Rossides, who himself had grand ideas of expanding the Treasury's role in the drug war, decided that the Treasury Department's customs bureau should take the lead in the offensive against Mexico. To this end, he appointed his assistant, G. Gordon Liddy, the imaginative man of action, to the task force as his personal aide. In the summer of 1969, under Liddy's guidance, Task Force One issued a report submitting that the highest priority should be "an eradication of the production and refinement in Mexico of opium poppies and marijuana. . . ." Not only was Mexico deemed to be a source of heroin entering the United States, but marijuana was asserted to be the critical "stepping stone" to one's becoming a heroin addict. The task force asserted that "85% of heroin addicts . . . started their use of drugs with marijuana" (no evidence was provided for this assertion, however).

The plan for direct action, known as Operation Intercept, was devised by Liddy and others on the working group drawn from the Treasury Department and the Department of Justice. It called for pressures to persuade the Mexican government actively to suppress the opium and marijuana traffic. (In the early planning stages it was even hoped that private American foundations might finance chemical defoliants to destroy the marijuana and opium crops, if the Mexican government would agree to use them.) Accordingly, the first pressure came on September 8, 1969. The Eleventh Naval District declared the city of Tijuana, Mexico, off limits to military personnel. A news story provided by the task force to the press suggested this would bring economic disaster to all the bars, brothels, and other border businesses dependent on the American military. Egil Krogh, who was sitting in on the task force as the White House representative, later recalled that after "it was leaked to the military . . . that we were planning to shut down the border . . . a number of U.S. sailors

[were] beaten up in Tijuana [by outraged Mexicans] a week before the President was to meet President Díaz [of Mexico] at Friendship Dam." Of course, this distressed the State Department, but Operation Intercept continued to unfold.

In September, 1969, two thousand customs and border-patrol agents were deployed along the Mexican border for what was officially described as "the country's largest peacetime search and seizure operation by civil authorities." Automobiles and trucks crossing the border were delayed up to six hours in hundred-degree temperatures; tourists appearing suspicious or recalcitrant were stripped and bodily searched. Although more than five million citizens of the United States and Mexico passed through this dragnet during the three-week operation, virtually no heroin or narcotics were intercepted from the tourists. But as Kleindienst pointed out to reporters, the ultimate objective of Operation Intercept was not to seize narcotics but to pressure Mexico to control it at the source by eradicating the production of marijuana and opium poppies in Mexico. Privately, Kleindienst explained to the president and concerned officials of the Department of State that the real purpose was to make the Mexican government more cooperative.

However, such crude and overt pressures caused a furor of indignation in Mexico. Mexican officials protested that Operation Intercept was undermining the Good Neighbor Policy in Latin America, and that the Mexican government would not submit to such harassment on its borders. Though the State Department looked at Operation Intercept as dangerously undercutting our diplomatic efforts in all of Latin America, and Henry Kissinger's National Security Council became concerned that the continuing search-and-seizure operation on the Mexican border might interfere with hemisphere defense arrangements, White House officials, according to Krogh, were impressed with the wealth of publicity that the administration's effort was receiving in the nation's press. The Justice Department's BNDD thus continued to brief reporters on the tools and techniques that would be later activated, including a remote sensor device capable of detecting the presence of marijuana and opium poppies from planes flying over fields in inaccessible mountainous regions. The device was to be further perfected by the National Aeronautics and Space Administration under an agreement with the Mexican government. The Associated Press was supplied with aerial photographs of tens of thousands of cars backed up in

Mexico and customs inspectors searching cars at border crossings. The Customs Bureau briefed the press on the operations of its patrol planes and ships as if it were a wartime operation, and periodic announcements were made of the seizures of marijuana. The Associated Press reported, "Pleasure boats, fishing vessels, cargo ships and ocean liners are being searched." By the end of September, however, the State Department's press office counterattacked by briefing reporters on the damage that Operation Intercept was wreaking on United States–Mexican relations. Incidents were described, as later reported in the New York *Times,* where "delays as long as six hours have kept outraged motorists waiting in line in the broiling sun . . . some travelers have been obliged to strip naked . . . thousands of Mexican workers have lost their jobs in the United States because of the customs inspection delay . . . millions of innocent people have been harassed. Border cities are facing economic collapse and tempers are wearing thin. . . ." President Díaz was even quoted as saying that Operation Intercept had created "a wall of suspicion" between Mexico and America. By mid-October the State Department had won that battle of the leaks, and the White House recognized that Operation Intercept was now generating negative publicity, according to Krogh. The task force thus was quietly withdrawn from the Mexican border, and, in return for $1 million in aid for the purchase of light aircraft, the president of Mexico agreed to sign some protocols which changed Operation Intercept in name to Operation Cooperation, which was then totally abandoned without further fanfare.

Although Egil Krogh later noted in a White House memorandum (July 23, 1970) that "Operation Intercept . . . received widespread media coverage," he did acknowledge to Ehrlichman that it had had no effect on the drug traffic. Others in the White House doubted the public-relations value of the Mexican adventure. To demonstrate the danger of such undertakings, Daniel Patrick Moynihan cited New York *Times* stories that suggested that Operation Intercept, by temporarily interrupting the marijuana traffic, had caused children to switch to heroin. Though there was little reason to believe that children would addict themselves to heroin because marijuana was temporarily more expensive, Moynihan used these stories to temper White House enthusiasm for such foreign adventures. Nevertheless, the inner circle at the White House continued to recommend the more highly dramatized crackdowns with code names like Operation Intercept. A 1970 crime-control memorandum circulated by the

Domestic Council noted that the "feasibility of mounting major operations with code names against heroin trafficking [would] create an aura of massive attack on our most feared narcotic." The memorandum recommended launching an election-year Operation Heroin modeled after Intercept. Moynihan, still worried about more Operation Intercept fiascoes, proceeded to persuade President Nixon that heroin control should be elevated to the status of a national-security problem. The president agreed and created the Ad Hoc Cabinet Committee on Narcotics, which was to be chaired by Henry Kissinger, then his national security advisor.

The ad hoc committee included the more illustrious figures of the early Nixon administration: Pat Moynihan; John Mitchell and his deputy, Kleindienst, who held that all law-enforcement matters should be the business of the Justice Department (which would include IRS as well as narcotics operations); the ambitious Eugene Rossides; John Ingersoll, the Democratic-appointed director of the BNDD; Richard Helms, the independent-minded director of the CIA; and Elliot Richardson, the undersecretary of state. Myles Ambrose was not a member, but he attended a couple of the meetings as an observer. Kissinger, who evidenced little interest in the heroin problem, rarely attended the committee meetings, which were then chaired by his deputy, General Alexander Haig. (On one typical occasion Kissinger arrived an hour late, joked about his having to translate the Vietnam peace negotiations from German to English for the president, then promptly left.) Though Moynihan at times sparred with Mitchell, most of these officials, though impressive in their own spheres of action, had little special knowledge about heroin and therefore had to rely on working groups to establish facts—all of which added to the confusion.

Kissinger, Richardson, and Haig spent most of their efforts dampening the enthusiasm of White House zealots to launch a new heroin crusade which might again threaten diplomatic relations with important allies. Meanwhile, the White House, usually through John Mitchell, made it known to the ad hoc committee that it wanted another dramatic effort. The crusaders thus sought another country in which to crusade.

8

The War of the Poppies

In 1970, more than five centuries after the Christian knights had abandoned their ill-fated crusade against the Turks, the Nixon administration moved to renew the ancient hostilities. Unable to uproot the marijuana plant from Mexico, the Ad Hoc Committee on Narcotics next turned its attention to the Turkish connection. To be sure, Turkey was by no means the sole, or even the largest, producer of opium. The opium poppy *(Papaver somniferum)* had been cultivated for centuries in virtually every country between Yugoslavia and Japan. And according to CIA estimates compiled for the ad hoc committee, India, Afghanistan, Pakistan, Thailand, Laos, and Burma all produced substantially more illicit opium than did Turkey. Moreover, after a thirteen-year prohibition, the Shah of Iran had decided in 1969 to plant 20,000 hectares with poppies, which was a 50-percent-greater area than Turkey had in cultivation. In all, the CIA estimated, Turkey produced only from 3 to 8 percent of the illicit opium available throughout the world. Nevertheless, Turkey was chosen as the most feasible target by the committee for several reasons. For one, Turkey was assumed to be the most convenient and proximate source for the European heroin wholesalers in the various scenarios, or "systems," worked out by the Bureau of Narcotics and

Dangerous Drugs. The putative distribution routes—from Afyon to Beirut to Marseilles to Montreal to New York, etc.—were neatly marked out on the bureau's maps, as if they were readily available tourist itineraries. (For the most part these maps reflected locations where the BNDD already had agents, and did not necessarily include all the smuggling routes.) According to these scenarios, all opium routes led to the Turkish province of Afyon, and alternative routes in Southeast Asia, which were not on the bureau's maps, were deemed of less importance. Second, and more important, Turkey was a NATO ally, dependent on United States military aid, and it could therefore be expected to be more vulnerable to American pressure than "neutral" countries such as Burma and India. Although India was still the world's largest producer of opium—both licit and illicit—the ad hoc committee considered it unlikely that it would bow to American diplomatic or military pressure. Indeed, Elliot Richardson warned that it might respond by denouncing United States "imperialism." (It was therefore necessary to promote in the press the myth that India's opium was tightly controlled by the government, even though the committee's analysis showed enormous leakage of Indian opium into illicit markets.) In the case of Burma (as well as of Afghanistan and Laos), it was recognized that the central government had virtually no control over the tribes growing and smuggling poppies, and that any American pressure—or incentives given to the central government— would be at best unproductive. Iran presented another problem: given the realities of oil politics, it was considered impolitic (and futile) to attempt to restrain the Shah from replanting the poppy in his country. This left Turkey. As one member of the committee put it, "Turkey was the only country where we could expect dramatic results, and that was what the president wanted."

The opium poppy had grown on the rich, shaly plains of Afyon for a millennium or so before the Ad Hoc Committee on Narcotics considered the problem, and it had become an integral part of peasant life in that province of Turkey. The poppy seed provided the oil for cooking, the protein-rich husks of the poppy plant provided nourishment for livestock, the leaves were used in salads, the stalks were burned as heating fuel in the cold Anatolian winters, and the gummy juice of the unripened capsule served as a remedy for most ailments and as a pain-deadener. This substance, which became known as "afyon" in Turkey and as "opium" in the rest of the world, could also be bartered or sold to passing caravans. Although in the twentieth century Turkish farmers were required by law to sell their entire opium harvest to the government at a fixed price for resale to pharmaceutical manufacturers all over the world (who used it to manufacture morphine and codeine), many farmers clandestinely siphoned off part of their harvest and sold it at higher prices to black marketeers. William Handley, the American ambassador to Turkey, warned the ad hoc committee that since the suppression of opium in Turkey could deprive tens of thousands of Anatolian farmers of their livelihood, it would prove difficult to persuade the Turkish government that opium should be banned in Turkey while India and other countries expanded their production.

Five thousand miles away, in Washington, however, the Nixon administration decided to escalate the pressures on Turkey to conform to American domestic policy. Initially, in early 1970, it was proposed only that the United States make "preemptive buys" of opium in Turkey and use it to build up the United States government stockpiles of codeine and morphine. State Department representatives on the committee argued that if the licit price for opium were raised, Turkish peasants would be better able to resist the temptation of selling part of their harvest to illicit traffickers. However, Eugene Rossides, who had taken an active part in Operation Intercept, was a Greek-Cypriot American with little sympathy for the Turks, and he vehemently objected to any plan which would subsidize the Turkish opium farmers. He reasoned that higher prices for licit opium would simply encourage more farmers to plant poppies, and therefore more opium would be produced for both licit and illicit markets. "We are at war," Rossides said metaphorically. "If the Turks refuse to go along with us in this crusade against heroin, we have to consider them enemies rather than allies." At this and subsequent meetings of the ad hoc committee, the rhetoric became more and more that of the first crusade against the infidel Turks. Myles Ambrose subsequently recalled that "they seemed to be totally divorced from the reality of the situation, and I felt like Alice at the Mad Hatter's tea party." What was the "reality"? Ambrose continued perceptively, "The basic fact that eluded these great geniuses was that it takes only ten square miles of poppy to feed the entire American heroin market, and they grow everywhere." At one point it was even suggested that Turkey be purged from NATO. Whatever suggestions were made at the committee, however, Krogh insisted that President Nixon realized the strategic importance of Turkey, and would not have allowed NATO to disintegrate over the opium question. Krogh explained, "Nixon was a poker player, and didn't expect the Turks to call our bluff."

Thus, in the spring of 1970, the Ad Hoc Committee on Narcotics decided to make an all-out effort to discourage Turkish production of opium. Through congressional testimony and news releases, Turkey was accused of supplying "up to 80 percent of the heroin smuggled into the United States." Even though the 80-percent estimate quickly became established as a journalistic "fact," it was predicated on a set of very open-ended assumptions. It was assumed, first of all, that about one quarter of Turkish opium was diverted to the illicit market (an estimate largely based on the difference between the expected and the actual yield per acre in 1968), and, second, it was assumed that almost all of this diverted opium was converted into heroin for the United States market. This in turn was based on the third assumption that there was no domestic consumption of opium in Turkey nor any demand for it in countries other than the United States. These assumptions were all extremely problematic. Despite the elaborately articulated systems and colorful maps that the Bureau of Narcotics used in its relations with Congress and the press, it had at the time no reliable means of identifying the source of American heroin. George Belk, the program manager of the bureau's international division, acknowledged in 1972 that scientifically "there is no way known of chemically tracing heroin seized in the United States back to the country, no less area, of its origin." It is all done, the bureau's director explained, "by deductive reasoning." In reality, John Ingersoll explained candidly, "We know that substantial opium goes from Turkey to the wholesalers in Europe, but we don't know what percentage of this ever reaches America."

When in late 1970 Ambassador William Handley attempted to convince Turkish officials that they were responsible for most, if not four fifths, of American heroin, they sharply disputed the underlying assumptions. Turkey had formed, with American financing, a special narcotics field unit of its police force in 1968, modeled after the American agency, and it claimed that only a small fraction of the opium grown seeped into the illicit market, and that this was mainly diverted east, to Iran. Though sympathetic to their ally's heroin problem, Turkish officials insisted that it was politically impossible for them to curtail production at the cost of jeopardizing the livelihood of a large number of Anatolian peasants. The Turkish populace would hardly perceive a heroin problem in America as germane to them.

"The problem was further complicated by the fact that Turkey was a somewhat shaky parliamentary democracy," Osman Olcay, the foreign minister at the time, explained to me. "Even those in the government and military most sympathetic to the American position realized that no government that threatened a half million Turkish farmers with starvation could remain in power for a day." Not only was the American plan to eradicate the Turkish poppy unpopular with the conservative elements in Parliament, who drew their support from the peasants, but the left-wing parties openly attacked it as American imperialism and interference. Even many moderate Turks argued that the United States was employing a double standard by demanding that Turkey alone suppress its poppy crop while India, Iran, and other countries continued to grow poppy. In light of this political situation in 1970, the best the Turks were willing to offer was to intensify the policing of their fields and borders, and gradually to substitute other crops for poppies.

The White House, however, was not satisfied with Ambassador Handley's efforts to persuade the Turks, and the ad hoc committee ordered more pressures to be selectively applied against their new adversary. The president's emissaries to NATO maneuvered the alliance into converting its new adjunct, the Committee for Challenges to Modern Societies, into another American antiheroin agency. Since none of our Western European allies had much of a heroin problem, this new arm of NATO was used mainly to harangue the lone Turkish delegate on the committee.

Congress was also recruited into the new crusade against the Turks. Eugene Rossides, believing that Kissinger "was dragging his feet" because he was unwilling to jeopardize the alliance, pressed black congressmen concerned about heroin addiction in their districts to cut off military aid to Turkey. This "hyping-up" of congressmen greatly concerned some members of the National Security Council, since the military aid was being extended to Turkey in return for the use of air bases and radar installations that monitored and tracked Soviet missiles. Rossides's assistant, G. Gordon Liddy, who had moved from Operation Intercept to the working committee to curtail Turkish opium supplies, suggested to Ambassador Handley that the cadavers of heroin addicts who had died of overdoses be sent in body bags to Turkish diplomats. At the time, Handley did not take the suggestion seriously.

As the election drew nearer, the White House strategists made

Handley and other American diplomats uncomfortably aware of the administration's determination to achieve quickly some dramatic breakthrough on the opium front. Indeed, Handley was rudely summoned back to Washington from Ankara. Minutes after his arrival at the White House, a presidential assistant told him, in front of Arthur Downey, a staff member of the National Security Council, "To show you how seriously I view the matter ... I intend to recommend to the president that unless we have an agreement, he should order the Sixth Fleet through the Dardanelles and shell Istanbul. They are committing naked aggression, why shouldn't we respond?" Handley, still not recovered from the seventeen-hour flight, left the room somewhat dazed. Downey, who was present at this meeting in the White House, later explained to me that the president's aide was merely trying to "build a fire under Handley" and the military threat was meant only metaphorically. At another point during this brief visit, Handley was called aside by Liddy, who said in his deadly quiet voice, "Mr. Ambassador, how many bodies have you picked off the streets of New York?" Again Handley fell speechless, while Liddy continued, "I have personally loaded overdosed victims into ambulances, and the Turks are responsible. Tell them that!" Still later, as Handley prepared to return to Ankara, President Nixon personally handed him a press clipping reporting growing concern over "heroin-related deaths" (a broad and somewhat deceptive category which included virtually all deaths of narcotic users, even if they died of old age or were hit by an automobile). The president told him to present the clipping to the Turkish prime minister immediately upon his arrival. When he returned to Ankara, Handley heard from his chief of mission that members of the ad hoc committee were demanding that the State Department fire any "ambassadors who failed to achieve the president's objectives in the drug program."

Fortunately, for Handley at least, the Turkish military forces overthrew the elected government of Turkey in 1971, and installed a government which was less willing to jeopardize American military aid and goodwill over the poppy issue. The new premier, Nihat Erim, told Handley that he was willing to suspend poppy cultivation temporarily before the American election if the United States would agree to compensate the farmers for the lost income and assist them in finding alternative crops and livelihoods. Handley continued negotiating with the Turkish military government through the spring of 1971 and, in June, finally achieved a tentative agreement. With the first victory in sight in his new crusade, President Nixon approved the idea of providing $100 million in aid over three years to Turkish farmers. When Rossides heard of the impending deal, he bitterly opposed "paying a dime" to Turkish peasants, but the president, not willing to allow this major coup to slip from his grasp, immediately authorized Handley to accept the Turkish terms, and invited Premier Erim to America for a joint announcement by the end of the month. (In a last-ditch battle Rossides managed to reduce the amount of aid to $35 million, which was finally approved by the Treasury Department.) Although in fact this victory would cut off only a small fraction of the opium growth in the world—less than 8 percent—and even this amount would quickly be replaced by opium from Southeast Asia, India, and other sources, White House strategists realized that if the announcement were properly managed in the press, it would be heralded as a decisive victory against the forces of crime and addiction.

9

The French Connection

When Arthur Watson, the former chairman of IBM World Trade Corporation, became ambassador to France, in May, 1970, President Nixon told him, "Your job is to clean up the heroin problem in France. . . . That is the most important priority today." Thus Watson left for Paris, taking along a copy of the book *The French Connection.* He was accompanied by Thomas P. Murphy, a former writer for *Fortune* and general aide-de-camp to Watson, who was to serve as drug coordinator for the embassy in France. On his arrival in Paris, Watson quickly discovered that the French were wholly indifferent to heroin addiction, which they considered "the American disease." Although American intelligence estimated that the vast preponderance of heroin reaching the United States passed through Marseilles, where "labs" converted morphine base into heroin, the Police Judiciaire drug force, which was charged with policing all illicit drugs in France, had only thirty-two members, who were doing mainly administrative work. Watson believed that in order for any real action to be taken by French officials, heroin would have to be hyped into a French problem. Stories were therefore ingeniously planted in French newspapers about French heroin addicts. (Watson himself went on walking tours through the place de la République and suspicious bars on the boulevard Saint-Michel, looking for addicts.) The United States Information Service, at Watson's request, had a gory American drug-addiction film adapted to a French version and put on French television. The embassy even imported a priest from New York to lecture on drug abuse. "The public-relations hype really worked," Murphy later told me. "Heroin went in French polls from being a nonexistent problem to being the number-one problem perceived by the French public."

Although the press campaign led to a doubling of the drug force in France and more cooperation from French officials, Washington was demanding more concrete results. Ambassador Watson received telegram after telegram from the State Department and the White House asking when a "major lab in Marseilles would be seized." Watson gradually learned that the highly prized labs were in reality "no more than dirty kitchens" where trays of morphine base were cooked with acetic anhydride until heroin precipitated out. Virtually any house in France, or in the world, with running water could have a lab. Bureau of Narcotics agents in France were also doubtful of the value of seizing labs, since the operation could be moved to another kitchen in a matter of days. Nevertheless, President Nixon wanted labs seized, congressmen and American journalists persistently asked to be taken on tours of the seized labs, and Watson was determined, with or without the French police, to seize as many "dirty kitchens" as he could.

A strong believer in the magic of technology, the ambassador ordered the science attaché at the embassy, Dr. Edgar Piret, to devote his full time and resources to the problem of detecting labs. Almost every week, the ambassador, piloting his own propjet plane, would fly Dr. Piret to Marseilles, where they would lunch with French police in a restaurant at the harbor (shown, coincidentally, in the opening sequence of the film of *The French Connection)* and discuss the modus operandi of the mysterious labs. Finally Dr. Piret came up with the idea for "sniffing out" the acetic anhydrides used in manufacturing heroin. A California firm, Varian Associates, which had developed a technique in Vietnam for chemically detecting the presence of drugs in urine, was given the contract for the "heroin sniffer," while Dr. Piret worked out the anticipated wind plumes and frequency of the fumes. Then, in 1971, the sniffer, concealed in a brand-new Volkswagen camper with a snorkel mounted on its roof, rolled into Marseilles. An American agent drove this not entirely inconspicuous sniffer through the streets, while another agent inside charted all the beep signals on a street map. Unfortunately, the signals given out by the acetic acid being sought were indistinguishable from the odor frequency of salad dressing, and when the map was analyzed, Watson found that they had inadvertently detected all the restaurants and salad-dressing concentrations in Marseilles—but no labs. To the great amusement of the French officials, the sniffer departed, and Dr. Piret was sent back to the drawing board.

Dr. Piret's next foray was into the sewers of Marseilles. Since the excess water used in the production of heroin eventually finds its way into the sewage system and contains telltale traces of the materials used in the process, Dr. Piret reasoned that a system of scientifically sampling the sewage might identify the elusive labs. "It was like *Les Miserables;* they had men wading in the sewers looking for clues," Paul Knight, a high-ranking Bureau of Narcotics official recalled. Since no budget was provided to the embassy for such underground projects, Watson, willing to try anything in his quest for the labs, obtained financing from "secret and unorthodox channels," which were presumed by some former narcotics officials to mean the CIA. Though monitoring the sewers failed to pinpoint the labs (because of a plethora of effluents and a certain difficulty in keeping agents in the sewers undetected), it helped convince French officials of American determination to seize labs. With the help of informers who seemed to materialize magically, the French raided a half dozen lab-kitchens in short order—thus satisfying Washington, or at least touring congressmen.

Thomas Murphy explained:

We knew we were dealing with a chain of finite length stretching from Afyon to Harlem; we first thought we could sever the link between Afyon and Marseilles by suppressing the poppy, but that proved hopeless, as there was an infinite amount of opium available elsewhere or in the pipeline. We next thought we could sever the link in Marseilles by closing the labs, but we found that the labs were portable. Then we realized that the real weak link was the couriers in the smuggling rings.

By resorting to more or less standard police procedures and recruiting informers in those rings, "the Paris task force was able to hamstring, though not eliminate, the heroin traffickers in France."

10

The Panama Canal

They track their quarry to the mountains of Mexico, the jungles of Southeast Asia and the arid dunes of the Middle East. They negotiate at the highest levels with foreign governments.

—National Observer, *December 18, 1971, describing the putative activities of agents of the Bureau of Narcotics and Dangerous Drugs.*

In Washington the White House strategists made it manifestly clear to John Ingersoll that the Bureau of Narcotics and Dangerous Drugs was expected to arrest and bring to trial at least one major international trafficker, to give the entire foreign crusade credibility. Up to this point, Ingersoll's agents had not netted any such international trafficker because, as Ingersoll explained to Attorney General Mitchell, "Major traffickers do not usually violate the laws of the country that they reside in, and even if they do, they are usually protected there by local officials whom they pay off." According to the bureau's deputy director, John Finlator, the attempt of two American narcotics agents to "snatch" a major heroin supplier in Mexico had resulted in the agents' fatally shooting five Mexican traffickers with M-1 carbines; but since the agents had no authority to be in Mexico, the shoot-out had to be hushed up (and Mexican police were given credit for killing the bandits). To achieve the visible success that the White House strategists desired, Ingersoll realized that a foreign trafficker would have to be legally lured to American soil.

The opportunity presented itself in December, 1970, when two United States narcotics agents, posing as members of the Mafia, made a "connection" in Panama with Joaquim Him Gonzales, who was then chief of air traffic control and deputy inspector general of civil aviation in Panama. The forty-two-year-old Panamanian had also been identified by the BNDD as "the man everybody had to know in Panama" to transship narcotics through Panama's Tecumen International Airport. The undercover agents thus arranged to have Gonzales witness an arrangement they made with a Texas pilot to obtain one hundred kilos of cocaine for them. Although they never received their cocaine, they flew back to Dallas, Texas, where they presented their evidence of a "conspiracy" to a federal grand jury, which promptly indicted Him Gonzales as a member of the conspiracy. Although Ingersoll initially hoped that the indictment of a major trafficker would suffice, the White House made it clear that they still wanted the traffickers arrested and tried in the United States, with all the attendant publicity that it would create. Panama, however, did not have a conspiracy law, and was unwilling to extradite the chief of air traffic control to the United States for trial. A few enterprising officials of the Bureau of Narcotics and Dangerous Drugs thus carefully arranged a trap for the Panamanian official. Since Him Gonzales frequently played in a softball game between Panamanian aviation employees and American officials stationed in the Canal Zone, a narrow strip of land along the Panama Canal which is administered by the United States government and policed by a United States Army military garrison, the agents arranged to arrest him during one of the softball games. Thus, when Him Gonzales arrived at the softball field on February 6, 1971, a narcotics agent pointed a gun at him and announced, "You are on United States territory and we are putting you under arrest on a charge of conspiring to smuggle narcotics."

The American ambassador to Panama, Robert Sayre, was not told of the plan to arrest a high Panamanian official in the Canal Zone. At the time, he was in the midst of delicate negotiations for renewing the United States lease on the Panama Canal, and one of the main issues to be resolved was the question of sovereignty over the Canal Zone. When the Panamanians read in their newspapers that their air traffic controller had been arrested by American narcotics agents in the Canal Zone, they exploded, Ambassador Sayre later recalled. The Panamanian negotiators demanded that Him Gonzales be released and that American police control in the Canal Zone be limited and put under the supervision of Panamanians. Suddenly the whole Panama Canal treaty was beclouded by the act of narcotics agents trying to deliver to the White House an international trafficker. The State Department advised the White House of the new crisis in Panama, but the BNDD refused to release the alleged conspirator. Meanwhile, the narcotics agents placed Him Gonzales on a Super Star jet Air Force plane and delivered the bewildered Panamanian to U.S. marshals in Dallas. Newspapers in Panama reacted by charging that the United States had kidnapped an official of their government. Panama's foreign minister protested to Ambassador Sayre not only that the arrest was illegal but that United States undercover agents had come to Panama with false identification papers in order to entrap a Panamanian official. Letters from Attorney General Mitchell and an "embassy" from the director of the Bureau of Narcotics and Dangerous Drugs failed to mitigate the anti-American campaign generated by this incident. Ambassador Sayre said he found that it became difficult "to renegotiate ... the Panama Canal in this atmosphere." With the government-controlled press of Panama featuring stories about how Joaquim Him Gonzales's ten-year-old daughter was waiting for America to return her kidnapped father, it became difficult for Panamanian politicians to agree to a new treaty which granted the United States de facto sovereignty over the Canal Zone. Unable to complete the renegotiations of the treaty, the dispute dragging on, Ambassador Sayre returned to Washington in 1973 to become inspector general of the State Department. (Gonzales was sentenced in Texas to five years in prison.)

In less than two years the Nixon crusades managed to interfere seriously with the objectives of American foreign policy. In Mexico the Good Neighbor Policy was confused by Operation Intercept. In Turkey the NATO arrangements to defend the eastern Mediterranean area were undercut by our demands that the Turks suppress poppy-flower cultivation. In France the American embassy was embarrassed by the attempts to find local heroin laboratories. And in Panama the vital Panama Canal was nearly lost by the pirating away of one alleged international trafficker.

PART FOUR

The War Within ★

. . . in sophisticated political units, power is diffuse and therefore difficult to seize in a coup.

—EDWARD LUTTWAK, *Coup d'Etat*

11

The Narcotics Business:
John Ingersoll's Version

In July, 1970, John Ehrlichman approved a memorandum by Krogh's staff that suggested "mounting [a] major operation with [a] code name against heroin traffickers . . . to create [an] aura of massive attack on [the] most-feared narcotic." Krogh specifically suggested the code name Operation Heroin for the domestic crusade. Such an operation required, however, the cooperation (and manpower) of established investigative agencies in the federal government, especially the Bureau of Narcotics and Dangerous Drugs in the Justice Department and the Bureau of Customs in the Treasury Department. This presented a bureaucratic problem, however, since both agencies considered themselves to be semi-independent entities and both attempted to define the narcotics business in terms that extended the domain of their agency.

When the Nixon administration assumed office, the effort to control narcotics comprised only a minute part of the police activities of the federal government. Although the government first became involved in narcotics control in 1914, when Congress enacted the Harrison Narcotics Act, the federal enforcement efforts tended to be more symbolic than substantial for at least a half century. Since the Harrison Act was theoretically a revenue law, which required all traffickers in opium, cocaine, and their derivatives to register with the government and pay an excise tax on their total sales, the responsibility for enforcing the law was originally assigned to the Treasury Department. Initially, the handful of agents in the Narcotics Division, headed by Colonel Levi G. Nutt, focused their attention on doctors and pharmacists who were dispensing opiates. (Between 1914 and 1938, some 25,000 doctors were arrested for supplying opiates, and some 40 heroin-maintenance clinics were closed.) Most criminal narcotics traffickers were left to the resources of the local police. In 1930, however, in what was to become a recurring theme in federal narcotics enforcement, a grand jury found that the federal narcotics agents in New York City had falsified their records to take credit for arrests made by the New York City Police Department, and that some of the agents were themselves involved with narcotics traffickers. In the midst of the scandal Colonel Nutt resigned, and the Narcotics Division was reorganized into the semi-independent Bureau of Narcotics. In August, 1930, President Hoover appointed Harry Jacob Anslinger, a career diplomat, as the director of the new bureau. For the next three decades Anslinger was content to wage only a rhetorical campaign, periodically citing lurid examples of the crimes of "dope fiends" to arouse public concern over narcotics and marijuana. Little effort was made to expand the size of the bureau or its law-enforcement activities. Indeed, until 1968, the Bureau of Narcotics never had more than 330 agents (most of whom were used in an administrative capacity), or, for that matter, an annual budget of more than $3 million.

The ascendancy of the narcotics agency within the federal government really began only in the final months of the Johnson administration, when it was decided to move the Bureau of Narcotics from the Treasury to the Justice Department. As part of this belated reorganization the fledgling Bureau of Drug Abuse Control, which had been created only three years earlier in the Food and Drug Administration to regulate amphetamine and hallucinogenic drugs, was merged into the Bureau of Narcotics and Dangerous Drugs, or BNDD, in the alphabet-soup world of Washington acronyms. The Johnson administration justified Reorganization Plan Number One, as the transfer was officially called, in terms of efficiency: by consolidating the drug police into a single agency within the Justice Department, investigators and prosecuting attorneys would be able to coordinate their work more expeditiously. Since this same reorganization plan had been resisted earlier by President Johnson (when Robert Kennedy was attorney general), and was now being rushed through in an election year, Eugene Rossides and other officials in the Treasury Department believed that the move was politically motivated. "Drugs have always been a political football," Rossides commented. "Johnson's main reason for moving the Bureau [of Narcotics] from Treasury was to strengthen the crime-busting image of Ramsey Clark."

As it turned out, there was little political profit for Johnson to gain from this move. Ramsey Clark selected John M. Ingersoll, a thirty-nine-year-old law-enforcement officer who had helped him plan the crime-control legislation, as the director of the new agency, and asked him for a realistic appraisal of its potential for enforcing the laws. Ingersoll found that the old Bureau of Narcotics, despite a flamboyant public image (which derived in large part from television series such as *T-Men),* lacked the intelligence-gathering means and techniques for disrupting the major channels of heroin distribution in the United States. At most, its few agents could at times make sensational arrests, which might satisfy the press and politicians but would have little effect on the narcotics business that Ingersoll had a professional interest in curtailing. The other part of the consolidation, the Bureau of Drug Abuse Control, had even fewer trained agents, almost no informers, and little experience outside of tracking down pharmaceutical products. As impressive as the reorganization might have looked on paper, it was of little use in launching the sort of national campaign against drugs required by the election-year White House.

Far more serious, however, as Ingersoll and Clark learned to their dismay, agents of the old bureau were heavily involved in a major drug scandal which was being investigated by a special group of Internal Revenue Service agents. Ingersoll immediately assigned nine special inspectors to the case. As the evidence unfolded, in 1968, it became clear to him that a number of federal agents in the New York office were in the business of selling heroin or protecting drug dealers, and that the bureau itself had been the major source of supply and protection of heroin in the United States. Under interrogation, many of the agents openly admitted to being "owned" by dealers. All of this was set forth in the Wurms Report, which was never released by the government. In December, 1968, Ramsey Clark disclosed that various agents were indicted for their part in this illicit activity (most of them were subsequently convicted). Eventually, almost every agent in the New York bureau was fired, forced to resign, or transferred.

In examining more closely the roots of the corruption, Ingersoll found that the nefarious working relationship between narcotics agents and traffickers was deeply ingrained in the system used by the Bureau of Narcotics to assure a constant number of arrests every year (which was the agency's main index of performance). In this system every agent had a quota of arrests he was supposed to make, and his promotion and tenure depended on his fulfilling this quota. Agents, however, could not fulfill their arrest quotas with any degree of certainty without the active collusion of persons who were in the narcotics business. Such illicit help was necessary because the sale of narcotics is a crime for which there is no complainant to alert police: both the buyer and seller are willing participants in the transaction. Nor are federal agents likely to be in a position to observe such transactions: most heroin users buy their supply from a relative, friend, or fellow addict they have known for several years in extremely private circumstances. (The pusher who lurks vampirelike in schoolyards and other places, and approaches strangers with his wares, is largely a television myth.) And the possibility of searching suspects for heroin at random is limited by court rulings which require a search warrant.

Under these circumstances federal agents found that they could fill their monthly arrest quotas only with the collusion of an informer, who could arrange to have street addicts attempt to sell them heroin. The informers in the best position to make such an arrangement with a narcotics agent were traffickers in the heroin business who, in turn, needed the agents' protection. Like the Athenians who sent a sacrifice of a set number of youths to the Cretan Minotaur each year, heroin dealers supplied the quota of arrestees for federal agents, and, eventually, went into business with the agents.

State and local narcotics agents were similarly dependent on the informer. For example, the chief narcotics officer in Baltimore claimed in a conference on narcotics informants, sponsored by the Drug Abuse Council in 1975, that there were 800 active *criminal* narcotics informers working with the police in Baltimore, and most of these informers were in fact dealers who had a de facto franchise from the police department which they preserved by turning in "competitors" not on the police payrolls. If this was the case in other large cities, as most of the narcotics officers at the conference suggested, then many, if not most, of the established narcotics distributors were probably in the employ of local police departments.

Since street arrests would always be difficult—if not impossible—without informers, Ingersoll reluctantly came to the conclusion that the quota system would almost ineluctably tend to corrupt agents in the field. After studying the problem, Ingersoll was determined not only to replace all the agents who had become entangled with their informers but also to do away with the informer system itself.

When the Nixon administration came into office, Ingersoll therefore presented the problem to the new attorney general, John N. Mitchell, and proposed that the bureau abandon the policy of arresting street addicts and dealers (which necessitated using informers) and instead concentrate its efforts on the major traffickers who smuggled the bulk of the heroin supply into the United States. Under this strategy the bureau would change its index of performance from arrests made to the value of heroin shipments seized. Mitchell, ever sensitive to the dangers of another scandal in the Department of Justice, readily approved this approach. (Subsequently he was able to explain in press conferences the low level of arrests by the bureau by saying, "the Bureau of Narcotics and Dangerous Drugs . . . changed their mode of operation to concentrate on the large international and interstate distributors, leaving to the states and localities the responsibility for the enforcement of the drug laws with respect to the pushers on the street.")

Since the new strategy required deploying American narcotics agents overseas, where bulk seizures could easily be made, Mitchell sent new guidelines (actually drafted by Ingersoll) to the Customs Service, which traditionally had the responsibility for interdicting contraband. It designated the BNDD as the agency that should control narcotics smuggling abroad, and instructed Customs to support the bureau's efforts.

By 1970, the bureau was fully engaged in the business of international narcotics seizures. With the help of computers and intelligence experts Ingersoll identified nine "primary systems" of heroin distribution throughout the world. Scores of agents, with large amounts of "buy money," were dispatched to Marseilles, Naples, Hamburg, Hong Kong, and Bangkok to make contact with foreign traffickers. By stationing agents abroad, the bureau was able to claim credit for "cooperative" arrests that occurred in these countries (even if they had not participated in them). Thus the bureau reported in 1970 total worldwide seizures (the bulk of which took place in France, Italy, and Thailand) of 1,593 pounds of heroin, morphine, and opium with a street value of $311 million. The street value was estimated by calculating the retail price at which the heroin would have been sold if it had reached the United States and been fully diluted into the maximum number of portions that could be sold on the street.

Ingersoll was fully aware that these seizure statistics were somewhat misleading. Most of the heroin had actually been confiscated by foreign police in foreign countries, and it could not be definitely established that it was ever destined for the American market. Moreover, the value of the confiscated heroin was exaggerated manyfold by using the street-level calculus. For example, a kilogram of heroin seized in France in 1970 could be replaced by the trafficker in France for about $5,000; yet the Bureau of Narcotics would report the street value for that same seized kilogram at $210,000, or roughly forty times what the heroin was actually worth to the trafficker. Measuring the value of confiscated heroin in terms of street value is analogous to measuring the value of rustled cattle in terms of the price per pound of steak in the finest New York restaurant (in both cases, the retail price reflects distribution costs and profits that never actually occurred). Ingersoll was concerned that inflating the value of heroin could eventually encourage amateurs to enter the business as dealers, but when he suggested using a more realistic measure of the value of seizures, such as replacement cost, both White House and Bureau of Narcotics press officers strenuously objected. Any such change, they claimed, would be disastrous, since the press would presume that the lower figure indicated a sharp decline in the bureau's performance. For example, after *U.S. News & World Report* revealed in 1970 that only 3 percent of the drugs being seized were "hard drugs," as opposed to marijuana (in what appeared to Ingersoll to be a leak from the Treasury Department in the ongoing interagency war), Krogh asked Ingersoll in a memorandum, "How can 'hard drugs' be defined to show that much more than 25% of the seizures were of hard drugs?" The problem was that the magazine was defining seizures in terms of the *weight* of the seizures. Ingersoll replied in another memorandum, "Rather than redefine 'hard drugs' to suit our purposes, perhaps we could approach the situation by redefining our seizures in terms [of] . . . specific units for each drug. . . . A unit of hard drugs could be one injection and a unit of marijuana could be one cigarette. This method would deflate the marijuana figure by a factor of 50–100 in relation to heroin." The ever-present G. Gordon Liddy attempted to solve this same problem by suggesting the development of an "index of successful performance." This novel criterion would divide the total weight of the drug seized in the year by the total number of estimated users in the population. Since there were presumed to be 100 times as many marijuana users as heroin users, it would appear that the government was, according to Liddy's calculus, twenty-five times as successful in seizing heroin. In any case, Ingersoll continued reporting the higher street value of seizures.

The strategy also proved quite successful with Congress. When Ingersoll was questioned by members of the House Appropriations Committee in 1970 as to why his bureau produced substantially fewer arrests despite a 50-percent increase in its operating budget, he cited the hundreds of millions of dollars' worth of seized heroin (measured by its street value) as evidence that his agency was becoming increasingly effective against the higher-level heroin wholesalers. The committee apparently was persuaded by his argument, since it recommended a further increase in the bureau's appropriation for the following year. By 1971 the BNDD had grown considerably, with a force of 1,500 agents and budget of some $43 million (which was more than fourteen times the size of the budget of the former Bureau of Narcotics).

Although Ingersoll had been successful in expanding the Bureau of Narcotics from a minor domestic law-enforcement agency to an international agency, the White House had some different objectives for the bureau. Krogh pointed out to Ingersoll that a series of private polls, commissioned by the White House staff, indicated that the American electorate considered heroin "to be a prime problem," and believed that the Nixon administration was not doing enough to control it. In particular, Krogh believed that this lack of public awareness of the Nixon administration's efforts—and successes—in reducing narcotics traffic stemmed from the bureaucratic inertness of Ingersoll's agency. Not only had the number of arrests made by federal officers actually decreased during the Nixon administration, but the BNDD press-relations officers were no longer emphasizing federal police operations against domestic drug pushers and "drug fiends." Instead, stories were being fed to the press about seizures of heroin in faraway and exotic countries. Even more distressing to the White House, in 1971 the BNDD began revising upward its estimates of the number of heroin addict-users in the United States: the number escalated from 69,000 in 1969, to 322,000 in 1970, and then to 560,000 in 1971. All three estimates, however, were based on the same 1969 data, the higher numbers being projected by using different statistical formulas rather than discovering new addicts. In Ingersoll's view the inflated estimates served the bureau's interests by showing Congress a greater need for appropriations to control the narcotics business. But with an election only one year away, such an "escalation" of addicts during the Nixon tenure was not the publicity the White House wanted. Geoffrey Sheppard, one of Krogh's young assistants, complained, "Those guys in the Bureau of Narcotics were creating hundreds of thousands of addicts on paper with their phoney statistics." But Ingersoll proved impervious to a barrage of phone calls from Krogh and his staff. Krogh then intervened by ordering that all press statements and public speeches on narcotics be coordinated and cleared by his office (Richard Harkness, a former NBC correspondent, was appointed as the White House press coordinator for matters concerning drug abuse). Krogh further suggested that a large number of well-publicized arrests by narcotics agents would be most helpful in calling public attention to the administration's new war on drugs. Though Ingersoll agreed to coordinate his public statements with the White House, he adamantly refused to change the bureau's policy of deemphasizing street arrests. He again argued that such "revolving-door" arrests would relieve neither crime nor the drug problem, and would only serve to lead federal agents into working again with underworld informers. Krogh cut the discussion short by saying, "We cannot accept your thesis." Ingersoll, who was concerned that his professional reputation might be severely tarnished if he reverted to the policy of mass-produced arrests for political purposes, appealed to John Mitchell for support. Mitchell, who, at least to Ingersoll, seemed concerned about the "long arm" of John Ehrlichman bypassing his authority in the Department of Justice, told Ingersoll that he, "not Krogh, [was] in charge of the bureau's policy." Since Ingersoll had acquired supporters both in Congress and in the law-enforcement establishment, he could not easily be fired. Thus, in 1971 Krogh was stymied, at least temporarily, in his attempt to control the narcotics police.

12

The Border War:
Eugene Rossides's Version

The rapid expansion of Ingersoll's Bureau of Narcotics and Dangerous Drugs into the field of international narcotics control cut directly into the territory of the Bureau of Customs, in the Treasury Department. Until Attorney General Mitchell declared new guidelines in 1969, which expanded the Justice Department's role in narcotics control and gave Ingersoll's bureau preeminence in foreign (as well as domestic) narcotics intelligence and operations, Customs had a major responsibility for tracking foreign shipments of narcotics, as well as other contraband, so that they could be intercepted at the borders. Rossides interpreted these new guidelines as Mitchell's initial move in a "grand plan [to] centralize all the government's law enforcement activities—IRS included—in his Justice Department." When Mitchell first broached this idea of consolidating law-enforcement agencies, at a cabinet meeting in 1969, Rossides was concerned that this could upset the "separation of powers and checks and balances" in government and, he noted in a subsequent memorandum, raise "the spectre of a national police force." At a less theoretical level, Rossides was also concerned that the stationing of BNDD agents overseas would limit his ambitions for expanding the Bureau of Customs.

He thus began a quiet but effective campaign in Congress and the press (through surreptitiously authored leaks) asserting that the Mitchell guidelines would both seriously undercut the antismuggling role of Customs and wreak irreparable confusion in the entire program to curtail narcotics. He argued in a memorandum, "The Department of Justice, and its Bureau of Narcotics, are supposed to enforce Federal law within the United States, not usurp the job of Customs in intercepting contraband shipments from abroad." Even from a practical point of view, it made no sense to Rossides for the BNDD, which had neither experience in foreign relations nor bilingual agents, to conduct overseas investigations and intelligence gathering which formerly had been conducted by Customs. "We certainly would not tolerate foreign agents working cases in the United States," he wrote in the same memorandum. Instead of "Americanizing the narcotics problem by sending American narcs abroad," Rossides suggested an interagency approach which would involve the Department of State, the CIA, Customs, and the BNDD. He eventually won the support of Secretary of State William Rogers, who agreed it would be "ludicrous [to send] a policeman in the Bureau of Narcotics to negotiate opium production with the President of Turkey." Mitchell, however, remained adamant, insisting that "all law enforcement functions be located in the Department of Justice."

Rossides remained equally determined to win a role for Customs in the heroin crusade, which, even at this early date, seemed to Rossides to be "the main area of action" in the Nixon administration. He had appointed in 1969 two hard-driving and ambitious former prosecutors, both of whom were very well acquainted with the Rockefeller crusade in New York State, to assist him in developing the Treasury Department's antinarcotics program—Myles J. Ambrose and G. Gordon Liddy. Ambrose, a charming New York lawyer, had devoted his career almost exclusively to law enforcement and politics—twin pursuits that are not always completely separable—working his way up from an assistant U.S. prosecutor in the Southern District of New York, to a commissioner on New York's Waterfront Commission. After working behind the scenes in President Nixon's 1968 election campaign, but not being offered an appointment as U.S. attorney (his first preference), he accepted the offer from Rossides to be the commissioner of Customs—and, at forty-three, he was the youngest person ever to hold that position. Despite some doubts about his extreme politics, Rossides acceded to a White House request and appointed Liddy as his special assistant for law enforcement, with special responsibility for coordinating the Treasury Department's narcotics program.

Continuing the head-on confrontation with the BNDD, Rossides and Ambrose actively campaigned in Congress for additional funds to modernize Customs' attack on the narcotics problem. Ambrose was particularly effective when he argued that the Bureau of Customs had the "same size force as in Calvin Coolidge's days," and still had not received modern equipment. Congressman Thomas Steed, a Democrat from Oklahoma and an admirer of Rossides, championed Customs' cause in the House Appropriations Committee. Consequently, between 1969 and 1970 Customs' budget for narcotics interdiction was quadrupled. The new resources were invested in a computerized system, known as CADPIN, for collating intelligence on narcotics traffic throughout the world; helicopters and other interception equipment (including heroin-detecting dogs); and an expanded force of agents to pursue international smuggling investigations.

With Ambrose pressing in his public speeches and press releases for the interagency approach to narcotics, and Customs receiving increased appropriations for its international investigations, Ingersoll found that the BNDD and Customs were still on a collision course. Rather than acting as the supportive agency in narcotics matters, as it was required to be by the 1969 Mitchell guidelines, Customs was becoming increasingly expansive in its antinarcotics policy, and often not even informing the BNDD of its arrest plans. In a number of cases Customs officers arrested BNDD informers who were attempting to make a "buy" of heroin from a Customs informer, and vice versa. Through Mitchell, Ingersoll appealed to the White House to settle the issue once and for all.

On February 5, 1970, President Nixon, accepting Mitchell's counsel, issued a memorandum which designated the Bureau of Narcotics and Dangerous Drugs as the agency with prime responsibility for controlling narcotics smuggling anywhere in the world, and Customs was thus to give BNDD preeminence in narcotics control. There was to be no further increase in the number of Customs investigators overseas, and any jurisdictional disputes between the two agencies were to be resolved by Mitchell, who was Ingersoll's main supporter. Clearly Ingersoll had won a battle, at least in his struggle to expand his agency.

Rossides, though blocked in the international arena, decided to move into an entirely new area of narcotics control: tax auditing and collection. After several discussions with Mitchell and J. Edgar

Hoover, it became clear to him that the FBI and the Department of Justice's strike forces, which had been established to pursue organized crime, had not been involved at all in the suppression of the domestic narcotics business. When he suggested at a meeting of Department of Justice officials in 1970 that the FBI and the strike forces might be redeployed against heroin traffickers, he received only an icy stare from the FBI executives, and the matter was not further discussed. Rossides realized, however, that the Internal Revenue Service, which came under his purview in the Treasury Department, was in a unique position to fill this gap and pursue the major domestic traffickers in heroin. The instrument would be the net-worth audit, a procedure by which IRS accountants, rather than examining the books and records of a suspect, reconstruct his total expenditures by examining his standard of living and comparing it with his reported income. By subjecting suspected narcotics wholesalers to such audits, Rossides believed it would be possible for the IRS immediately to freeze their assets with "jeopardy judgments" without waiting for trials, and thereby to paralyze their business.

In early 1971 Rossides proposed to John Connally, who had just been appointed secretary of the treasury, that the IRS organize a pilot project in Baltimore for scrutinizing the assets and returns of narcotics suspects. Connally, a man of action, replied, "Don't bother with the test program. Go national." In the next few days Connally won the approval of the director of the federal budget, Roy Ash, for two hundred additional IRS agents who would be employed in the antinarcotics program (the necessary appropriation was eventually forthcoming from Congress). Rossides implemented the plan by establishing a target-selection committee which included representatives from BNDD, Customs, and the IRS intelligence unit. All federal and local law-enforcement agencies were requested to pass on to the committee the dossiers of suspects. The committee would then evaluate each case and pass back to the IRS those cases selected for a complete tax investigation and net-worth audit. Initially, executives at the IRS objected to the agency's being used for any purpose other than tax collections. They argued that the use of an outside committee to select targets for IRS investigations was fraught with the potential for political abuse, and that it would establish a dangerous precedent. Rossides agreed in principle, but believed that narcotics control was crucial to the nation, and convinced the reluctant IRS officials that he could effectively insulate the target-selection committee from the influence of any other agency, including the White House.

The Narcotics Trafficker Program, as the IRS campaign was officially called, proved to be an immediate success. In its first year of operation IRS agents levied tax penalties of more than $100 million against individuals suspected of being in the narcotics business by local, state, and federal law-enforcement agencies. In many cases, as soon as a suspect was arrested on any charge, an IRS inspector immediately filed a jeopardy assessment based on what he estimated very roughly the suspect might have earned from the sale of narcotics. If the suspect could not instantly pay the assessment, the IRS would confiscate all his property and savings (some $25 million was thus confiscated in the program's first year of operation). Even if the charges were subsequently dropped against the suspect, the IRS did not necessarily restore the seized property. In one case, for example, a National Airlines stewardess suspected of dealing in drugs was arrested in Miami for speeding. The police found a bottle in her possession containing four pills. The IRS immediately filed a $25,549 lien against her, and confiscated her jewelry and savings. Although the charges were dropped against the stewardess (the pills were prescribed by her doctor), and neither the police nor the IRS was able to produce any evidence that she was involved in the narcotics business, under the existing tax law she was unable to have the $25,549 tax assessment dismissed. In a very real sense the IRS was converted into a highly unorthodox arm of narcotics-law enforcement to strike at the "Achilles' heel of the drug business," as Rossides put it.

The success, and unrestrained effectiveness, of the IRS did not escape the notice of the White House. Egil Krogh and the White House staff pressed Rossides for a "more coordinated approach" in which the Treasury Department's enforcement units would be "aligned with White House policy."

Krogh repeatedly warned Rossides that "we are at war," and that the president "would not tolerate bureaucratic maneuvering" in an area as important as narcotics. But the stubborn assistant secretary of the treasury steadfastly refused to allow the White House to have any control over the operations of the IRS and Customs, even to the point of denying information to Krogh's staff. "My job was to protect the autonomy of the Treasury Department's law enforcement agencies," he explained subsequently. "If Krogh or Ehrlichman wanted to run them, they would first have to get Connally to fire me." And that was not a feasible alternative. As relations between the White House staff and Rossides deteriorated, Krogh turned to Rossides's staff for assistance. Myles Ambrose, impressed with Krogh's "efficiency in cutting through bureaucratic red tape" and, more important, his proximity to the center of power in the White House, became increasingly attracted to the White House group. Gordon Liddy, who was, according to Rossides, "looking to head a law enforcement agency," became an active ally of Krogh's. (He was actually proposed in 1970 by the White House for the directorship of the Alcohol, Tobacco and Firearms control division of the Treasury, but was rejected by senior Treasury officials.)

Not only was Liddy dealing behind Rossides's back with Krogh, but he was openly flouting the established policy of the Treasury Department on a whole range of issues, including gun control. "The situation was intolerable," Rossides explained. "Liddy was acting as if he had independent authority from the President." In the spring of 1971 the deputy undersecretary of the treasury, Charls R. Walker, decided that Liddy could no longer be retained in the Treasury Department; he was given time to find a new job, though. Krogh vigorously protested the firing of Liddy, but to no avail—Rossides, Walker, and Connally all stood firmly by the decision. After Liddy resigned in July, 1971, Rossides, with powerful support in Congress, intensified the effort to establish "an autonomous role for the Treasury in the war against heroin," even if it meant continued skirmishes with Attorney General Mitchell, Ingersoll's BNDD, and the White House.

13

Conflict of Interests:
Egil Krogh's Version

Despite continuing efforts by Egil Krogh and his young staff on the Domestic Council and increasing pressures from their superiors in the White House for "dramatic results," the embryonic war on drugs soon dissolved into open bureaucratic strife. There were no fewer than fifteen different federal agencies, with different programs, involved in the government offensive against drugs, and each tended to view the problem from the perspective of its own particular programs and interests. By early 1971 Krogh found that the administration's entire effort was leaking like a sieve, with the various agencies releasing to congressional subcommittees and the press, information which advanced their own programmatic interests and undermined those of competing agencies. In this morass of conflicting claims and statistics it became impossible for the White House to sustain its initiative for long.

For example, after the Bureau of Customs succeeded in obtaining tens of millions of dollars' worth of new airplanes and patrol equipment on the assumption that much of the narcotics in America came from Mexico, and could therefore be intercepted by intensified border surveillance, the Bureau of Narcotics and Dangerous Drugs released information to Congress and the press which suggested that

Turkey, not Mexico, was the crucial source of supply. When the White House then succeeded in pressing the State Department into action against the Turkish poppy fields, the CIA released its "survey," which showed that Turkey produced only a small fraction of the world's illicit opium, and that if this supply were curtailed, it would rapidly be replaced through other countries in Asia and the Middle East. In another case John Ingersoll had hired systems analysts to demonstrate to the public that there were nine primary systems of narcotics distribution in the United States. When the BNDD was focusing almost all its efforts on these nine systems rather than on the small trafficker, Eugene Rossides and the Bureau of Customs found a tenth system, unlisted by the BNDD in its charts. More embarrassingly, it was the largest single supplier of heroin to United States markets.

Nixon called Ingersoll and Krogh to his office to clarify the situation, and after Ingersoll presented a number of bar graphs depicting the increased value of seizures of narcotics through this systems approach, Krogh recalled that the president responded, "Now this is very impressive, but does it have anything to do with solving the problem of narcotics . . . are there less narcotics on the street? Are there fewer addicts? Is there less crime related to the use of narcotics? Can you show me that the problem itself is being corrected by these operational indices of success?" Since Ingersoll could not specify the number of addicts in the United States, or the total amount of heroin that was consumed, Nixon realized that there was no way of knowing what proportion of the heroin traffic passed through the nine systems that Ingersoll was concentrating his forces on. Even Rossides readily admitted to anyone who asked that less than one fifth of all narcotics shipped into the United States was intercepted before it reached its ultimate customers. At one point, when Ehrlichman brought him a report on bureaucratic charges and countercharges, the president shook his head in dismay and asked, "Why are they fighting each other . . . instead of drug traffickers?" Yet the continuing conflicts between the law-enforcement agencies involved in the war on drugs were relatively minor compared to the "bureaucratic in-fighting," as Krogh put it, among the nine agencies involved with the problem of treating narcotics addicts—and thereby reducing demand.

The federal government had first become involved in the treatment of addicts in 1929, when Congress established facilities at Lexington, Kentucky, and Fort Worth, Texas, to treat the large number of imprisoned addicts in federal penitentiaries and to provide an alternative to the private clinics that had recently been outlawed by the federal government. These "narcotic farms," as they were called, detoxified addicts by gradually reducing their daily dosages of heroin until they were completely withdrawn from the drug under the supervision of government-employed psychiatrists. Detoxification proved unsuccessful in permanently changing the behavior of those who underwent the treatment—more than 70 percent of those who were committed to the government's narcotic farms eventually resumed the use of heroin. It was debatable whether this resumption was due to the environment to which they returned or to the chemical lure of the drug itself. In any case, detoxification became the central focus for government research and data collection on narcotics addiction. By the time the Nixon administration assumed office, the National Institute of Mental Health (NIMH), which administered the "farms" and employed the psychiatrists engaged in the detoxification programs, had developed a "bureaucratic interest in maintaining the status quo," as Egil Krogh explained the situation. Despite White House pressures, NIMH resisted the idea of using treatment as part of the law-and-order campaign which focused on the ghetto population. It claimed that this was because the methods of treatment were untried and possibly unsafe. Krogh, however, saw this as a bureaucratic problem. He explained in a memorandum to John Ehrlichman that the "primary orientation of NIMH is towards professionals and psychiatrists not other approaches; the Institute's target populations have historically been non-poor; . . . philosophically, NIMH orientation could not accommodate non-mental health approaches. . . ." In September, 1970, the president himself became concerned over the "independence" of NIMH, when its director, Bertram Brown, was quoted by the Washington *Post* as recommending that marijuana violations be treated no more seriously than traffic violations and that offenders simply be given a ticket. Since this conflicted directly with the administration's bête-noire strategy, to appear merciless and unrelenting in prosecuting crimes, Krogh recalled, "The president hit the ceiling." He even wrote Krogh a personal note suggesting "that clown Brown" be fired immediately, and then angrily reiterated this demand in a meeting a few days later with Ehrlichman, Krogh, and Krogh's assistant, Jeffrey Donfeld. According to Donfeld, Krogh then asked him to prepare a memorandum for the president which would provide "evidence of incompetency." Donfeld investigated and found that Brown was a close friend of Elliot Richardson's, and that Richardson would not be easily persuaded to fire Brown to please the White House. Realizing that Richardson was not a man to be trifled with, the president ordered the matter dropped. And by December, 1970, as Krogh and Donfeld watched in complete frustration, Bertram Brown managed to gain effective control over an interagency study group which was supposed to promulgate national goals for the war on drugs. Brown steered the group into recommending that his agency, NIMH, take the lead in government efforts to reduce addiction. To counter these recommendations, Krogh immediately set up another study group of experts not in the government.

The administration was also having problems with the Department of Health, Education, and Welfare, which through a number of its other agencies was funding treatment programs throughout the United States. Secretary Richardson took the position that the criterion for allocating funds to programs should be the "size of the local drug problem." Although this may have seemed like a rational way of allocating federal money to the neediest areas, it would mean that New York City, which then had approximately half of the drug addicts in the nation, and Chicago, which also had a large addiction problem, would receive most of the federal money. In political terms, H. R. Haldeman pointed out, reaching two cities that were "Democratic strongholds" was "unacceptable." Donfeld reminded Krogh of this consideration in a May 17, 1971, memorandum criticizing the submission of drug-abuse "initiatives" from the Health, Education, and Welfare Department. In the section on "Selection of Recipient Cities," Donfeld noted, "If 'size of the local drug problem' is a key criteria for funding, then most of the money will be poured down the insatiable holes of New York and Chicago with no likely visible reduction in crime. Let's dream up a non-formula where some political mileage can result from visibly achieving a reduction in crime." On the other hand, two agencies created by Lyndon B. Johnson in his war on poverty, the Model Cities Administration in the Department of Housing and Urban Development (HUD) and the Office of Economic Opportunity (OEO), wanted a large part of the "drug money" invested in counselors and other jobs in the ghettos which would be administered by their agencies. The White House staff feared that such money would not go for treating addiction or reducing the crime problem in the inner city but for hiring more organizers in the poverty agencies who would ultimately work against the interests of the Nixon administration. Adding to the confusion, NIMH proposed that "community mental health centers be the focal point for drug rehabilitation projects." The White House staff viewed this as simply an attempt by NIMH to expand its empire, and commented in a memorandum, "Community Mental Health Centers are brick buildings in primarily middle class neighborhoods ... how many young blacks now go to psychiatrists or would want to go to mental health centers for their addiction?" The staff warned that such a program would strengthen the NIMH dynasty to the detriment of the administration's law-and-order programs. (NIMH was also muddying the waters by releasing multibillion-dollar estimates of the amount of crime being committed by drug addicts; and the Domestic Council, according to a staff report authored by Krogh and Donfeld, attributed these exaggerated figures to NIMH's "desire to evidence [a] need for treatment programs, thereby aggrandizing their territory.")

There was also "a growing White House concern with coordinating treatment programs for soldiers returning from Vietnam," according to Krogh. In the summer of 1970, both Egil Krogh and John Ehrlichman visited Vietnam and discovered that it was an open secret that a large number of American servicemen in Saigon were using heroin. The Department of Defense, however, refused to accept Krogh and Ehrlichman's findings and claimed that there were "only a few dozen" confirmed cases of heroin addiction in the Army. Meanwhile, Krogh found out that congressional investigators in South Vietnam were being told by unit commanders that between 10 and 15 percent of all U.S. troops in South Vietnam were addicted. The specter of several hundred thousand addicts returning from Vietnam convinced the president that the federal government would have vastly to expand its treatment facilities. At one point Krogh suggested that funds could be provided to the Veterans Administration to allow it to expand its treatment facilities for returning soldiers. The president, demonstrating some insight into the escalating nature of bureaucracies, decided against building new "Veterans Administration capacity to handle heroin addicts because once they are built, one can never get rid of that capacity," according to a memorandum of the conversation. (Such memoranda were assigned to what was known as the President's File.) Since there seemed no other way out of the bureaucratic tangle, the president agreed with Krogh and his staff that the only answer was to "reorganize into a central agency the separate efforts of the nine federal agencies dealing in these areas. . . ." Krogh later explained, "We felt we couldn't get control of policy unless we put it all together."

The idea of placing all the federal treatment and rehabilitation programs for narcotics addicts under the umbrella of a single agency was first proposed in 1970 by the President's Advisory Council on Executive Organization, which was headed by Roy L. Ash. The Ash Council, as it was known in the government, suggested that this new umbrella agency be created within the Department of Health, Education, and Welfare. It became clear, however, in early 1971 that this new agency would, if located in HEW, fall under the influence of Bertram Brown's NIMH rather than that of the White House. Since hundreds of millions of dollars were to be channeled into selective cities and programs by this new agency, and it was hoped that such treatment might bring about dramatic results before the 1972 election, Ehrlichman decided that the new umbrella agency should be under the direct control of the White House. "There was a strong feeling that it should span everything, be accountable to the president and be in the president's office," Krogh later stated. Thus, in the spring of 1971, President Nixon approved plans to create a special-action office which would allow the White House staff radically to revamp all the government's narcotics treatment programs and use them for novel purposes.

14

The Magic-bullet Solution

It was Jeffrey Donfeld, the youngest member of Krogh's staff, who discovered what appeared to be a magical solution to both the narcotics and law-and-order problems. Donfeld first became involved in politics in 1965, when he was elected president of the student union at the University of California at Los Angeles, where he majored in political science. When he went on to law school at Berkeley, he made a name for himself by opposing the free-speech movement there. Then, in the summer of 1967, he interned with the New York law firm of Richard Nixon and John Mitchell. He impressed Nixon with sharp questions about the war in Vietnam, and after working briefly in California Republican politics, he was asked at the age of twenty-five to join the administration as a staff assistant in the field of drug control. Initially working on such projects as inviting disc jockeys to White House conferences and arranging drug propaganda for the administration, he acquired the belief that "all government is 75 percent PR."

In June, 1970, Krogh sent Donfeld on a whirlwind tour of New York and Chicago to evaluate treatment programs in those cities. Donfeld said that the doctors operating the various programs tended to be zealots, with each "believing that his program is the true panacea." When he demanded some statistics to confirm the effectiveness of the treatment program in terms of "drug recidivism arrest [records], employment or schooling, program drop-out rates and per patient costs" he found to his dismay that "most programs . . . did not have, or would not provide, these statistics because their programs were 'too new.' " He added sarcastically in his report to Krogh, entitled "Different Strokes for Different Folks," "If they [the treatment programs in New York and Chicago] were 'too new' it is because prior efforts proved to be failures and the current program is the latest hopeful effort." Moreover, he reported that there was no agreement at all in the medical community about what the goal of drug rehabilitation should be. Donfeld found, however, that one form of treatment promised to reduce crime statistics for the administration—methadone maintenance.

Methadone, a synthetic opiate which can be manufactured in laboratories, was developed by German scientists during World War II as a substitute for heroin and morphine, since these natural opiates could not be obtained from the prewar suppliers in the Middle East. After the war the formula for this synthetic drug was given to American drug companies, and it was subsequently manufactured for "investigative use" by Eli Lilly and Company. In distributing the drug to doctors, the Lilly Company described it as a "synthetic narcotic analgesic with multiple actions quantitatively similar to those of morphine" and warned that it was "a narcotic with significant potential for abuse with dependence-producing characteristics." Although methadone was slightly less powerful than heroin, it produced virtually the same sort of pain-deadening and sedative effects and was no less addictive than a natural opiate. Because of its similarity to heroin, methadone was initially used in government hospitals for detoxifying addicts—a procedure in which doctors gave addicts progressively decreasing dosages of a narcotic until they were drug free. Since methadone could be administered to patients orally every twenty-four hours, it proved to be a convenient detoxifying agent in hospitals. However, it was hardly viewed as a cure—the vast majority of detoxified addicts eventually returned to the use of illicit heroin.

In 1964 two New York City doctors found a radically different means of using methadone to treat addiction. Under the auspices of the prestigious New York Health Research Council, Dr. Vincent P. Dole, a research associate at the Rockefeller Institute, and Dr. Maria E. Nyswander, a psychiatrist, initiated a series of experiments which laid the groundwork for what was to become known as "methadone maintenance." Rather than using methadone to withdraw addicts from heroin progressively, Dole and Nyswander actually increased the dosages of methadone for twenty-two addicts participating in the experiment until they were stabilized on a higher daily dosage of methadone than they had previously used of heroin. Since methadone was as addictive as heroin, Dole and Nyswander merely succeeded in substituting the methadone for heroin as the addictive agent. The idea of attempting to cure one form of drug addiction with another, it will be recalled, was not new. Dole and Nyswander, however, provided a medical rationale for maintaining patients on methadone rather than heroin. They postulated that the use of heroin caused a permanent and irreversible metabolic change in the nervous system of an addict. This meant that an addict could never be normal unless he had a narcotic in his system that compensated for this metabolic disease. According to their theory, there was no possibility of an addict's being permanently withdrawn from drugs: it was simply a question of which narcotic he would use. Even though methadone had all the pharmacological properties of heroin, Dole and Nyswander found that an addict needed less-frequent administrations of the dosage—that is, every twenty-four hours rather than every four hours—and he could live a more normal life on methadone than on heroin, working normal hours. The objective of their rehabilitation program was not to render the addict drug-free but to make him socially useful. They justified maintaining addicts on extremely high dosages of methadone—80 to 150 milligrams, a dosage previously given only to terminal cancer patients—on the basis that this established a pharmacological block against the addict's returning to heroin. They also claimed that since addicts received their methadone free, they had no further reason to steal money or property. In 1966, the medical team reported, "The blockade treatment ... has virtually eliminated criminal activity [among the patients in the program]."

In this original experiment Dole and Nyswander were treating a few dozen middle-aged addicts who for the most part had begun using heroin during or just after World War II; each volunteer demonstrated a strong motivation to give up his life of addiction (and crime) before he was selected for the experiment. Working with such a small and well-motivated group, it was not especially surprising that Dole and Nyswander achieved successful results. As more patients were admitted for methadone maintenance, Dole and Nyswander resorted to using various forms of statistical legerdemain to make their results appear more impressive than they were in terms of reducing crime and narcotics addiction.* Indeed, other doctors tried to replicate Dole and Nyswander's program of methadone maintenance but found that many of the methadone patients continued their criminal careers despite the fact that they were receiving free dosages of methadone to take home with them every night.

In reviewing these programs, Donfeld fully realized that the data were seriously flawed, if not intentionally distorted, to gain additional funding, and that most of the claims of dramatic crime reduction resulted from evaluations by self-interested parties. And though he doubted that methadone maintenance would provide a permanent solution to the problems of either drug addiction or crime, he did think it possible that it could temporarily alleviate the administration's law-and-order problem by bringing about a reduced crime statistic in urban centers with large addict populations. The distribution of free methadone would lessen the need for addicts to steal, he reasoned, and furthermore, local police departments had adopted the policy of not arresting, where possible, addicts who were enrolled in rehabilitation programs (thus, massive enrollment of street addicts in methadone programs would automatically reduce arrest statistics in some cities). Donfeld therefore recommended to Krogh, "Drug rehabilitation is a virgin, yet fertile area for social and political gain."

As liaison with the District of Columbia government, Krogh had already been briefed by Dr. Robert DuPont on the possibilities of using methadone in Washington, D.C., based on a "filling-station" principle, in which addicts would have the same easy access to acquiring methadone as motorists have to gasoline. However, any sort of a national methadone program presented a problem, as Krogh explained to Donfeld, because it implied that the administration sanctioned the use of an addictive and highly controversial drug. Donfeld nonetheless suggested a way around this political problem. In his June 11 visit to Chicago he spent a full day with Dr. Jerome Jaffe, who was then director of the Illinois State Rehabilitation Program, and found him to be not only an impressive administrator but also "politically sensitive" to the emotional issues involved in methadone maintenance. To avoid the charge that he was forcing

* For an analysis of the various statistical artifices employed by Dole and Nyswander, see my article "Methadone: The Forlorn Hope" in *The Public Interest* magazine, Summer 1974.

addicts to become dependent on methadone, Dr. Jaffe offered in his programs "modalities" of treatment, including detoxification and drug-free therapy as well as methadone maintenance. This "mixed-modality approach," or what Donfeld called "different strokes for different folks," effectively masked the methadone program from political criticism. Donfeld noted in a memorandum, "Jaffe sells his mixed modality approach, though he believes that 90% of the addicts will require methadone . . . the balanced program is political protection." One month later Donfeld argued in a policy paper that "it goes without saying that the primary goal [of treatment] should be to create law-abiding citizens and thereby reduce crime" and that "methadone maintenance is the modality which can best fit our needs." He also recommended disguising the policy of maintaining heroin addicts on another addictive drug, explaining:

> I believe that there are a number of sound reasons for describing any new drug rehabilitative initiative of the Nixon Administration in terms of a multi-modality approach rather than a methadone maintenance approach.
> Implicit in the multi-modality approach is the notion that we are still searching for effective techniques to rehabilitate the drug abuser. If, therefore, there is not a perceptible decrease in the rate of crime once this rehabilitation program is introduced, we can always claim that the effective modality has not been found yet.

Krogh, who himself had never used any drug—not even cigarettes, alcohol, or caffeine—felt some reluctance about recommending a massive methadone-distribution program, but he was persuaded by Donfeld that it might be the only answer to the law-and-order problem. Moreover, New York City's Mayor John V. Lindsay, who then seemed a possible candidate for the Democratic nomination in the 1972 election, was implementing a major methadone program in his city—certainly a concern to Nixon's political strategists. Krogh thus ordered Donfeld and his Domestic Council staff to consider the option of a massive federal methadone program. The resulting 1970 Domestic Council summary option paper stated:

> Mayor Lindsay has recently announced a 4.4 million dollar methadone program in New York City. . . . If methadone does prove to be successful in New York on a large scale, Lindsay can claim credit for taking a bold step while the Administration remained cautiously skeptical.

Is the goal of decreased crime more important than the inevitable outcry from some people in the medical community, liberals, and black militants that the Administration is subjugating the black addict to the white man's opiate?

In 1972 citizens will be looking at crime statistics across the nation in order to see whether expectations raised in 1968 have been met. The federal government has only one economical and effective technique for reducing crime in the streets—methadone maintenance.

John Ehrlichman, like Krogh, expressed serious doubts about the "morality and wisdom" of distributing an addictive narcotic in the ghettos as part of an administration program. Nonetheless, persuaded by Donfeld's assertion that this was the only means of reducing crime before the 1972 election, he recruited Dr. Jaffe to organize a drug review for the Domestic Council which would develop the methadone strategy. After Jaffe completed the study, Donfeld was assigned the task of analyzing this report and comparing it with an earlier in-house study prepared by the National Institute of Mental Health and other government agencies with an interest in the subject. In December, 1970, less than six months after he first learned about the possibilities of rehabilitation, Donfeld discredited in the resulting Domestic Council staff report virtually all the reservations expressed by other government agencies about the proposed massive methadone scheme. NIMH objected to the "government . . . sanctioning one addiction in order to reduce the burden on society of heroin addiction." Donfeld effectively attacked the objectivity of NIMH by writing, "It would be an overt admission that the profession of psychiatry has failed to deal with heroin addiction if the National Institute of Mental Health endorsed methadone chemotherapy"; for good measure he characterized NIMH as "privately [believing] marijuana should be legalized." Similarly, the Food and Drug Administration (FDA), which objected because "the long-term physiological effects of methadone are not known," was depicted as a bureaucratic morass. The staff report commented, "FDA bureaucrats have not made it clear to researchers precisely what data will suffice. The researchers, who are arrogant egocentrics, are incensed at anyone who questions their research." The failure of either the government or researchers in private programs to produce satisfactory data about the effects of methadone on the health of long-term users was thus cavalierly dismissed as "bureaucratic intransigence."

The most serious objections came from the Bureau of Narcotics and Dangerous Drugs, which suggested that methadone from government programs would inevitably be diverted into the black market and thus lead to an entirely new drug as well as a new law-enforcement problem. Donfeld granted that there was no way to prevent such leakage into the illegal market, but argued that even if this happened, it would work, at least in the short run, to the advantage of the administration. He explained, "Though non-addicts may die from methadone overdoses, one must question whether the costs to society are greater than the certain deaths from heroin and attendant crime or the potential death of innocent people." He even suggested that the leakage of methadone from treatment programs to the black market would undercut the price of heroin, thereby diminishing the addicts' level of criminal activity. He reasoned in the staff report: ". . . if heroin addicts were to obtain supplies of methadone [illegally], society is not hurt in a direct way because methadone will help to sustain an addict until he gets his next heroin fix: The addict will have less compulsion to commit crimes to obtain money to buy that fix."

One important objection to the massive distribution of methadone remained: the American Medical Association (AMA) still expressed doubts as to the medical safety and effectiveness of the drug itself. Since John Ehrlichman believed that there would be great political risks attached to the government's distributing a drug that did not have the sanction of that powerful medical group, Donfeld met on February 4, 1971, with Raymond Cotton, whom he described in a memorandum to Krogh the next day as "second in command of the American Medical Association's congressional liaison office . . . in Washington." Donfeld then reported on this meeting to Krogh:

> The gist of his conversation was that in view of the fact that in the last election the AMA gave 85% of its money to the Republican party and 15% of its money to Democrats who usually support the President on key issues, he felt that there was no reason for the AMA ever to be in the position to oppose the substantive proposals of the Administration and Congress. He made it quite clear that he wanted to be in the position to support the Administration on any issue on which we might want AMA's assistance.

Donfeld responded by asking for help on the methadone problem.

> He [Cotton] said that a committee of AMA was currently preparing a

position on methadone. I told him that it would meet with great favor at the White House if the position paper concluded that initial results in methadone projects seemed to indicate that it is efficacious and safe for the treatment of heroin addiction. He got the point and said that he would keep in touch with me on the progress of the documents. . . .

In March, 1971, after trying to influence the scientific findings on methadone by the American Medical Association, Donfeld proceeded to draw up a final Domestic Council decision paper, which discounted all objections to launching a national methadone-maintenance program. In the rush to prepare analyses for the Domestic Council on this issue, Donfeld found there simply wasn't time to commission any independent studies or statistical evaluations of the existing methadone programs in various communities. The data which he originally found unacceptable because it was shaped by the self-interest of the various local programs was presented to the Domestic Council as "suggestive though not conclusive" that methadone "may significantly reduce arrest and crime records." Ehrlichman, who was never apprised of the vulnerability of the data, accepted Donfeld's and Krogh's logic on methadone in April, 1971.

Though Donfeld and the White House staff easily overwhelmed the muted resistance to methadone of the discredited bureaucrats in NIMH, FDA, and BNDD, there still remained the problem of convincing Mitchell, Richardson, and President Nixon of the political merits of the Domestic Council plan to distribute a highly addictive drug in urban centers. Krogh subsequently explained:

> With the President as well as Mr. Mitchell and Mr. Richardson there was a basic hostility to developing this kind of [methadone] program. . . . The President in fact expressed himself that methadone was, if anything, more dangerous than heroin itself. . . . There was at first quite a strong feeling that the government should not be funding drug addiction. . . . Why should we be actually funding programs that addict people to methadone if it is nothing more than a synthetic opium? . . . It took some time to persuade both Mr. Mitchell and John Ehrlichman that it was better to have a person on methadone maintenance where he was identified, where he could be counselled, where he could hopefully get a job, than to have them on the streets using heroin. . . .
>
> There was a feeling that it was moving too fast and more time was necessary to study the effectiveness of it. Nevertheless, we [were] persuaded . . . that it was a doable program, that it could be on line within a year, and that some very direct results could be presented to the President in time for the 1972 election.

When John Mitchell and Elliot Richardson received the Domestic Council decision paper on methadone, they both reacted, as Krogh predicted, "negatively." According to a memorandum to John Ehrlichman written on March 30, 1971, Mitchell recommended instead a small pilot project monitored by "a prestigious independent committee with a staff of highly qualified experts who have full access to the data generated by methadone and possibly other treatment programs." Secretary Richardson expressed his opposition even more forcefully and eloquently in a memorandum intended for the president:

> All the professional agencies involved (NIMH, FDA, BNDD) are extremely wary of a greatly expanded federal emphasis on methadone maintenance. Their fears of an expansion of federal activities in this area must be treated with great respect, particularly given the conjunction of these views coming from greatly different programmatic interests.
>
> My own view is that embarking on a national program of methadone maintenance may court potential disaster. We would be forced into the posture of pushing this program without the support of a generally accepted consensus of scientific knowledge and in the face of a judgment of our professional advisors.

The resistance was not sufficient to stop the methadone project in an election year. On April 28, 1971, Ehrlichman arranged a high-level meeting including himself, Mitchell, Richardson, Krogh, and their respective staff members to resolve the methadone issue. Before the meeting Krogh met with Mitchell and primed him on the political importance of launching the methadone program in time to obtain results for the election; the attorney general then reluctantly agreed "not to oppose." Handwritten notes of the meeting, taken by Krogh's assistant, reveal that Richardson counseled against anything more than "a careful pilot study," while Mitchell tried to assure him that methadone was "not the answer . . . but only an interim measure."

In the days following that cabinet-level meeting Krogh and Donfeld became increasingly concerned that Richardson's articulate opposition to a crash program would undercut their plans for reducing crime statistics. As the time came for a presidential decision, however, Ehrlichman reassured them that Nixon was now haunted by the specter of "hundreds of thousands of heroin addicts returning from the wars in Vietnam." He would thus be disposed to approve of a White House–controlled treatment program, especially if it could be defined as a positive step toward restoring law and order. In writing the briefing paper for the president, Krogh and Donfeld skirted around the criticisms of Richardson and Mitchell, stating only: "Although controversial on moral, social, and medical grounds, and although not the answer to heroin addiction, methadone is the most effective technique now available for reducing heroin and criminal recidivism and increasing the employment of drug dependent persons. . . ." The stage was thus set for the White House to direct millions of dosages of methadone into treatment centers in selected cities in the hope that it would bring about the dramatic results that the president demanded.

PART FIVE

Triumph of the Will ★

As long as the execution of the coup is rapid, and we are cloaked in anonymity, no particular political faction will have either a motive or an opportunity to oppose us.

—EDWARD LUTTWAK, *Coup d'Etat*

15

The June Scenario

In June, 1971, G. Gordon Liddy, a man possessed with a purpose, ascended to the inner circle of power at the White House. His attempt to take over the thousand-man Alcohol, Tobacco and Firearms enforcement unit of the Treasury Department on behalf of the White House group had been successfully resisted by the Treasury Department earlier that year, and his immediate superior, Eugene Rossides, had moved to ease him out of that department entirely. But Liddy foresaw that the heroin issue could be the very instrument that the White House group needed to consolidate power within the bureaucracy, and thereby extend its police power. To demonstrate how a few determined men could manipulate the emotions of an entire nation by invoking a few highly visual symbols of fear, Liddy invited his new cohorts in the White House to a series of propaganda films being shown in the National Archives that June. The "inner circle" that Liddy persuaded to view these films included John Ehrlichman, whose Domestic Council had assumed by now undisputed control over all domestic issues; Egil Krogh; Donald Santarelli, who was then slated to head the billion-dollar Law Enforcement Assistance Administration (LEAA), which disbursed money to local police departments; Robert Mardian, who headed the internal-security division of the

Department of Justice; and a number of Krogh's young assistants on the Domestic Council. The cycle of films was climaxed on June 13 by the showing of *Triumph of the Will,* a Nazi propaganda film made under the auspices of Hitler and Goering which graphically depicted the way a "national will" could be inculcated into the masses through the agency of controlled fear and frenzied outrage.

Krogh later recalled that he had "considerable apprehension" about hiring Gordon Liddy to work for the White House on the drug program. Rossides had warned him that Liddy was both disloyal and "potentially dangerous." Indeed, these were the reasons Rossides tendered for dismissing Liddy from the Treasury Department. Disloyalty to a bureaucracy might mean loyalty to the president, Krogh reasoned. Moreover, given Rossides's record of bureaucratic infighting, Krogh interpreted the potential danger of Liddy as simply his will to act decisively and cut through red tape. Krogh later came to the realization that Liddy had "simply a higher energy level than anyone else" and that therefore he could be extremely persuasive in moving others to action. And as Krogh gradually became persuaded that the drug issue was the best available lever for moving and reorganizing entrenched bureaucracies in the government, Liddy, with his ideas for mobilizing popular support on the drug issue, seemed an "invaluable addition" to his staff on the Domestic Council.

Nixon's Domestic Council analyzed the implications of launching a heroin crusade for more than a year but found that their plans were always undercut by bureaucrats in the various agencies of the government. With the 1972 election quickly approaching, Krogh decided the time was right for presidential action. Due to a fortunate turn of events earlier that year, a military coup d'etat in Turkey had swept into office Nihat Erim, who was willing to suspend temporarily the cultivation of opium poppies in Turkey—a long-term objective of the Nixon administration—in return for some token compensation. It seemed feasible for the president to pull a publicity coup of his own by meeting with Prime Minister Erim and jointly announcing what the media would assume to be, if properly prepared by the White House staff, a brilliant victory over heroin addiction and crime in America (even though Turkey at the time produced only a small portion of the world's illicit opium).

On another front, Ehrlichman had finally been persuaded by Krogh and Donfeld that a massive federal program to distribute the synthetic narcotic methadone was the only real hope the administration had of reducing crime statistics, if not crime, before the upcoming election. Despite the tough rhetoric of the Nixon law-and-order campaign, crime had actually risen in the United States, even in Washington, D.C., where the federal government had direct control over the police, according to the FBI's Uniform Crime Reports. Substantive measures, such as court reform or reorganizing police departments, could not possibly have an effect on crime statistics in time for the 1972 election, Krogh cogently argued. One of the largest categories of arrests in urban centers was narcotics violations—which in most cases merely meant the revolving-door arrests of junkies and their subsequent release a few days later. Donfeld pointed out that if large numbers of addicts received legal methadone rather than illegal heroin, and were enrolled in some sort of treatment program through which the methadone was distributed, narcotics violations could be expected to decrease dramatically in major cities, and this alone might bring about diminished crime reporting by local police departments. Moreover, if addicts received free narcotics from the government, their financial motivation for stealing might be diminished, and this might show up in police reporting. A month earlier, John Mitchell had objected to the methadone scheme on the grounds that there would undoubtedly be enormous leakage of methadone into illegal markets, and it then would become another illegal drug for the Justice Department to deal with. Krogh agreed that a large amount of methadone that was given to addicts to take home with them over weekends would be resold illicitly, but he held that such a diversion of methadone into the illegal market would serve to undercut the price of heroin and thereby both disrupt the illicit market and again reduce the financial burden of the criminal addict. Doubts regarding any large-scale distribution of this untried narcotic by the government remained, but Mitchell agreed not to oppose the election-year plan, if Ehrlichman believed that the methadone program would dramatically reduce crime statistics.

Elliot Richardson was another problem. Despite Krogh's fervent arguments, Richardson prudently refused to accept methadone as a mere election-year expedient. However, as Ehrlichman controlled access to the president, he was confident that Richardson's objections could be watered down and bypassed. According to the "outlines of the discussion with the President" kept by Krogh that month, Ehrlichman effectively skirted the real objections of both Mitchell and Richardson and only told the president, "Although controversial on moral, social, and medical grounds, and although not the answer to heroin addiction, methadone is the most effective technique now available for reducing heroin and criminal recidivism. . . ." Nixon was thus never fully apprised of the depth of dissent among his highest-ranking cabinet officers on the methadone question. Advised instead that methadone was the only means at the administration's disposal for reducing crime statistics by election time, the president tentatively approved the methadone program.

At one meeting in early June, with H. R. Haldeman, John Ehrlichman, and others, Krogh noted that the president expressed a desire to have changes in personnel through the federal agencies dealing with the drug problem. According to the memorandum in the President's File of that meeting, "he wants people brought in from outside of the government . . . and he wants a sense of urgency injected throughout the whole program. The President said that no one's feelings should be spared . . . the President wants the Department of Health, Education, and Welfare to be shaken up; he wants budgets cut and government hacks fired." This was also the moment Krogh and Ehrlichman were waiting for to reorganize the government bureaucracies. A "special-action office," operating directly out of the White House under the aegis of Krogh, would take over the operations of various agencies in the Department of Health, Education, and Welfare. Such a move would particularly undermine NIMH and HEW, which had advocated a scientific rather than a law-and-order approach to the drug problem. Krogh advised Ehrlichman that "bureaucratic sluggishness has made it difficult for NIMH to accept and implement new ideas . . . note the philosophic direction of NIMH and why it has not helped development." Ehrlichman in turn told the president, "There is no mechanism to insure concerted action. Efforts and coordination of the seven agencies dealing with drugs failed even at the Domestic Council level." He thus recommended to the president at the beginning of June that a joint-action group on drugs be established by executive order and include members of both his Domestic Council and Henry Kissinger's National Security Council. This group, according to the outline of the discussion with the president, was to have responsibility for the "inter-relations of law enforcement agencies" and for coordinating "international considerations to domestic considerations."

Before a heroin crusade could be properly launched, however, public attention had to be focused on the drug menace. Krogh thus planned a scenario which would begin in early June with the deliberately leaked news of American ambassadors in various countries being recalled over the drug issue. It would then reach an exciting climax with President Nixon's proclaiming to both houses of Congress a national emergency over the heroin epidemic. And it would finally be resolved on June 30 by the well-publicized announcement that Turkey had agreed to an opium ban. According to the June scenario, heroin crises would be periodically intensified as the president was proposing new legislation to Congress. When Krogh asked Haldeman in a memorandum on June 7, "Should new drug abuse legislation be introduced (1) to [create a more] unified authority (2) to add new authority in the area or (3) to add visibility to the President's program?" Haldeman, always businesslike, answered that the purpose of proposing new legislation was (3)—in other words, public relations. The second stage in the June scenario was to convene an emergency cabinet meeting. Ambassadors were to be urgently recalled from Turkey, NATO, Thailand, and France, with someone leaking to the press that "the president has a plan" to eradicate opium. Three days before the meeting, it would further be officially announced that the ambassadors were on their way home, and that "the president would propose new initiatives." An arrangement was made with ABC Television secretly to televise portions of the cabinet meeting, so it could later be released to the American public, with the White House reserving the right to edit the tape for its own benefit. It was also planned that at the meeting Ingersoll would brief the cabinet on the dimensions of the epidemic, and the president would ask Ingersoll, who was proving increasingly troublesome to the White House group, some embarrassing but difficult questions, according to the handwritten scenarios prepared by Krogh and his staff.

The president's declaration of a national emergency was to be a masterpiece of fear-mongering, rivaling the rhetoric of Governor Nelson Rockefeller in New York State, which had provided Nixon's speech writers with vivid metaphors for public hysteria over heroin. Nixon's speech would compare "the epidemic" to a cancer spreading across the youth of the nation. This cancer would threaten the safety of every citizen, not only through the possibility of addiction but also by precipitating a national crime wave. The very nation would be imperiled by this new threat. The president would then propose a sweeping reorganization of government and supplemental appropriations for the law-enforcement agencies. After the speech, according to the scenario, high administration officials would brief members of the press on the emergency and the president would meet privately with media executives. Meanwhile, Charles Colson, a special counsel to the president, was to arrange major leaks—to *Time, Newsweek,* and *U.S. News & World Report*—of the spreading heroin crisis.

Finally, at the end of June, the scenario called for the prime minister of Turkey be flown to the United States to meet with President Nixon and jointly announce the opium ban. If all went well, the scenario planners hoped that the public—and the news media—would accept this as a first victory in the war against heroin and endorse other elements in the president's crusade, including the reorganization of the bureaucratic agencies of the government. The scenario assumed that congressmen would not be able to resist the drumfire of publicity about the "drug menace" or to vote against any element of the president's crusade without appearing to their constituents to be soft on drugs. As one of Krogh's assistants later explained to me, "If we hyped the drug problem into a national crisis, we knew that Congress would give us anything we asked for."

The carefully orchestrated scenario unfolded as planned during the first two weeks in June, 1971. Surreptitious news stories about the emerging heroin crisis began surfacing in the nation's press. Congressmen demanded immediate action. On Monday, June 14, as scheduled, five American ambassadors were recalled to Washington and harangued by President Nixon about the threat of a national drug crisis. On June 13, 1971, with the final draft of President Nixon's speech declaring a national emergency over the heroin issue, the White House planners had seemingly succeeded in manufacturing a crisis to which Congress would respond with funds and reorganization authority. That night, however, an unforeseen event preempted their publicity drive: the New York *Times* decided to begin publishing the Pentagon Papers.

16

Bureau of Assassinations

Even in the most enlightened Hollywood films (not to mention Transylvanian folklore) it is perfectly justifiable to execute vampires summarily—or even their victims, when they're transformed into vampires—without the benefit of any legal process, presumably because they embody an evil so easily transmittable to others and destructive to society that there is no time for a fair trial. For similar reasons it is generally accepted in more contemporary dramas for heroin pushers (often cast as updated versions of Dracula) to be disposed of summarily by extralegal means. In the early seventies a number of films and television dramas centered around the execution of pushers by vigilantes reenacting the role of crusaders against the vampire. For example, in the movie *Hit* a former CIA agent puts together an assassination team for the express purpose of murdering a dozen or so heroin dealers in France, which the film justifies as appropriate action.

The unconventional liquidation of those suspected of participating in the narcotics business was not limited to films or fiction. When Ingersoll continued to report that "our enforcement agencies are not getting the top traffickers," Krogh demanded an explanation. Ingersoll replied that although his agency was able to identify the top traffickers in foreign nations, the local police in those countries were unwilling to move against these wholesale dealers, apparently because they had their protection. The only way to get immediate results, he suggested defensively, was to assassinate the traffickers. He assumed, at the time, that such an alternative would be "completely unthinkable"—at least, that is how he explained it to me two years later.

Unknown to Ingersoll, the Ad Hoc Committee on Narcotics, also under the aegis of Egil Krogh, was receiving information that made such an alternative "less unthinkable." The CIA reported that there were only a handful of kingpin traffickers in Latin America, who could be eliminated very swiftly. Two new advisors to Krogh, E. Howard Hunt and G. Gordon Liddy, were also pressing for unconventional actions. Liddy told William Handley, then our ambassador to Turkey, that he was for liquidating top traffickers by any means available. By mid-May, Ingersoll was asked by the White House to prepare a plan for "clandestine law enforcement"—as if law enforcement could be clandestine. What Ingersoll suggested was a fund which could be used for various clandestine activities and "which would be set up along the lines of the CIA," meaning that only a few Congressmen—the majority and minority members of the appropriate subcommittees—would know the actual details of the expenditures of this fund. Ingersoll subsequently explained to me that he intended to use this fund mainly for "disruptive tactics," such as planting misinformation among various drug-dealing factions and purposely misidentifying informants in the hope of inciting some kind of gang warfare. But at the time, at the White House, at least, assassination was "a very definite part of the plan," according to Jeffrey Donfeld, who drew up most of the memoranda concerning the "clandestine law enforcement" program.

The fund also grew in White House planning to assume proportions far beyond the original plans, according to Ingersoll. A May 27 memorandum for the president from John Ehrlichman (written by Krogh) noted that one decision the president would be required to make would concern "$50 million for overseas operations in the Bureau of Narcotics and Dangerous Drugs, for such clandestine enforcement." Later that week, John Ehrlichman met with President Nixon. According to Krogh's detailed "Outline of Discussion with the President on Drugs," the president agreed to "forceful action in [stopping] international trafficking of heroin at the host country." Specifically, the memorandum of the meeting noted, "It is anticipated that a material reduction in the supply of heroin in the U.S. can be accomplished through a $100 million (over three years) fund which can be used for *clandestine law enforcement* activities abroad and for which BNDD would *not be accountable.* This decisive action is our only hope for *destroying or immobilizing* the highest level of drug traffickers." (Emphases added.) Though the word "assassination" was never used by the president, it is clear from the context of the "Outline of Discussion" that clandestine operations in the host country could accomplish the destruction of drug traffickers, who were assumed to be under the protection of police and politicians abroad. As one of Krogh's young assistants facetiously explained when I showed him the outline of the presidential discussion, "one hundred million dollars would buy a lot of contracts on a lot of major heroin dealers." Ingersoll doubted that such a "staggering sum" was ever intended to be used for any sort of narcotics enforcement, but was possibly some sort of clandestine slush fund. In any case, it was clear that this fund was not meant to be controlled by the Bureau of Narcotics and Dangerous Drugs. (Indeed, the $100 million proposed for unaccountable clandestine activities abroad was more than the bureau had received in its entire budget in 1970 for overt and legal law-enforcement activities.) Ehrlichman suggested that an executive order be issued establishing a "Domestic Council–National Security Council Joint Action Group" on drugs which, among other things, would "set policies which relate international considerations to domestic considerations." In the accompanying decision paper the president tentatively approved the "flexible law enforcement fund . . . for clandestine activities," for which there would be no accountability. According to Krogh, this would be used for underworld contacts and disruptive tactics, with the eventual goal of destroying those deemed to be heroin traffickers.

Whatever happened to this clandestine fund is not entirely clear. Ingersoll recalls that the amount appropriated "without account-ability" was far less than the $100 million, three-year program, and was used mainly to buy informants and information abroad. Egil Krogh recalled in 1973 that after the secret fund was approved by the president, Ingersoll, who by then had lost favor with the White House, was no longer trusted to disburse it. Krogh claimed that the only narcotics assassinations actually carried out were in Southeast Asia, where the CIA arranged to have various traffickers lured into traps by their enemies. Krogh's assistants, however, strongly intimated that a great deal more was done with the program and that it resulted directly in disrupting the Latin American connection. At the suggestion of Howard Hunt, a part-time consultant to Krogh on narcotics, Lucien Conein, a CIA colonel of Corsican origin who had been deeply involved in the coup that resulted in the assassination of Premier Diem of South Vietnam, was brought into the BNDD as the head of its strategic intelligence.* That fall, Hunt also approached the Cuban exile leader Manuel Artimes in Miami and, according to Artimes, asked him about the possibility of forming a team of Cuban exile hit men to assassinate Latin American traffickers still operating outside the bailiwick of United States law. The idea of assassinations also became quite popularly applied to the French connection in Marseilles. In September, 1972, for example, the idea was broached to members of the National Commission on Marijuana and Drug Abuse during their "heroin trip" through Europe. Dr. J. Thomas Ungerleider, a member of that commission, reported in a memorandum of his conversations with BNDD officials:

> There was some talk about establishing hit squads (assassination teams), as they are said to have in a South American country. It was stated that with 150 key assassinations, the entire heroin refining operation can be thrown into chaos. "Officials" say it is known exactly who is involved in these operations but can't prove it.

If "150 key assassinations" were actually being considered by the BNDD or others in the Nixon administration, then the $100 million fund would be more easily explained. (At the time, Professor Ungerleider and other members of the commission were being shepherded through Marseilles by BNDD and embassy officials in what became a regular packaged tour for Congressmen, journalists, and other VIPs interested in narcotics.)

Meanwhile, back at the BNDD, Colonel Conein was being briefed on assassination equipment. The now-defunct B. R. Fox Company,

---

* Ingersoll believed that Conein had access to the files and modus operandi of Corsicans involved in heroin traffic. At the time he did not suspect that the White House had placed Conein there for a purpose of its own—although he considered this a possibility later.

which was then incorporated in Virginia and which provided such lethal equipment, sent a salesman to see Colonel Conein and demonstrate a wide range of devices.* Colonel Conein subsequently denied that any of this equipment was used for narcotics assassinations, saying, "That stuff is only good in a war and who's got a war?" **

* On January 23, 1975, the New York *Times* printed excerpts from a photostat of one of the company's spring, 1974, catalogues. Available items included:

Telephone handset insert. Miniature activator with time delay . . . use inside telephone handset. Automatic charge fired at–SEC following lifting of instrument handpiece.

Cigarette pack–antidisturbance explosive. Electronics and explosive module packed inside cigarette pack. When the pack is lifted or moved in any manner, the explosive is set off.

Modified flashlight . . . antidisturbance unit. Standard Everready 2D cell flashlight has antidisturbance electronics concealed inside where batteries have been removed. Remainder of the batteries have been removed. Remainder of the battery space is packed with explosive.

Remote-controlled, light-activated sensor. Unit delivers a predetermined charge from a remote location according to its pre-set code. Use with explosive for firing upon the occurrence of certain conditions relating to light intensity.

Booby-trapped, M-16 explosive clip. Use: A mechanically activated electronic charge circuit is built into a common military item. Upon removal of the single round in the magazine, either by firing or by hand removal, the explosive concealed in the magazine is detonated.

Fragmentation ball–anti-disturbance unit. Unit is similar in its operation as the anti-disturbance flashlight, BRF model FD-2. The exception is in the type of explosive charge. . . .

Explosive black box modules. . . . Flat black finish on metal rectangular modules. One screw at each end secures top on unit. Top is removed to pack inside with explosive.

** Colonel Conein was used in a character assassination. E. Howard Hunt, after forging a State Department telegram implicating President Kennedy in the murder of Diem, showed the forged document to Conein, who then appeared on an NBC documentary and divulged its contents. (Hunt also briefed the producer of the program, Fred Freed, on the secret telegram, which shaped the program in such a way as to imply Kennedy's complicity in the murder.)

However, in an interview with the Washington *Post* on June 13, 1976, Conein acknowledged that he had been brought to the Bureau of Narcotics and Dangerous Drugs to superintend a special unit which would have the capacity to assassinate selected targets in the narcotics business.

17

The Screw Worm

On June 10, 1971, at 3:10 in the afternoon, President Nixon met a "miracle worker"—at least that was the way that Egil Krogh, Jr., introduced Dr. Jerome Jaffe, a well-respected pharmacologist and psychiatrist with immaculate liberal credentials in his home city of Chicago. The president, already briefed by Krogh on how Jaffe had single-handedly reduced the crime rate in Chicago through the magic of distributing methadone and other treatment services to drug addicts, asked Jaffe why, if his program had been so successful, Mayor Daley was not aware of it. Dr. Jaffe, always exuding confidence, replied, according to the memo in the President's File, "Daley did not have to know about the program because I was taking care of the mayor's city" (apparently meaning that his drug program had succeeded in reducing the number of drug addicts in Chicago). "What was your bag in terms of treatment?" the president asked. Jaffe replied by describing a complex series of programs including "therapeutic communities ... methadone detoxification ... methadone maintenance [and] occasionally psychiatry," which produced, according to Jaffe, a "40 percent decrease in crime." The president, obviously impressed, though uninterested in the details of the program, suggested the possibility of the death penalty for those in the narcotics business. Jaffe, distressed, attempted to change the subject by suggesting that as law enforcement became more efficient, the price of heroin would increase, and therefore there would be a need for an enormous "treatment capacity"—the type he could provide—as an alternative to crime for heroin addicts. Attempting to impress the president with the possibility of a technological solution, the miracle doctor reported that work was progressing on a saliva test to detect heroin which would replace the urine test presently being used in Vietnam. (He explained, according to the memo, "It is easier for men than women to get urine into a bottle.") The president seemed unimpressed. Jaffe next suggested that with more money they might be able to develop a "narcotic antagonistic" which could "block" addicts from receiving any sensation from heroin. He further suggested, at another point, that Naloxone, an already existing antagonist, could be used to demonstrate to servicemen the dangers of heroin addiction, since it would bring about a precipitous set of withdrawal symptoms. The president "opted for using this method [in Vietnam] even though there was the remote possibility of a few fatalities."

As the meeting drew to a close at four o'clock, Dr. Jaffe suddenly came up with a technological solution that caught the president's fancy—"an insect which could consume poppy crops." According to the memo in Krogh's file, "The President became excited about the idea and called Secretary of Agriculture [Hardin] in order to get information on the insect which he had heard to be bred in such a way as to insure its own destruction. . . . The President remarked that the insect died after intercourse. A member of the group suggested that this insect be called the 'screw worm.' " The president then spent fifteen minutes discussing the screw worm with Dr. Jaffe, according to Krogh. The president wanted Edward Land, the founder and developer of the Polaroid camera, and William Lear, the founder of Lear Jets, "brought in to help develop this concept." He ordered Secretary Hardin, still on the phone, to move ahead at full speed in developing the screw worm, promising to obtain a special appropriation for it from Congress. Private millionaires and the Agriculture Department would thus all be part of a secret project to develop an insect that ate the poppies that produced the opium that supplied the heroin that obsessed President Nixon.

On June 17, less than a week after President Nixon heard of (or invented) the screw worm, the president asked Congress for a special supplementary appropriation for the war on heroin which, among other things, would provide "two million dollars to the Department of Agriculture for research and development of herbicides which can be used to destroy growths of narcotics-producing plants without adverse ecological effects." Since a herbicide is defined simply as a "substance used to destroy plants," Nixon's speech writers were at least temporarily able to disguise the screw worm as an innocent-sounding ecological weed-killer.

With the screw worm being biologically designed at the Department of Agriculture's Stoneville (Mississippi) laboratories, where scientists experimented in producing various mutations of weevils by manipulating their life cycles, President Nixon was finally able to launch a worldwide campaign, under the supervision of Krogh, to eradicate all the poppies in the world. Although Turkey had already agreed to eliminate the poppy cultivation in its Anatolian provinces, most of the world's poppies grew in countries which were not vulnerable to the sort of political pressures put on Turkey by the United States (and NATO). Krogh fully realized that if the demand for heroin continued, other poppy areas would rapidly fill the vacuum left by Turkey—especially at the then current market price of $500 a pound for morphine base in Europe. The new coordinator for international narcotics control, Nelson Gross, argued that "it wasn't enough to eliminate opium in one country. The cultivation of the opium poppy had to be ended throughout the world." Nixon tentatively agreed with Gross and endorsed the idea of possibly using the screw worm in the so-called Golden Triangle, an area including parts of Burma, Laos, and Thailand.

Before the poppies of the Golden Triangle (and elsewhere) could be eliminated through biological warfare, they first had to be located and scientifically charted. Gross managed to enlist the support of Secretary of Defense Melvin Laird and of the Air Force, which supplied specially equipped SR71 planes, the successor to the U2 spy planes, and Air Force reconnaissance Phantom planes for mapping out the poppy fields of Burma, Thailand, Laos, and other nations. Finally, after all the bad publicity the Department of Defense had received in Vietnam, it appeared to Laird that Phantoms and SR71s could be used to alleviate a domestic problem—heroin addiction. But the planes came precariously close to the Chinese border, creating more than one potential incident and threatening the détente with China that Henry Kissinger was then busily working on. As much as Kissinger and the National Security Council would like to help in the war against the poppy, the word came down from Kissinger himself that the overflights of Burmese poppy fields would have to be curtailed.

The gap was quickly filled by the National Aeronautics and Space Administration (NASA), which was determined to demonstrate that the space program could be used to help society fight domestic problems such as heroin. NASA offered to make the Earth Resources Technological Satellite available for photographing poppy fields all over the world, thereby eliminating the overflight problem. To obtain an authentic "signature" for photoreconnaissance from the satellite, the Department of Agriculture obligingly planted poppy fields in Louisiana and Arizona (photographs of which would be compared with photographs taken of the suspected poppy fields by the spy satellite).

While NASA prepared to search for poppy fields from outer space, the Department of Agriculture actually created a voracious screw worm that would rapidly proliferate and destroy any poppy field in the world. Dr. Quentin Jones, Agriculture's man on the case, modestly explained that the poppy weevil "might be offered to such countries as Laos and Pakistan whose poppy fields border on those of Burma and Afghanistan," and suggested to Gross and Krogh that the Department of Agriculture had two alternatives: Plan A or Plan B. Plan A would entail a crash program of all the resources of the department and would be put to the task of getting a poppy weevil airborne within six months. It could be expected to destroy the world's poppy crops within a year. Plan B involved continued experiments for a year to determine whether the screw worm was host specific. Krogh inquired what "host specific" meant. Dr. Jones explained that if the screw worm was host specific, it would eat the world's poppy crops and then die when it had exhausted the supply of poppies. If, on the other hand, the weevil—or any mutation of it—was not host specific, it would adapt to another host, such as rice or wheat. The specter of an American screw worm eradicating the wheat and rice crops as well as the poppies of Asia was sufficient to dampen the enthusiasm of the president for the crash weevil-development program. Even if the screw worm and its mutants were host specific, the State Department argued, they still might cross international boundaries and work themselves into the licit poppy fields of the Soviet Union, thereby undermining détente. Given these drawbacks, the screw worm was relegated to a long-term experimental program which would be made operational only if it produced a categorically host-specific weevil that would also stop at international borders.

18

The Celebrity File

As well as providing funds for clandestine operations and assassinations, the new heroin crusade promised to fulfill a cherished political objective of the Nixon administration: the recruitment of celebrities into the Nixon camp. In 1969, immediately after he assumed office, President Nixon had attempted to mobilize the disc jockeys of the nation into an antimarijuana campaign, which would give his administration considerable exposure on the nation's airwaves. Art Buchwald, the noted humorist, invited the leading disc jockeys to the White House at the president's request. Egil Krogh, coordinator of the event, explained, "Murray the K came and Cousin Brucie came and others. . . . We asked them to incorporate into their hip language between the playing of hip tunes sort of an antidrug theme. . . . They tried to tell us that perhaps they weren't the best vehicle for . . . an antidrug pitch." The president was slightly more successful in recruiting Art Linkletter into his anti-LSD campaign, after the entertainer's daughter committed suicide in 1969. An Air Force plane was sent to fly Linkletter from California to the governors' conference in Washington in December, 1969, and after an emotional session with the assembled governors, Linkletter agreed to head a national advisory council on drugs.

Now the White House sought a more charismatic celebrity, according to Krogh, and in December, 1970, Elvis Presley, the rock star, was brought to the White House to cooperate in the drug program. Egil Krogh described the encounter between Presley and the president: "Elvis showed up at the northwest gate of the White House with velvet pants and his silk shirt opened to his waist. . . . He wanted to tell the president how strongly he felt [about the drug problem] because he loved his country . . . but he said he'd also like to have a BNDD badge, because he collected badges. . . . His gift to the president was not appropriate—a .44 Colt automatic pistol with bullets. . . . He went into the president's office and it had to be the most bizarre meeting I'd ever seen. . . . He said, 'Mr. President, I really believe in what you are doing, I love my country, I love my family, I think law enforcement is great.'. . . The president suggested that he use an antidrug theme in his songs and Presley responded by showing the president his badge collection, and asked the president for a BNDD badge. The president shook his head in disbelief . . . and Presley ended the interview by suggesting that they keep this meeting secret. Nixon responded, 'Absolutely! Don't tell anybody; preserve your credibility at all cost.' " Elvis later received his BNDD badge, but the White House staff decided that he would not make an appropriate campaigner for the president.

It was not until the spring of 1971, when the White House strategists were writing the scenario for a national heroin crusade, that the appropriate celebrity was found—Sammy Davis, Jr. John Ehrlichman broached the subject to President Nixon on May 28. The details of that discussion, transcribed by Krogh for the President's File, note, "It is suggested that the President consent to an interview with Sammy Davis, Jr. on the subject of drug abuse as an introduction to a ninety minute drug abuse television special M.C.'d by Sammy Davis, Jr. and participated in by well known musicians and actors." Ehrlichman cited the advantages of such a connection, saying, "In view of the fact that Davis will be taking over a number of talk shows over the next four months, the administration would get continuous mileage out of the fact that Davis is involved with this production. Furthermore, Davis could be asked to bring a live production to our troops in Viet Nam and in NATO countries." (Donald Rumsfeld, then ambassador to NATO, had sent Egil Krogh a memorandum a few days earlier mentioning that President Nixon had suggested sending "Art Linkletter . . . to do a world tour of military bases . . . linked with the drug program because he could talk so effectively about his daughter and the problem.") Ehrlichman finally persuaded the president to use Sammy Davis, Jr., by arguing, "As a result of this special, the President could cultivate a friendship with the top artist for 1972 campaign purposes."

To further the plan, President Nixon personally met with Sammy Davis, Jr., on July 1, 1971. According to the memorandum on the meeting, Davis said that he was "honored and thrilled to be with the President." Nixon quickly came to the point and said, "As a celebrity the country would listen to [your] caution about drugs much quicker than they would to the cautions of politicians.... Kids would be turned on by [you]." He further assured Davis that the administration was for kids and it was not trying to repress them. Knowing that Davis was interested in the fate of black colleges, Nixon added, "The Administration is behind black colleges and has thus far given more than a hundred fifty million dollars to them." As the discussion continued, Nixon showed progressively more venom toward the "elite." He said that "the elite of the United States are least capable of governing the United States," and then paraphrased Tolstoy, saying, "Every individual is basically two people; he has creative and destructive instincts.... The secret in life is to sublimate the destructive instincts, for the same energies that can build can destroy." Davis, obviously impressed, agreed to help the president—although he had no way of knowing at the time exactly what it would entail.

On August 20, after Sammy Davis, Jr., had agreed to go to Vietnam for the administration, Jeffrey Donfeld sent a memo to various agencies of the government stating that Davis "will integrate into his show the anti-drug items which are of special importance to our government. I would therefore like to ask you to submit to me brief vignettes or brief messages or even anecdotes which will get across messages of particular concern to your department." Officials of the government responded to the White House by writing sketches for Davis. John Ingersoll suggested such anecdotal situations as the following:

A known drug abuser appears at a large conference on drug abuse prevention. His dress was extreme in the hippie sense and he insisted on taking the floor to criticize all printed information available to the public. He was particularly incensed by an Ad Council piece entitled

"Diagram of a Drug Abuser" . . . he took it apart item by item. What was cynically amusing was that he personally mirrored every fact he challenged. He wore dark glasses, his nose was noticeably red, he sniffed at every verbal pause, he was emaciated, and wore a long-sleeve hippie costume. He lit a cigarette with hands shaking so badly that he had to hold the match with the other hand. He closed with the impassioned statement, "I say they should tell it like it is. . . ."

Ingersoll also enclosed a "tongue-in-cheek quiz" and a *"Laugh-In* format" for a film entitled *Pot Is a Put-On.* The Defense Department suggested "incorporating a comedy routine around one of Davis' more well known themes, "Here Comes De Judge," but, more modest than the BNDD, it also suggested employing the talents of "a professional comedy writer."

While Sammy Davis's October trip to Vietnam was being planned, the White House attempted to arrange a television show for Davis, with presidential participation, on drugs. To sponsor this program, Jeffrey Donfeld approached Ira Englander, of the Hoffmann–La Roche pharmaceutical company (which manufactures Valium), and Perry Lieber, the president of the Hughes Sports Network (Hughes being a long-time supporter of President Nixon's campaigns). Although both showed great interest in the Nixon–Sammy Davis program, they were unwilling to provide all the funds for production costs. Donfeld thus stated, in a rather pessimistic memorandum to Egil Krogh, on October 21, 1971, "Unless someone on Chuck Colson's staff can come up with the production costs and arrange for network time, this project may never be launched." Colson, however, showed little enthusiasm for raising money for the television spectacular— especially since it would be to the credit of Egil Krogh rather than himself. All President Nixon eventually received from the Sammy Davis connection was a loving embrace on television at election time.

The lack of a slush fund to finance such activities as the Sammy Davis special concerned John Ehrlichman. Donfeld had suggested in an earlier memorandum that "there is a feeler by the drug industry to donate funds to a drive to be used in the fight against drug abuse." Although the government was restricted by law from accepting these funds for a specific purpose, Donfeld suggested that "if a foundation existed, we could recommend that such profits go there." Ehrlichman became interested in the idea of creating such a foundation, not only for the funds which it would attract but because it would increase the president's visibility on the antidrug issue. He thus recommended to Nixon that "in order to firmly and continually place the President in the forefront of those concerned with drug abuse, it is suggested that the White House encourage the establishment of a drug abuse foundation to which the President would have close association. The concept is similar to Franklin Delano Roosevelt's association with the March of Dimes." The president immediately approved the idea of creating a March of Dollars for a national drug foundation, and assigned the project to Egil Krogh. In his June 30 (1971) proposal for creating the foundation, Krogh estimated "that three million dollars would be available from industry sources as feed money. It is reasonable to assume that the foundation could raise twenty-five million dollars over three years. These funds would not come from traditional political sources." In asking for direct presidential involvement on the board of directors of the planned foundation, Krogh noted that "drug abuse is of paramount concern in the public mind. . . . Presidential involvement would crystallize support on a positive issue." Since presidential involvement meant in practical terms being photographed by the press, Haldeman approved the "photo opportunity . . . in a location other than the White House, such as the National Press Club." Bruce Kehrli, another White House public-relations strategist, commented on the proposal, "Although . . . it isn't the ultimate solution in terms of substance, it should provide a hype for the P.R. side of the drug abuse issue, since the President's initiative [June 17, 1971] got only moderate coverage because of the breaking of the New York Times [Pentagon Papers] story." This promising project, however, was jettisoned when Tex McCrary, who was to be the fund-raiser for the foundation, inadvertently told a journalist about the plan to raise money from the drug industry to wage the heroin crusade. As Donfeld pointed out in a February 4, 1972, memorandum, "Once it becomes known that we are courting the pharmaceutical industry, the integrity of the project is impugned," and he recommended that "someone turn off McCrary." Even though by this time Gen. William Westmoreland and Tricia Nixon had been mobilized for the March of Dollars, Haldeman decided reluctantly to "turn off" the foundation idea.

As it turned out, narcotics did not prove to be as great a lure for attracting celebrities and finances as the Nixon strategists had hoped.

As the 1972 election approached, and corporations contributed, illicitly, tens of millions of dollars to the Nixon reelection campaign, and celebrities joined the political bandwagon, the "celebrity file" was closed.

19

World War III

On August 2, 1971, Nelson Gross, of Saddle River, New Jersey, was chosen to lead a worldwide attack on illicit drugs. As a New Jersey politician, Gross had been successful in staging a quiet revolt against the older wing of the Republican party in New Jersey, thus gaining a modicum of power for himself in 1968. He failed to win elected office as a congressman or senator, even though he ran loyally on President Nixon's law-and-order theme. After his defeat for the Senate in 1970, Gross asked Nixon for a position in foreign policy, and Nixon appointed him senior advisor and coordinator for international narcotics matters at the Department of State. In theory, the "global war" against drugs was to be coordinated by the newly created (September, 1971) Cabinet Committee on International Narcotics Control, which held its first meeting on network television and included such illustrious figures as Secretary of State William Rogers, who nominally chaired the new committee, Attorney General John Mitchell, Secretary of the Treasury John Connally, Secretary of Defense Melvin Laird, newly appointed Secretary of Agriculture Earl Butz, and CIA director Richard Helms. The committee met on only three other occasions before it was phased out after the 1972 election, and most of the day-to-day tactical decisions were left to Gross and

Egil Krogh, who was, in addition to his other duties, executive director of the cabinet committee.

Although a battle had temporarily been won in Turkey, the war against heroin was anything but over—at least as far as Gross and Krogh were concerned. The 1972 election was little more than a year away, and there was the dramatic possibility for further victories in the war against heroin. The rapidly expanding BNDD (its budget had trebled in four years) advanced the theory that there still remained a large Turkish stockpile of opium, which would explain the need for drug agents in the foreseeable future. According to the convenient stockpile theory, every Turkish poppy farmer had squirreled away a hoard of opium as a dowry for his daughter's marriage and for other future emergencies. Even though they were now being forced by their government to plow under their opium crops, they could reach into this presumed hoard and sell it to traffickers for the American market.

President Nixon had already publicly demanded the eradication of the poppy flower from the entire world, and Gross concluded that America could not wait for the screw worm to be developed. The Golden Triangle was not only producing ten times as much illicit opium as Turkey ever produced but supplying about 20 percent of the American soldiers in Vietnam with pure heroin. Gross foresaw that it was only a matter of time before this Golden Triangle heroin found its way into the American market, and he decided to consult Graham Martin, who had been ambassador to Thailand and to Italy before becoming ambassador to South Vietnam. Much to Gross's surprise, but not necessarily to the White House staff's, Ambassador Martin, in a state of exasperation, reported in no uncertain terms that the only way of disrupting the supply of opium from the Golden Triangle was to organize assassination teams to kill the few key traffickers that controlled the trade. Though New Jersey politics in Gross's day were fairly tough, assassinations seemed extreme.

Instead, Gross decided to make heroin a primary foreign-policy objective of the United States. He ordered fifty-odd American embassies around the world to draw up action plans which specified how American diplomats in those countries could stimulate interest in the heroin problem to persuade the host government to conform to American narcotics objectives, and to detail ways in which the CIA and State Department intelligence could be used to discover and intercept heroin traffic. Gross further wanted American diplomats to threaten any country that refused to cooperate in the effort with an immediate cutoff of economic and military aid. He even suggested the use of the American veto to prevent the World Bank and other international financial organizations from extending credit to such countries. There was considerable concern in the higher councils of the State Department that such "heroin diplomacy," as Gross called it, would lose more friends for the United States than it would net traffickers, and might endanger what they considered more long-term foreign-policy objectives, such as the safety of the United States. Henry Kissinger's National Security Council also had its doubts about heroin diplomacy, especially since less than two months before Gross assumed his command in the new global war, the secret report of a White House task force with representatives from both the National Security Council and the State Department concluded, "application of aid sanctions would be ineffective and counterproductive except where degrees of U.S. support establish overwhelming diplomatic dependence (Vietnam)." The White House task force recognized that aid sanctions might result in favorable publicity for the president, but listed against this advantage six drawbacks:

1. . . . would exasperate relations and make cooperation even less likely.
2. . . . may create internal political repercussions making it difficult for governments to cooperate (Turkey, Pakistan, India).
3. Would be counterproductive to other major U.S. security and foreign policy needs (Southeast Asia, Turkey).
4. Cannot be applied to countries where we provide no aid (France, Burma, Lebanon, Bulgaria).
5. Could not be applied easily within international financing institutions . . . unless we invoke extreme action of veto.
6. *All threats subject to our bluff being called.*

When Gross read the "international working group report," as it was called, he knew he was playing with fire in threatening to cut off American aid, but he also believed that "our bluff" wouldn't be called. He thus began the main counterinsurgency effort against heroin by inducing Laos and Thailand, which were militarily dependent on the United States, to form mobile strike forces with American advisors. These strike forces could then be employed against narcotics traffickers in the Golden Triangle. In Laos, "irregular" narcotics police, as the State Department put it, burned a group of huts suspected of being used for converting opium into heroin, before a more formalized *groupe spécial d'investigation* was created to enforce the newly promulgated narcotics laws (written by the American embassy in September, 1971).

In Thailand, U.S. aid financed the creation of a task force known as SNO (or, less acronymously, the Special Narcotics Organization), which attempted to intercept opium caravans in northern Thailand and to intimidate Thai officials involved in the traffic. For example, one SNO colonel, recruited by the CIA, simply went to leading Thai officials and told them in a quiet voice that they would be killed if they continued in the opium business. (Many withdrew, and others were killed, according to the unverified claims of CIA officials.) Among the traffickers in the Golden Triangle were private armies of Nationalist Chinese. Gross and his CIA advisor on the working committee believed that it would be more effective to buy them out of the opium business than to threaten them. Despite the cabinet committee's stated policy against preemptive buying of opium, which Eugene Rossides and John Connally in the Treasury Department insisted on, a deal was struck in March, 1972, with a band of Chinese in northern Thailand. In return for land in Thailand for "farming" and "assistance," which was to be financed mainly through the United States, though laundered through the United Nations, they delivered twenty-six tons of brownish material that supposedly constituted their entire opium stockpile, and pledged to remain out of the opium business for several years. The deal subsequently appeared somewhat embarrassing when unevaluated CIA reports were leaked to columnist Jack Anderson by some American missionaries interested in arranging opium purchases for competing Nationalist troops. These reports said that the brownish material which was delivered and incinerated in front of news cameras was in fact heavily weighted with cow fodder. The BNDD, which had sampled the narcotics randomly and found a "high content" of opium, disputed Anderson's charges. (If the bureau's samples were indeed random and accurate, it would seem that the CIA reports which emanated from the missionaries were inaccurate.) In any case, the possibility for counterinsurgency warfare was ultimately limited by the always-present danger of embarrassing leaks about the United States government's buying opium or arranging the intimidation (or assassination) of our allies in Southeast Asia.

Gross also attempted to spread the American heroin crusade to the rest of the world by convincing underdeveloped nations that narcotics was a major problem for them as well as for America, and that they should immediately create a special narcotics police force modeled on the American Bureau of Narcotics and Dangerous Drugs. The United States would provide the equipment, propaganda, and necessary narcotics agents to train the local forces. Cambodia, for example, was given $20,000 to create the Khamir Narcotics Unit and received "technical guidance provided through bi-monthly visits of Bureau of Narcotics personnel from Saigon." Afghanistan received training for one Afghani police officer and $60,000 for "an aerial survey of opium poppy cultivation areas." The number of narcotics advisors in American embassies abroad proliferated at such a rate that Daniel Patrick Moynihan complained in a telex, when he was ambassador to India, "One can scarcely enter an American embassy in some parts of the world without being surrounded by narks. The cable traffic that crosses an American ambassador's desk concerns drugs more than any other single issue of domestic importance. Visiting bureaucrats are more likely—on a statistical basis—to be concerned with drug matters than any other subject."

In the midst of his far-flung global war against heroin, Gross became the target of a grand jury in New Jersey investigating corruption in his former bailiwick. As his own indictment grew nearer, he reluctantly had to return from his peripatetic travels to Afghanistan (where he helped arrange the return of Timothy Leary from Kabul) and other opium-producing regions, to prepare his own defense. In early 1973 Gross was indicted and convicted of several felonies, including conspiracy to bribe and evasion of taxes. Without his irrepressible enthusiasm, the global war was quietly disassembled by the State Department, which now returned to its more traditional role.

PART SIX

Production of Terror ★

Control over the flow of information emanating from the political center will be our most important weapon. . . .

—EDWARD LUTTWAK, *Coup d'Etat*

20

The Manipulation of the Media

The extraordinary measures that the White House planned to undertake in its war against crime depended heavily for their success on the organization of public fears. If Americans could be persuaded that their lives and the lives of their children were being threatened by a rampant epidemic of narcotics addiction, Nixon's advisors presumed they would not object to decisive government actions, such as no-knock warrants, pretrial detention, wiretaps, and unorthodox strike forces—even if the emergency measures had to cross or circumvent the traditional rights of a suspect. To achieve this state of fear required transforming a relatively small heroin addiction problem—which even according to the most exaggerated estimates directly affected only a minute fraction of the population in 1971—into a plague that threatened all. This in turn required the artful use of the media to propagate a simple but terrifying set of stereotypes about drug addiction: the addict-dealer would be depicted as a modern-day version of the medieval vampire, ineluctably driven to commit crimes and infect others by his insatiable and incurable need for heroin. The victims would be shown as innocent youth, totally vulnerable to the vampire-addict. And the federal law-enforcement officer would be shown as the only effective instrument for stopping the vampire-addicts from contaminating the rest of society. The most obvious medium available for projecting these stereotypes on the popular imagination was television.

The plan to mobilize the media developed in March, 1970. President Nixon had instructed his chief domestic advisor, John Ehrlichman, to "further utilize television as a tool in the fight against drug abuse." Ehrlichman then turned the project over to Egil Krogh, his assistant, and Jeb Stuart Magruder, the deputy director of the Office of Communications in the White House. Magruder, a thirty-six-year-old former advertising salesman and merchandise manager for a department store, found initially that officials in the various federal agencies resisted his plans for a publicity hype of the drug issue. He recalled in his autobiography, "The first meeting we called was hilarious—I couldn't believe those people [in the federal agencies] were working on the same problem. . . . We encountered the usual hostility the White House people meet in the bureaucratic world." But eventually "everyone agreed that television was the single most effective means to reach young people and alert them to the hazards of drugs." On March 11 the White House held a press conference, and the memorandum by Magruder summing up the "feedback" noted that

> the media interest sparked by the press conference has been favorable. . . . We have been getting calls from all over the country . . . ranging from network television to rural weeklies to professional journals. . . . A good many of those calling indicated enthusiastic support for the Administration [press] programs and inferred [*sic*] that they would be doing supportive and follow-up pieces, including editorials.

The White House strategists, however, were more interested in prime-time television. On March 18, 1970, Jeffrey Donfeld, the enterprising assistant to Krogh, sent a memorandum to the White House proposing that since "the President expressed his desire to have more anti-drug themes on television," the president should personally attend a meeting of television producers that Donfeld was arranging for April 9, 1970, at the White House. Among those being invited, Donfeld noted, were:

> 1. The vice-presidents in charge of programming of the three networks.

2. The vice-presidents in charge of continuity acceptance [who approve the contents of the programs] of the networks.
3. The heads of production of the six major television production companies.
4. The producers of select programs which can accommodate narcotics themes . . . this group will represent at least 90 percent of prime-time shows.
5. Television programming vice-presidents of the three major advertising agencies.

Donfeld explained that the day-long program would be held in the White House theater and that the purpose of the meeting would be to "stimulate these producers to include in their fall programming anti-drug themes." In a March 19 memorandum John Ehrlichman recommended personally that the president meet the television executives in his office for a "photo opportunity." On April 2 a detailed scenario was drawn up for the meeting of the following week. "To expedite the meeting and give it a little novelty," it recommended:

> The Attorney General will just be finishing his remarks before the group in the White House theatre [at 9:30 A.M.]. At that time Steve Bull [the White House assistant] would enter and hand the Attorney General a note. The Attorney General would then announce that the President has asked us to step over to his office. Prior to that time, the men attending the conference would not know when they would be seeing the President. Therefore, the Attorney General's announcement would be the first indication that they were about to go over and meet with the President.

H. R. Haldeman approved this spontaneous moment in the scenario, even though it broke "the President's rule of not doing something before 10:00 A.M." After this minor success, Magruder sent a background paper to Attorney General Mitchell, stating:

> We intend to make available to the television industry information on anti-drug themes that could be used in a broad expanse of appropriate television programs. . . . The President thought that an effort should be made to have one television series with a drug theme analogous [*sic*] to the *FBI Story* [a continuing series on ABC television]. . . . As a consequence, invitations to forty-eight persons who were responsible for over 90% of prime-time television between 7:30 P.M. and 11:00 P.M.

were sent over your signature on behalf of a President greatly
concerned over the drug problem.

Magruder further explained, "The individuals being invited think in
dramatic terms. We have therefore tailored the program to appeal to
their dramatic instincts. Your personal presentation will be virtually
the only 'straight' speech. The remainder of the program will consist
of audio-visual and unusual presentations." The unusual presentations that Magruder had planned were described as follows: "The
Bureau of Narcotics and Dangerous Drugs will have one of its special
agents interview one of its undercover agents"; "The Bureau of
Customs will bring in shepherd dogs to demonstrate how they are
used to detect concealed marijuana"; "The National Institute of
Mental Health will conduct a group therapy session with addicts";
"The Department of Defense will present a slide and film presentation depicting the relationship of . . . dissent and drugs." One specific
goal of this program was to "provide a telephone number in
Washington which television writers [could] call in order to obtain
information for inclusion in their scripts, plus access to federal
activities (training sessions, Customs Inspection points) so that their
scripts would have a high degree of realism." Finally, Magruder
sycophantishly reminded the attorney general, "National attention
will properly be focused on you as the principal individual in the
Nixon administration whose concern is with drug abuse." Mitchell
agreed to give the "straight" speech and announce that he had just
received an impromptu message from the president.

John Ehrlichman got a slightly different explanation for the
purpose of this "White House Theater." Jeffrey Donfeld stated in an
April 3 memorandum, "The government has a difficult time changing
the attitudes of people. . . . Television, however, is a subliminal
stimulus." In other words, viewers would receive a hidden, or
subliminal, message, which they would not be conscious of receiving
but which would all the same stimulate their fear of heroin addicts.
"If indeed television is a subliminal stimulus," Donfeld suggested to
Ehrlichman, "you are urging the producers to focus their creative
genius to effect changes in people's attitudes about drugs . . . [and
offering] to guide them in presenting efficacious programs." The
talking points Donfeld prepared for Ehrlichman included such
instructions as: "Program content should be carefully designed for the
audience that is likely to be tuned in at a given time"; "It would not

be accurate to portray the drug problem as a ghetto problem. . . . It is a problem which touches all economic, social and racial stratas of America"; "You will receive a drug information kit. . . . Included in that kit will be a telephone contact list so that you or your script writers can call government officials for clarification and additional information"; "Television subtly and inexorably helps to mold the attitudes, thinking and motivations of a vast number of Americans."

The remarks that the president made to the television producers were prepared by Buchanan, the speech writer who delighted in writing hard-line speeches which closely paralleled the rhetoric then being used in New York State by Governor Rockefeller. In this "impromptu" speech the president warned ominously that "the scourge of narcotics has swept the young generation like an epidemic. . . . There is no community in this country today that can safely claim immunity from it. . . . Estimates of it are somewhere between five and twelve million people in this country have used illicit drugs." (When Buchanan redrafted this speech for Nixon six months later, he increased the estimates to "between twelve and twenty million people"; he thus added some seven million new drug users to government estimates. The president then pointed out to the television producers that "between the time a child is born and he leaves high school, it is estimated he watches about 15,000 hours of television. . . . The children of this country are your captive audience for a good segment of their growing years in which their whole future can be determined." Then he warned, "If this nation is going to survive, it will have to depend to the great extent on how you gentlemen help raise our children." Finally, the advanced scenario called for the president "spontaneously" to summon the press to the Oval Office to photograph the television producers.

The conference went precisely as scheduled by the scenarists. The executives and producers, rounded up for the president by John Ball, of J. Walter Thompson advertising agency (where Haldeman had formerly been employed), met at the White House and were greeted by the attorney general. At 9:30 A.M., in the midst of his introductory remarks, Mitchell received an "urgent message" from the president, summoning the television producers to the Oval Office, where he delivered the "off-the-cuff" remarks prepared by Buchanan. The production then adjourned to the White House Theater, where the German shepherds demonstrated how they could sniff out marijuana in mail pouches. At lunch, in the State Department dining room, John

Ehrlichman added drama by saying that the dogs had actually discovered a packet of hashish during the demonstration. Afterward, the forty guests were shown one and a half hours of "shocking" films of narcotics addiction in the president's private projection room. The carefully staged demonstrations were highly successful, as Krogh recalled. One television producer at the conference, Robert Lewis Shayon, later commented, "Up front in the fifth row I sensed that there was hardly a dry eye in the whole hard-boiled crowd—so genuine, touching and fraught with universal significance [was the program]." Meanwhile, the advertising agency executives, who provide sponsors for most of the programs on television, were brought into the East Room by Jeb Stuart Magruder. To their surprise they were greeted by the president himself, who listened attentively as Magruder explained how the advertisers could use their influence to encourage television producers to incorporate the drug-oriented scenes, selected by the White House, into their programming. Never fully realizing the extent to which they themselves were part of a production, most of the television producers and executives left the White House that night believing, at least according to subsequent interviews, that they were part of a war on drugs.

"The producers loved it, and in the weeks following they flooded us with letters about new drug-related programs," Magruder later noted, and added, "Shows like *The Name of the Game* and *Hawaii Five-O* added segments on the problem, new series were planned, and dozens of documentaries were produced." Such programs as *The FBI, Mod Squad, Marcus Welby, M.D., Matt Lincoln, Room 222, The Young Lawyers,* and *Dan August* all promised to produce segments on the narcotics problem. In addition, producer Jack Webb began negotiations with the Treasury Department for an entire television series called *Treasury Agent,* which would give continuous coverage to the administration's heroin crusade. On September 21, 1970, Magruder advised Ehrlichman in a memorandum, "At least twenty television programs this fall will have a minimum of one anti-drug theme in it as a result of our conference" and recommended in the following month that there be a "White House Conference on Drugs for the radio industry."

The purpose of the meeting with radio-station owners and managers would be "to urge increased drug education programming and to curb pro drug music and jargon of disc jockeys," according to an October 13 memorandum for the president prepared by Egil Krogh.

"This conference is a continuation of the effort to enlist mass media's support . . . to fight against drug abuse," Krogh further explained. In the press plan for the conference he advised the president that there would be "no press coverage of your remarks to the group in the Cabinet Room, but there will be press coverage of the German Shepherd marijuana sniffing demonstration." To add weight to the conference, Dean Burch, chairman of the Federal Communications Commission, which regulates the broadcasting industry, agreed to attend this meeting of seventy leaders of the radio industry. The scenario further suggested that "the President will have a colorful opportunity to emphasize the stepped-up federal law enforcement effort against illicit drug traffic and can praise the initiative of law enforcement people" on news cameras that would televise the event.

As scheduled in the press plan, the White House conference on the radio industry began promptly at nine, the morning of October 14, 1970, with a speech by Dean Burch on "The FCC and Public Service Time." He suggested that the Federal Communications Commission would look favorably on licensees who provided more time for antidrug commercials. Then came the same dog show that had been prepared for the television producers, complete with German shepherds, shock films, and demonstrations of law-enforcement techniques. John Ehrlichman repeated his lunch remarks. The president continued by telling the radio owners, "We have brought you gentlemen here today because we very much need your active help to halt this epidemic. . . . Ninety-eight percent of the young people between the age of twelve and seventeen listen to the radio. . . . No one is in a better position than you to warn our youth constantly against the dangers in drugs." Again, according to White House evaluations, the conference proved successful in injecting the drug menace into radio programming. "Our costs were minimal and the results, measured in terms of television and radio programming, were remarkable," Magruder concluded.

The media campaign continued with the highly publicized Drug Abuse Prevention Week; the National Drug Alert (to coincide with the opening of school); high-level briefings for media executives; drug seminars, in which dramatic law-enforcement stories were given to newspapers; and a White House meeting for religious leaders on the drug problem. By 1971, responding to continual White House pressure, television stations and sponsors had donated commercial time worth some $37 million (at times which may have gone unsold anyway) for administration messages about the war on drugs, according to an estimate done by the Advertising Council in 1972. In large part because of this massive "subliminal stimulation" campaign in the media, President Nixon could point out in his June, 1971, declaration of a national emergency that "the threat of narcotics . . . frightens many Americans." The generation of fear had succeeded: even in cities which had few, if any, heroin addicts, private polls commissioned by the White House showed that citizens believed the drug menace to be one of the two main threats to their safety.

21

The Movable Epidemic

We must now candidly recognize that the ... present efforts to control drug abuse are not sufficient in themselves. The problem has assumed the dimensions of a national emergency. I intend to take every step necessary to deal with this emergency. ...

—PRESIDENT RICHARD M. NIXON, in a message to Congress on
June 17, 1971

President Nixon justified his request for emergency powers to deal with drug abuse in 1971 by citing an uncontrollable heroin epidemic which, if not brought under immediate control, "will surely in time destroy us." According to official statistics supplied to the media by federal agencies, the number of addict-users had increased from 68,000 in 1969 to 315,000 in 1970 to 559,000 in 1971, or what Myles Ambrose declared in 1971 to be a "tenfold increase." Such a geometric progression threatened the entire American citizenry with "the hell of addiction" in a few short years, the president suggested, because every individual infected with heroin was in turn driven to infect at least six others. Nor could such an epidemic be brought under control by ordinary means: the president explained that the suppliers of heroin "are literally the slave traders of our time. . . . They are traffickers in Living Death [and] they must be hunted to the ends of the earth."

A tenfold increase in the number of heroin addicts would certainly be a cause for national concern; the magnitude of the 1971 epidemic was, however, more a product of government statisticians than of heroin traffickers.

Until 1970, official estimates of the number of heroin addicts were based on a register kept by the Bureau of Narcotics and Dangerous Drugs which, like the FBI's Uniform Code Reports, was simply a compilation of reports from local police departments. All police departments—and medical authorities—were supposed to report the names of known addicts to the bureau. And, on the theory that most, if not all, addicts eventually would come to the attention of some police department or hospital, it was assumed that the total number of names on the federal register constituted nearly the entire addict population (within "a deviation factor of less than two percent," Myles Ambrose explained to the National Commission on Marijuana and Drug Abuse in 1971). The pre-epidemic estimate of 68,088 in 1969 was based on this register. (By mid-1970 the addict population had grown to only 68,864, according to the register, which was not published that year.)

The prodigious increase from some 68,000 addicts in 1969 to 315,000 in late 1970 and 559,000 in 1971 came not from any flood of new addicts reported to federal authorities in 1970 or 1971 but from a statistical reworking of the 1969 data. Rather than continuing to publish estimates based on the federal register, the Bureau of Narcotics and Dangerous Drugs decided to apply a new formula to the old 1969 data, which produced first a quintupling, then an octupling, of the estimated number of addicts. Unlike the previous theory that almost all addicts would eventually come to the attention of authorities, the new formula was based on the belief that only a small fraction of the addict population would ever be reported to police or medical authorities, and therefore listed in the federal register. Joseph A. Greenwood, the statistician at the BNDD who devised the new formula, explained, "It is impossible to actually know the number of addicts in the United States. . . . The best we can do is make some assumptions"; he then proceeded to apply these assumptions to the data collected in *1969* to estimate the number of *unknown* addicts. "The estimate makes use of a technique similar to that by which the number of fish in a lake . . . is estimated," he noted.

To understand how this statistical artifact led to a tenfold ballooning of the number of addicts in America and provided the president with a national emergency, it is necessary to examine the so-called "tagged-fish-in-a-pond" technique. One way of estimating the number of fish in a pond would be to catch an initial sample of fish, tag them, then release them and allow enough time for a random redistribution of the tagged fish among the rest of the fish in the pond. A second sample of fish is then caught, and the proportion of tagged to untagged fish in this catch would allow an estimate to be made for the total number of fish in the pond. For example, if one out of ten fish in the second sample was already tagged, then the total population would be assumed to be ten times the number of fish originally tagged. In applying this concept to addicts, statisticians at the BNDD divided the total number of names on the federal register in 1969 by the number of names that were "tagged" (that is, reported in 1969) and rereported in 1970, and found only about one out of five of the tagged addicts was rereported. After some refinements were made in the statistical model, the 1969 total of 68,088 was multiplied by 4.626, the calculated ratio, and an estimate of 315,000 addicts was arrived at. This accounted for the 1969–70 epidemic. The same 1969 data were then, in 1971, further refined, and a new ratio was calculated of one known addict to 8.21 unknown addicts, which produced a staggering total of 559,000 in 1972, an increase of some 244,000 between 1971 and 1972. The total increase was in unknown addicts, who were not unlike the paper army of nonexistent serfs in Gogol's *Dead Souls.* In 1969 it was not assumed that there were a significant number of addicts not known to the police agencies; in 1970 it was assumed that there were 246,912 unknown addicts roaming the streets; in 1971 it was assumed that there were 490,912 unknown addicts at large.

Although this statistical device might work in the case of fish (when it is not assumed that a tagged fish is more cautious after being caught once), it presents problems in the case of drug users, who cannot be expected to follow the same random distribution pattern as fish. For one thing, the ratio is heavily affected by changes in the policies of police toward arresting addicts from year to year. In 1970 in New York, for example, Police Commissioner Patrick Murphy, deciding to increase narcotics arrests, authorized that each policeman be given a bonus of one day off for every narcotics arrest he made. Predictably, the number of arrests increased by almost 50 percent that year. Since these arrests produced few convictions, the policy was eliminated the following year, and by 1972, drug arrests fell by more than 60 percent.

Moreover, the entire tagged-fish estimate is predicated on the assumption that all those addicts tagged and reported by local authorities are in fact addicts who will be vulnerable to being arrested or reported the following year. However, a substantial portion of the names reported each year are not necessarily addicts but simply violators of the drug laws that prohibit possession of marijuana, cocaine, amphetamines, or heroin. And, of course, there is no reason for assuming that if these nonaddicts are not *re*reported the following year, they are "unknown addicts." In any case, although these tagged-fish estimates were reported to the public, they were never fully accepted by officials in the drug programs as a precise determination of the addict population. Myles Ambrose explained to the National Commission on Marijuana and Drug Abuse that estimates of 300,000 to 500,000 addicts were merely "ballpark figures." John Ingersoll, the director of the BNDD from 1968 to 1973, explained that the estimates were projected from police reports which did not employ uniform standards and therefore produced "an entirely unreliable picture of addiction." He suggested retrospectively that "there was no drastic increase in the addict population in the 1970s; it is just that we vastly underreported it until 1969 and then probably overreported it." Dr. Richard S. Wilbur, the assistant secretary of defense for health and environment, said that data amassed by the Army, which includes induction examinations of new recruits and compulsory urinalysis of all military personnel, did not indicate that there was any epidemic or sharp increase in heroin addiction in America between 1969 and 1972. He explained that the increase in deaths due to narcotics measured the quality of heroin as well as its prevalence, and the upsurge in heroin-related deaths was, as far as the Army could determine, "related to the deterioration of the heroin" after 1969. (Apparently the war in Vietnam and disruptions of normal channels of distribution by the federal government caused a shortage of quinine, which is used to dilute heroin.) This finding was essentially confirmed by the Special Action Office for Drug Abuse Prevention, which President Nixon had created in 1971 to coordinate the treatment programs of the federal government. In analyzing the data obtained from some 73,000 addicts seeking treatment, the special-action office found that the onset of heroin addiction in these cases peaked between 1968 and 1969, well before the Nixon administration's statistical epidemic began. This suggested that by 1971 there had actually been a decline in new heroin users.

Although White House officials had originally encouraged the BNDD in 1969 to reinterpret its statistics and find "higher numbers" in order to justify the entire drug crusade, Haldeman and Ehrlichman subsequently became "agitated and concerned" when the bureau continued to boost the estimated number of addicts in the election year of 1972, according to Director Ingersoll. It will be recalled that when the reinterpretations reached 559,000 and the press was reporting *increased* addiction under the Nixon administration, Krogh ordered Ingersoll not to release "any more numbers" and to clear all his public statements with a special White House press officer, Richard Harkness. The epidemic thus peaked at 559,000 addicts—and then was arbitrarily reduced to 150,000 addicts. The elimination of 409,000 addicts (who might never have existed) was subsequently cited as evidence of success in the Nixon crusade.

In any case, through the magical projection of a statistical "invading army of addicts," the White House strategists were able to manufacture an epidemic of crisis proportions, even though, as data from treatment centers indicated at the time, the number of new cases of heroin addiction had been on the *decrease* for several years.

22

The Crime Nexus

Drug traffic is public enemy number one domestically in the United States today and we must wage a total offensive, worldwide, nationwide, government-wide, and, if I might say so, media-wide.

—PRESIDENT NIXON, *in remarks before media executives at the Flagship Hotel, Rochester, N.Y., June 18, 1971*

The mobilization of public fears and anxieties to support the president's offensive was based not on the damage heroin addicts inflicted on themselves but on the damage they presumably inflicted on innocent members of society. "The real problem is that heroin addicts steal, rob, and commit every other kind of crime," Ambrose told *U.S. News & World Report* in 1971, "so we have this terrible problem of crime in the cities, much of which is related to heroin addiction." (This image was reinforced by the antidrug messages in television programming and commercials which depicted addicts as glassy-eyed fiends compulsively driven to commit violent crimes.) Nixon also postulated, in a speech to Congress, "Narcotics addiction is a major contributor to crime. The cost of supplying a narcotics habit can run from thirty dollars a day to one hundred dollars a day. This is two hundred ten to seven hundred dollars a week, or over ten thousand dollars to over thirty-six thousand dollars a year." The president went on to explain that since "addicts do not ordinarily hold jobs ... they often turn to shoplifting, mugging, burglary, armed robbery, and so on." Administration officials then calculated that "the total annual crime cost of the country—largely crime on the streets—is roughly 18 billion dollars." This staggering figure of $18 billion—which was based on a series of assumptions about what fraction of the value of stolen goods addicts receive from "fences"—was then released to the press and to Congress as the official estimate of crime caused by heroin, and was included in the government's "briefing book" used to inform reporters writing about the problem of drug abuse.

While such authoritative-sounding figures were widely reported in the press and no doubt added to public anxieties about crime and narcotics, they were not in fact related to any actual statistics compiled by the government. Indeed, the $18 billion worth of crime which government spokesmen claimed addicts were committing to buy their supply of heroin was actually more than 25 times greater than the total sum of property that was stolen and unrecovered throughout the United States in 1971 (including hijackings, embezzlements, automobile, fur, and jewelry thefts), according to the Uniform Crime Reports published by the FBI. (In New York City alone, where more than half of all of the nation's addicts were presumed to reside, addicts would have to steal goods worth more than $9 billion, if one used the calculus of the Nixon administration; yet the total value of property stolen that year according to police-department records was only $225 million—or one fortieth the amount that addicts alone were presumed to have stolen.) To be sure, not all theft is reported to the police—though the dollar value of stolen property is more often exaggerated, or overreported, than it is underreported. However, a study commissioned by the Law Enforcement Administration Agency in 1972, using census-taking techniques to poll the citizenry about crime, estimated that no more than one half the crimes in New York City and other urban areas with major addiction programs go unreported. Even if the total amount of crime was doubled in 1971, addicts would still be stealing more than twelve times all the property actually stolen in America in 1971. This 1200-percent discrepancy between the claims of the Nixon administration and government statistics was further compounded by the fact that the sorts of crimes

which accounted for the bulk of stolen and unrecovered property—
such as car theft, hijacking, bank robbery, embezzlement, and fraud—
were not normally attributed to addicts by law-enforcement officials.

The $18-billion figure did not correspond to reported or even actual
crime in America; it was merely another datum in the campaign to
brief the press and thereby better organize public fears about heroin
addicts. Though journalists widely reported such billion-dollar hyperbole as fact, Egil Krogh and the White House strategists fully realized
that the "magic numbers," as Krogh put it, were based on very
dubious assumptions about the relation of crime and drug addiction.
For one thing, the multibillion-dollar estimates were based on the
BNDD's projection of 559,000 addicts. This projection, in turn, was
based on a statistical artifact which was later revised downward (when
no evidence was found of the 400,000 or so unknown addicts).
Moreover, the $18-billion calculus assumed arbitrarily that each
addict required $16,750 worth of heroin every year to sustain his
habit; yet there was no hard evidence that the average heroin user
purchased even one tenth that amount of the drug. More important,
there was no reason to assume that all heroin users were compelled to
support their habit through crime rather than through part- or full-
time employment (or through support provided by friends, relatives,
or welfare programs). As Krogh readily admitted, the government
had no empirical basis for estimating the proportion of addicts who
supported themselves through theft. If all the projected 559,000
addicts committed two or three burglaries a day, as President Nixon
postulated, they would have to commit at least 365 million burglaries
a year. This sum would be two hundred times more than all the
burglaries committed in 1971 in America. (Nixon's speech writers
apparently borrowed this particular hyperbole from the rhetoric of
Governor Rockefeller in New York State.)

In computing the costs of addiction to the rest of society, the
administration's sharp departure from reality proceeded from the
myth of the vampire-addict that had been developed almost a half
century before by Captain Hobson. So long as it was assumed that all
heroin users were ultimately transformed into fiends who were driven
by their insatiable appetite for the drug to commit any crime or take
any risk to obtain enough money to satisfy their habit, it followed that
the total cost of their crimes could be computed simply by multiplying
the cost of their drug consumption by the number of addicts.
Although such a model of addict behavior became an integral part of

television dramas depicting themes of drugs and crime (partly owing to the efforts of the Nixon administration), such dramatic stereotypes grossly oversimplified the behavior of most heroin users. For example, a study prepared for the State of New York by the Hudson Institute on "The Economics of Heroin Distribution" concluded that 39 percent of those classified as addicts were either "joy poppers," "intermittent users," "apprentices," or addicts with otherwise "small habits." Less than one quarter of those classified as addicts used more than $25 a day worth of heroin and were considered to have "large habits." Moreover, the assumption that heroin users cannot work at legitimate jobs is questionable. Findings of the United States Army in Vietnam showed that hundreds of thousands of soldiers were able to perform their normal duties while using heroin (which is why the problem was not detected for three years). To be sure, a large number of addicts are engaged in illegal occupations, but even addicts engaged in theft tend to avoid the more risky crimes of robbery, mugging, and other crimes against persons. Instead they tend to concentrate on such low-risk crimes as shoplifting, boosting (that is, stealing from parked trucks), or burglarizing abandoned buildings. In a study of sixty-five active heroin users in New York City, Heather L. Ruth found that less than 10 percent of her sample ever engaged in robbery or mugging. Presumably, the reason why criminal addicts avoid high-risk crimes against persons is not that they have higher morals than other criminals but that the costs of being imprisoned and denied their drug are higher than for nonaddicted criminals. Since from the available data there is no way of knowing what proportion of heroin users support themselves through regular or part-time work, welfare, or dependence on other persons, any crime nexus or calculation of the amount of crime that addicts commit must be ultimately problematic.

The White House staff itself had little confidence in the huge crime numbers that were being supplied to the press through briefing officers in the various agencies. For instance, a 1970 Domestic Council staff report in Egil Krogh's file explains, "The National Institute of Mental Health estimates that addicts in the United States commit up to five billion dollars worth of crime in the country." Krogh's staff estimated that in fact the figure was "closer to one billion dollars," but explained that "the high figure of the National Institute of Mental Health can be attributed to their desire to evidence need for treatment programs, thereby aggrandizing their territory." In other words,

Krogh and his staff presumed that the multibillion-dollar numbers attached to drug crimes were simply a product of bureaucracy's attempting to excite the public. Nor was the Domestic Council staff unaware of the fragile nature of the connection between heroin and crime. On March 19, 1971, the Domestic Council decision paper, "Narcotic Addiction and Drug Abuse Program," drawn up by Krogh and Donfeld, stated, "Even if all drug abuse were eradicated, there might not be a dramatic drop in crime statistics on a national level, since much crime is not related to drug abuse."

23

Private Knowledge

While the Nixon administration was operating on the public front to inject fear-provoking stereotypes of incurable addicts into prime-time television, to disseminate authoritative-sounding statistics suggesting that there was an uncontrollable heroin epidemic sweeping the nation, and to inform journalists about the $18-billion crime wave being conducted in America by new hordes of addicts, on the private front it was receiving information from its own agencies which did not fit the picture of imminent national peril, and this information was kept private. As early as December, 1970, an interagency committee on narcotics and drug abuse composed of representatives from the Department of Defense, the Bureau of Narcotics and Dangerous Drugs, the Department of Labor, the Department of Housing and Urban Development, the Office of Economic Opportunity, the Veterans Administration, and the National Institute of Mental Health reported to the Domestic Council that "in terms of the size of the problem, for example compared to the problems of alcoholism, mental illness, automobile injuries and fatalities, the problem of drug abuse is relatively small." It further cautioned:

Hasty and ill-considered policies may not only be ineffective, but they may generate different types of casualties and adverse consequences of the medical, social, and legal nature, such as loss of respect for the law, extensive arrest records [for youthful violations] ... and accidental death and levels of dependence hitherto unknown as a result of leaks in widely dispersed or poorly conceived methadone maintenance programs.

Since there were then more than 9 million alcoholics compared to fewer than 100,000 known narcotics addicts, the White House strategists agreed that the problem could not be presented simply in terms of a menace to public health. A Domestic Council staff report on national drug programs was prepared in December, 1970, with the assistance of the National Institute of Mental Health and other government agencies involved in drug-abuse evaluation. It noted:

Alcoholism, though a much greater public health and safety problem than other forms of drug abuse, is not perceived in the public and political minds as a great social and moral evil. . . . If the misuse of all drugs—illicit drugs as well as alcohol and tobacco—was discussed in only medical and public health terms, the problem of drug abuse would not take on inflated importance requiring an undeserved federal response for political purposes.

This report further observed, "If the misuse of drugs is viewed with proper perspective, it is not in actuality a paramount national problem. . . . However, because of the political significance of the problem, visible, hard-hitting programs must be highlighted to preclude irrational criticism." In this private report the agencies of government dealing with drug abuse admitted not only that narcotics was not a paramount national problem but also that "the dimension of the drug-using population is not known with any degree of accuracy; we don't even know how many users are being treated. . . ." In the spring of 1971, the Domestic Council found that there were no "hard" estimates in any agency of the government of the number of addicts, the amount they spent on narcotics each year, the amount of theft they committed, or the effectiveness of law enforcement on reducing addiction or theft. According to Egil Krogh's recollection, the president himself closely questioned John Ingersoll, asking him such questions as "Are there less narcotics on the street [now]? . . . Are there fewer addicts? Is there less crime related to the use of narcotics? Can you show me that the problem itself is being corrected by these operational indices of success?" Ingersoll bluntly told the president that the government had not yet approached answering these questions, and the president, according to Krogh, "just shook his head in disbelief."

Since the data of other government agencies were equally elusive when it came to answering these central questions about addiction posed by the president, Krogh ordered the Office of Science and Technology, in August, 1971, immediately to commission a complete analysis of all available data on narcotics addiction and crime. He subsequently explained to me that because of the president's "sense of discomfort over . . . the statistical work" of the government agencies directly engaged in drug programs, "we wanted an independent unit under the Office of Science and Technology who were professionals at data collection and analysis to tell us whether or not the assumptions on which our programs have been based were in fact sound." The Office of Science and Technology (which is a part of the executive office of the president) contracted out the special presidential assignment to the Institute for Defense Analysis (IDA), a think tank established by the Joint Chiefs of Staff to analyze, independently, military strategies and problems. IDA was given complete access to all the data on drug abuse that the government possessed.

Unlike previous groups that had studied the problems of drug abuse in America, IDA had no bureaucratic or financial interest in the outcome of its study. The systems analysts at IDA began examining the assumption that addicts steal billions of dollars' worth of property to pay for their habit. They quickly found that "expenditures for heroin and the value of addict property crime is not known to within a factor of four or five," which meant, in effect, that the government estimates had no claim to being even a rough measure of reality. The IDA analysts then went on to test the truism, accepted for more than half a century by government agencies and private treatment centers, that addiction was a major cause of crime in America. Even though it was generally known that a "majority of heroin addicts have a history of criminality preceding their abuse of the drug," as John Ingersoll noted in a November 3, 1970, memorandum to Egil Krogh, and therefore were not innocent persons compelled to commit crimes, it was assumed that the cost of maintaining their heroin habit forced them to commit more crimes than they otherwise would have undertaken. To determine whether this time-worn assumption was valid, the IDA team focused on the summer of 1972, when a shipping strike temporarily interrupted the supply of heroin in Eastern cities and quintupled the street price of the drug when it was available at all. If heroin addicts had to finance their habit through theft, and psychologically and physiologically had no choice over the amount of the drug required to avoid physical illness and mental pain (which was the definition of "addiction"), then there should have been either a sharp increase in crime in these Eastern cities or an increase in the number of addicts enrolling in methadone-treatment programs (where they would receive a free substitute for heroin). The analysts found, however, that this elegant hypothesis was, as Lord Keynes put it on another occasion, "murdered by a gang of brutal facts." The crime rates did not go up, even though prices increased, and addicts did not enter treatment programs. The IDA report was thus forced to conclude:

> The little evidence available suggests that during a time of severe heroin shortage, addicts may not be willing or able to increase their crime commensurately with the price increase, and therefore they compensate by reducing their heroin consumption and/or substituting other drugs. Also the data *do not* suggest that entering treatment is the preferred option [italics in the original].

This conclusion undermined the entire theory of the heroin addict as it was developed by Captain Hobson and his successors in American politics: if heroin addicts could substitute other drugs, such as barbiturates and amphetamines—which were manufactured domestically and inexpensively—for heroin when it was unavailable, or even "mature out" of using it entirely in these periods of time, then they were not actually addicted to heroin but had simply chosen it when they could afford it. In this case, those addicts who committed crimes could not be considered to be physically compelled by their habit to commit crimes, but rather they purchased heroin as a consumer good with the proceeds from criminal endeavors.

By examining the records of the jails in Washington, D.C., in the summer of 1972, IDA analysts found cogent evidence that criminal-addicts could indeed switch from heroin to amphetamines and barbiturates when heroin became more expensive. All arrestees in the Washington jails were subject that year to urinalysis, which would show if they were using opiates (heroin or methadone), amphetamines, or barbiturates. During the East Coast dock strike that summer, IDA researchers found that heroin use in the Washington jails dropped from nearly 20 percent to 0, and commensurately that the use of barbiturates and amphetamines among the arrestees rose from 3 or 4 percent to nearly 20 percent. In other words, most criminal addicts simply replaced heroin with these other drugs without showing any discernible signs of withdrawal or physical discomfort. During this period in Washington, D.C., applicants for the methadone-treatment program actually decreased even though there were no waiting lists or other barriers to obtaining free methadone. (Apparently, illicit drugs, which could be taken intravenously, still had great appeal because of the "rush," or euphoric pleasure, they could provide.) Just as a cigarette smoker is not addicted to a single brand, but can switch to other brands if his preferred choice is unavailable, the data suggested that the criminal addict had great flexibility as to what drug, if any, he would buy at a given time and could adjust consumption to fit his current income. One evaluator of the IDA report commented, "There seems to be very definitely a significant number of addicts who have a choice of which drug they will use or not use, and if they have a choice about it, most of the projections we have been making about heroin epidemics and crime don't really work."

The IDA findings also provided at least some explanation for vexing data coming in from methadone-treatment centers in different cities. This data showed that even when addicts were given a free supply of the heroin substitute methadone, they did not reduce their theft activity, at least as it was measured by criminal charges filed against them. For example, 416 addicts enrolled in a New York methadone program sponsored by the Addiction and Research Treatment Corporation (ARTC) were evaluated by the Center for Criminal Justice at Harvard University. Among the addicts younger than thirty-one years of age, the only reductions in criminal arraignments one year after they had begun methadone treatment (compared with their records one year prior to treatment) occurred in three categories: drug offenses—by far the largest component of the total reduction; forgery; and prostitution. In all other categories the rate of criminal charges filed against these addicts actually increased, even though they were receiving daily dosages of free methadone. Robbery charges quadrupled; assault charges were up by almost 50 percent; and even burglary and property-theft charges increased after one year of methadone treatment. If the full period of a patient's addiction was taken as a measure, rather than merely his peak year, the level of criminal charges was actually higher after he used methadone for one year than it was during an average year on heroin. Since these addicts did not need to steal to finance their habit (which the government financed for them), heroin addiction could not be held to be the motivating force behind their continued (and even increased) criminal behavior. Instead this evidence strongly suggested that heroin use as well as the consumption of other illicit products was merely a by-product of a life of crime.

Finally, the data systematically collected by the Department of Defense in Vietnam in 1972 shattered what remained of the theory that most heroin users were inexorably dependent on heroin. In evaluating the effects of heroin on soldiers, the Department of Defense provided the sort of laboratory conditions that did not exist in civilian life: all soldiers were compelled to submit to urinalysis to determine whether or not they were using heroin or opiates. It turned out, it will be recalled, that several hundred thousand soldiers stationed in Vietnam used heroin between 1970 and 1972, and about 14 percent of these users were classified as addicts, since they met the standard criteria of both continuous heroin use and withdrawal symptoms should they stop using heroin. Yet, when faced with the threat of Army discipline (of not being allowed to leave Vietnam), 93 percent of those classified as addicts (and virtually all the rest of the users) managed to stop using heroin during their remaining months in the Army, where they were subjected to daily urinalysis tests; and when tested one year after their discharge, they were still abstaining from heroin. Dr. Richard Wilbur concluded from this data that "addiction is not a meaningful concept in the vast majority of the cases; most soldiers used heroin because of psychological and peer-group pressures, and because it was readily available. . . . When it was no longer available, or when they faced detection or penalty, they were able to simply give it up." From Vietnam the government was finally able to obtain massive data about the behavior of hundreds of thousands of heroin users, and virtually none of the findings supported the hoary myth of the "drug slave," or the addict who physiologically had no other choice than to do what was necessary to obtain a daily supply of heroin.

Despite the IDA report (which was never made public) and the other evidence that emerged from treatment centers in the United States and Vietnam, the Nixon administration continued to define heroin as "the root cause of crime in America," as Myles Ambrose stated in speeches on drug abuse in 1972. After it became unmistakably clear to the White House strategists that reducing the supply of heroin in the United States would not diminish crime (since, as the IDA report suggested, criminal addicts would simply move on to another drug), President Nixon continued to demand extraordinary powers to reorganize the investigative agencies of the government so that they could continue the crusade against crime and drugs. Between 1968 and 1974, the federal budget for enforcing narcotics laws rose from $3 million to more than $224 million—a seventyfold increase. And this in turn gave the president an opportunity to create a series of highly unorthodox federal offices. The production of threatening images of the vampire-addict which accompanied these executive actions, and created the atmosphere of fear in which Congress passed without consideration the necessary legislation and appropriations, could not be undercut by the private knowledge that was emerging in the reports and studies commissioned by the White House: far more was at stake.

PART SEVEN

The Coup   ★

Our behavior in the midst of the bureaucratic jungle will be purely defensive, unless we have a "direct line" to one or another of the security agencies. If that is the case, the security agency concerned would provide an ideal "cover" for our activities.

—EDWARD LUTTWAK, *Coup d'Etat*

24

The Liddy Plan

Richard Nixon's battle with the Central Intelligence Agency began in 1958. He was then vice-president, and the CIA was secretly financing and supporting an armed insurrection against the Sukarno regime, in Indonesia. When the CIA effort collapsed, to the embarrassment of the United States government, President Eisenhower ordered his vice-president to purge those in the CIA involved in the fiasco. Nixon personally arranged for Frank Wisner, the highly respected deputy director of plans for the CIA, and other top officials of the agency to be brusquely relieved of duty, according to Colonel L. Fletcher Prouty, then liaison officer between the CIA and the Air Force. Prouty notes in his book *The Secret Team*:

> Since the Indonesian campaign was . . . highly classified, most other government workers did not know why all these nice people [in the CIA] had been fired, and since they were cool to Nixon anyhow, they arose in unison to damn him when he ran for President in 1960.

Indeed, Nixon reportedly believed that the CIA was responsible for providing the press in 1960 with very damaging data on a "missile gap" between the United States and Russia—which turned out to be questionable, if not wholly fictitious. He held the agency's leaks to be at least partly responsible for his defeat in the close 1960 election. When he ran again for election, in 1968, it developed that the CIA was keeping his national security advisor—at that time, Richard Allen—under some sort of surveillance, and Nixon suspected that CIA officials were again trying to compromise him by finding embarrassing information (this time about his efforts to block a peace settlement in Vietnam). This suspicion did not end entirely when he was elected president: at an early meeting of the National Security Council, which superintends the Central Intelligence Agency, Nixon asked Richard Helms to brief the council and then leave. Helms, a Harvard-educated aristocrat of the intelligence community, could not believe that Nixon would break the long-standing practice of having the director of Central Intelligence attend National Security Council meetings.

As president, Nixon fully understood that those who opposed him in the executive branch of the government had the power to undercut any of his programs, projects, or appointees by leaking embarrassing information—or misinformation—to the press or to Congress. William Safire, a chief speech writer for President Nixon, has pointed out:

> ... the press has been frequently used by the bureaucracy to build its protective shell. An adept bureaucrat, his domain threatened by a cutoff of funds, is able to alert those interest groups about to be adversely affected and to zero them in to the appropriate newsmen. A judicious leak, a horrendous prediction of the homelessness, starvation, pestilence the cutback would cause, a follow-up reaction story about the interest group, a letter campaign by them to influence congressmen, a severe editorial or two, and the public interest [as represented by the president] gives way to the bureaucracy focused interest.

Since bureaucrats are entrenched in their positions by the traditions and tenure of civil service, or protected directly by powerful congressional subcommittees, a president has little power to countermand this insubordination unless he can first pierce the veil of anonymity provided to the bureaucrats by the press (or the staff of congressional committees). In order actually to rule over government, rather than merely reigning as a figurehead for the independent fiefdoms in the executive branch, Nixon needed to control at least one federal agency with investigative powers. As his staff quickly found out, this was no easy requisite to fill. Nixon feared not only the Central Intelligence Agency but also the Federal Bureau of Investigation while it remained under the directorship and control of J. Edgar Hoover. He told close associates in the White House that he believed that Hoover had used information he had acquired through wiretaps and investigations to blackmail Presidents Kennedy and Johnson, according to Krogh.* Although early in the administration, in 1969, Nixon had sought Hoover's help in wiretapping newsmen and government officials (after the attempt to wiretap a newsman's phone by John Caldwell, a private detective hired by the White House with campaign funds, was thought to produce very quick results), the president's concern that Hoover would use the transcripts of these wiretaps became acute when it was discovered that Hoover was keeping these transcripts in a private file in his office. (Subsequently, in July, 1971, John Ehrlichman authorized William Sullivan, then an associate director of the FBI, to remove this incriminating file from Hoover's FBI office; on July 12, 1971, it was brought to Ehrlichman's White House office.) In any case, by spring, 1970, the demands of Hoover that the White House provide him with written requests for its surveillance operations against leaks, and his shrewd maneuvers to gain control over the transcripts of wiretaps, convinced President Nixon that the FBI could not be relied on for more sensitive investigative work for the White House.

On June 5, 1970, frustrated by his inability to gain control over an established investigative agency or to stop the recurring leaks from the bureaucracy, President Nixon summoned the heads of the various intelligence agencies to the White House—including J. Edgar Hoover; Richard Helms; Gen. Donald V. Bennett, of the Defense Intelligence Agency; and Adm. Noel Gayler, of the National Security Agency— and described his dissatisfaction with them in reportedly "blistering"

---

* Nixon's suspicions about Hoover's blackmailing of President Kennedy were not, it turns out, baseless. The investigation of the Senate select committee chaired by Frank Church stumbled during the course of its inquiries on the intriguing fact that J. Edgar Hoover had himself been briefed on a liaison that the president was then having with a young woman who was also having liaisons with reputed racketeers involved in organized crime. After the FBI's electronic surveillance turned up this possibly embarrassing connection, Hoover had a luncheon meeting with President Kennedy; afterward, the telephone communications between President Kennedy and the young woman stopped. Subsequently, Attorney General Robert Kennedy intervened to block the investigations of a wiretap involving these organized racketeers on the grounds that they were involved in "dirty business," on behalf of the Central Intelligence Agency, directed against Fidel Castro.

terms. He demanded a new mechanism for coordinating intelligence activities, especially domestic ones that were extralegal, and he proposed that a committee be formed immediately to achieve this objective. Tom Charles Huston, a young speech writer at the White House and a Nixon loyalist, was assigned the task of directing this committee toward creating a new investigative structure which could bypass the authority of both Richard Helms and J. Edgar Hoover. After only three weeks of meetings, the ad hoc committee, under Huston's effective control, recommended that the president authorize secretly the use of illegal wiretapping, illegal mail covers, and illegal break-ins for domestic-intelligence purposes. In a highly classified document entitled "Operational Restraints on Intelligence Collection" the committee noted that surreptitious entries (break-ins) were "clearly illegal," and explained, "It amounts to burglary. It is also highly risky and could result in great embarrassment if exposed. However, it is also the most fruitful tool and can produce the type of intelligence which cannot be obtained in any other fashion." Although the "Huston Plan" was initially approved by the president, it ran into such powerful opposition from J. Edgar Hoover that after five days it was rescinded. Nixon and Ehrlichman did not believe that Hoover had opposed this plan because of any "qualms about civil liberties," as Krogh put it; the FBI had performed hundreds of illegal break-ins for other presidents, as well as illegal wiretaps (and had an entire program organized to harass Martin Luther King and other civil rights leaders through extralegal means). The CIA also had an ongoing program to open mail from foreign countries, and in certain instances engaged in domestic surveillance. The National Security Agency, which specializes in communications and codes for the government, had intercepted telephone transmissions for over ten years. The point was not that these were new or unprecedented transgressions but that the Nixon administration was proposing a new structure to direct them, and Hoover was not about to allow the FBI to be bypassed by such a committee. On August 5, 1970, Huston attempted to override Hoover's objections by recommending in a memorandum to Haldeman:

> At some point, Hoover has to be told who is President. He has become totally unreasonable and his conduct is detrimental to our domestic intelligence operations. . . . It is important to remember that the entire intelligence community knows that the President made a positive decision to go ahead. Hoover has now succeeded in forcing a review.

Huston apparently did not realize that Hoover already possessed incriminating wiretaps on newsmen, which he could leak, and that Nixon had no choice but to acquiesce. Although an interagency domestic-intelligence unit was temporarily set up, it was allowed to lapse a few weeks later into obscurity. "The whole thing just crumpled," John Dean, the president's counsel, explained to Nixon while discussing the need for "a domestic national security intelligence system" in 1972. (This conversation was recorded by Nixon's ubiquitous tape recorder.) Soon afterward, Huston was eased out of the administration. The first attempted coup had thus failed.

The quest for control of an investigative agency was not to be abandoned because of the objections (and temporary power) of J. Edgar Hoover. While John Ehrlichman and his staff attempted to discredit the FBI director by leaking stories to the press that he was senile and "losing his grip," President Nixon turned his attention to the Treasury Department, which had under its control such potent investigative agencies as the IRS, Customs (with its unhindered "search authority"), and the Alcohol, Tobacco and Firearms unit (which had an eight-hundred-man force and wiretap authority). Nixon was fully aware that the Kennedy administration had used the IRS for its own purposes. Under the cover of prosecuting organized crime, a list of names that the Kennedy brothers desired to prosecute was circulated within the executive branch, and this became the priority list for IRS investigations. The vast majority of crime cases during the Kennedy administration turned out to be revenue cases, according to the records of the Department of Justice. When Kennedy wanted to call attention to his war on crime, he persuaded the IRS to initiate investigations against gamblers in order to force the FBI to investigate. Indeed, Kennedy was so successful in commanding the loyalty of the Internal Revenue Service that he was able to persuade that agency to grant large tax deductions to American drug manufacturers who contributed to paying the ransom demanded by Premier Fidel Castro in return for the CIA-trained Cuban immigrants who had been captured in the ill-fated Bay of Pigs invasion in the first year of the Kennedy administration. (In fact, the drug companies participating were allowed to deduct the full retail price, rather than the actual cost, of the drugs as their contribution, which allowed them to make profits on the transaction.)

The White House strategists saw no reason why the IRS could not be made equally responsive to the special needs of the Nixon administration and in 1970 pressured the tax-collecting service into creating the Special Service Staff (SSS). According to a White House document, "The function of the SSS was to gather information on the finances and activities of extremist organizations and individuals, both left and right, and make this information ... available to the appropriate division of the IRS." The internal-security division of the Justice Department, then headed by Robert Mardian, an Arizona lawyer with close connections to the White House, provided the SSS with a computerized list of protestors (which was also provided to the CIA). However, despite constant prodding from Huston and the White House, the SSS refused to move against any organizations (for example, the Black Panthers) that the Nixon administration considered enemies. Huston noted in a September 21, 1970, memorandum to H. R. Haldeman:

> Nearly eighteen months ago, the President indicated a desire for IRS to move against leftist organizations. ... I've been pressing IRS since that time to no avail. ... What we cannot do in a courtroom via criminal prosecutions to curtail the activities of some of these groups, IRS could do by administrative action. Moreover, valuable intelligence-type information could be turned up by the IRS as a result of their field orders.

By the end of 1970 it became clear to the White House that the IRS was "dominated by Democrats" who could not be counted on to cooperate with the Nixon administration. The Treasury Department had also rejected the attempts of the White House group to place first John Caulfield and then Liddy in the job of chief of the enforcement branch of the Alcohol, Tobacco and Firearms unit. Randolph Thrower, then commissioner of the IRS, had testified that he opposed these White House appointments because of his concern about "the potential for a personal police force which would not have the insulation of the career staff." Finally, Rossides became very definitely the enemy in the eyes of the White House when, according to Krogh, he informed Ehrlichman in early 1971 that he planned to dismiss Liddy from his key position as his assistant for law-enforcement matters in the Treasury Department. Liddy, who had distinguished himself in both Operation Intercept and the crusades against Turkey, had become a main liaison with the White House staff and had reported to them frequently on what resistance Rossides and other bureaucrats at the Treasury Department were planning against White House actions and objectives. Krogh presumed that Liddy was being fired because "he was too loyal to the White House," and therefore obtained Ehrlichman's permission to hire him on the Domestic Council. Although Krogh continued to warn Rossides that the president "would not tolerate bureaucratic maneuvering," the intrepid assistant secretary of the treasury steadfastly refused to yield to the White House any control over the operations of the IRS and Customs, even to the point of denying Krogh's staff information. Krogh found that the former all-American football player "didn't know when his side had lost or when the game was over." Rossides subsequently explained, "My job is to protect the autonomy of the Treasury Department's law enforcement agency.... If Krogh or Ehrlichman wanted to run them, they first would have to fire me." Since they couldn't fire Rossides without a major struggle (and Secretary of the Treasury Connally apparently backed Rossides), White House strategists, temporarily, at least, suspended their ambition to gain control over the Treasury agencies.

Even though the White House staff had directly participated in hyping the so-called drug menace into a national emergency, they found that they had little influence over the independent-minded director of BNDD, John Ingersoll. When a private poll indicated in the spring of 1971 that the American public remained largely unaware of the law-and-order measures of the Nixon administration to eradicate narcotics, Krogh called Ingersoll into his office and demanded that Ingersoll increase the number of narcotics arrests before the 1972 election. The actual number of narcotics arrests had substantially decreased during the highly publicized heroin epidemic because Ingersoll had changed the focus of the bureau's efforts from street arrests in America to seizures of narcotics abroad. Although this policy may have made sense in terms of curtailing the amount of heroin entering the United States, it seemed a potentially damaging policy to the White House strategists in an election year. When Krogh suggested that some mass arrests of narcotics addicts by federal agents might help alleviate the situation, Ingersoll again argued that such revolving-door arrests would relieve neither the crime nor the drug problem, and again might tempt federal agents into working hand in glove with underworld informers. Although Krogh cut the discussion short by saying, "We cannot accept your thesis," Ingersoll, who knew he had the support of key congressmen, professional police organizations, and even John Mitchell, simply ignored Krogh's orders. The White House was stymied. Its attempts to seize control of one of the investigative arms of the government had been so effectively frustrated by the spring of 1971 that plans were made to establish a privately financed investigative organization that could do political work for the White House. John Caulfield, who was then doing private wiretaps and investigations for the White House, drew up plans for a private detective agency. As the plan finally developed,* it was modeled after Intertel, a "detective agency," formed by former members of the Kennedy administration's Department of Justice, that sold its services, at least ostensibly, to corporations concerned about organized crime. The new organization designed by Caulfield would perform security services for corporations supporting the Nixon administration (e.g., Hughes Aircraft, Northrop, Gulf Oil) but would actually use part of the funds it collected to perform covert operations for the White House, including wiretaps, break-ins, collection of political information, and surveillance of "enemies." According to Caulfield, the plan he had in mind involved Vernon Acree's and Roger Barth's resigning from the Internal Revenue Service in order to provide their services and contacts, and Joe Woods, brother of Nixon's personal secretary, Rose Mary Woods, would also join the firm, as a vice-president and head of the Chicago office. Caulfield would run the intelligence-gathering operation, which would be clandestinely based in New York City, on East Forty-eighth Street, and would infiltrate rival campaigns, steal embarrassing documents from opponents, and release derogatory information. Caulfield drew up a memorandum in June, 1971, which noted, "The offensive involvement outlined above would be supported, supervised, and programmed by the principals but completely disassociated (separate foolproof financing) when the corporate structure had located in New York in extreme clandestine fashion." Although this memorandum called for the new organization to be staffed by former FBI agents, the White House strategists were concerned that Caulfield would not be able to find an adequate number of former FBI agents for the task, and even if he could, these agents would have no effective cover if they were caught in any covert operations. Moreover, such a private organization, dependent on corporate financing, would not have the necessary authority to alert the Internal Revenue Service and other investigative agencies of the government to possible suspects.

* See Appendix, "Operation 'Sandwedge.' "

While the White House staff was debating the merits of creating this privately financed "detective agency," Liddy came up with a superior plan, calling for a new special narcotics unit which would report directly to the White House. In a presidential option paper that he drew up late in the summer of 1971, according to Krogh and others familiar with the plan, Liddy proposed more concretely that since neither Ingersoll nor Rossides could be easily fired from his position before the election, the president's most effective option for gaining control over the narcotics agents would be to detach agents and specialists who could be relied upon by the White House from the BNDD, the IRS, the Alcohol, Tobacco and Firearms division, and the Bureau of Customs. This new office would operate directly out of the executive office of the president. The beauty of the Liddy plan was its simplicity: it did not even need approval from Congress. The president could create such an office by executive decree, and order all other agencies of the government to cooperate by supplying liaisons and agents. Congress would not even have to appropriate funds, according to those familiar with the Liddy plan: the Law Enforcement Assistance Administration (LEAA), which was located in John Mitchell's Department of Justice, could funnel monies via local police departments to finance these new strike forces. The new office would have all the investigative powers of the privately financed detective agency: it would have wiretappers from the BNDD; Customs agents, with their unique "search authority"; IRS agents, who could feed the names of suspects into the IRS's target-selection committee for a grueling audit; and CIA agents for "the more extraordinary missions." In addition, since it would control grants from LEAA, this new office could mobilize support from state and local police forces in areas in which it desired to operate.

The most important feature of the Liddy plan, however, was that the White House agents would now act under the cloak of combating the drug menace. Since public fears were being excited about this deadly threat to the children of American citizens and their property, few would oppose vigorous measures against alleged pushers by this new office, even if its agents were occasionally caught in such excesses as placing an unauthorized wiretap. On the contrary, if the dread of drugs could be maintained, the public, Congress, and the press would probably applaud such determined actions. Krogh and the White House strategists immediately saw the advantages to having the new office operate its agents under the emblem of a heroin crusade rather than under the cover of a private security organization, and Liddy's option paper, much modified in form to remove any embarrassing illegalities, was sent to the president with the recommendations of Krogh and Ehrlichman. In the fall of 1971, with the election rapidly approaching, the president gave his assent to the plan.

25

The Secret of Room 16

On June 13, 1971, the meticulously planned scenario promulgating a national emergency over the putative heroin epidemic was rudely interrupted by the New York *Times*'s publishing an archive of national defense documents which became known as the Pentagon Papers. In the weeks that followed, the controversy over the publication of these classified documents dominated the covers of the national newsmagazines and the choice time on network television. Meanwhile, the disclosures from the White House about the drug menace, the recalling of ambassadors from France, Turkey, and other countries, the cabinet-level meetings to deal with narcotics, the agreement to suppress opium production in Turkey, and other highlights of the heroin crusade were relegated to the back pages of newspapers and newsmagazines and given only minor coverage on television. While the timetable for creating a White House–controlled office with unprecedented investigative powers moved slowly ahead under the direction of G. Gordon Liddy and Egil Krogh, the president demanded immediate action to remedy the massive leaking of the Pentagon Papers. When Krogh returned from an inspection of the drug problem in Vietnam in late June, he was summoned to the Western White House, at San Clemente, California, and told by Ehrlichman that the president wanted him to work on a special project. The president's assistant for domestic affairs explained more fully the next day that this project involved investigating the background of Daniel Ellsberg, a former Rand Corporation employee who had provided the New York *Times* with the Pentagon Papers. Ehrlichman stressed that this was a joint undertaking of his Domestic Council and Henry Kissinger's National Security Council, and that Kissinger, then a national security advisor to the president, was supplying a top investigator on his staff named David Young, who along with Krogh would direct this new investigative unit.

Krogh and Young established their Special Investigations Unit, which Young nicknamed "the Plumbers," in room 16 of the Executive Office Building, conveniently located on the ground floor near the narrow underground passageway leading directly to the White House. Since Krogh had little experience in spy work, he brought his more experienced assistant on the Domestic Council, Gordon Liddy, into room 16 as his deputy. Liddy, then working to develop a more permanent investigative capacity in the White House under the cover of a narcotics office, seemed to Krogh "a natural choice" for the Plumbers, who would engage in "all sorts of national-security work." Since the White House assumed that the FBI would not cooperate fully in investigating what was then thought to be a possible conspiracy of "establishment Democrats" involved with Ellsberg in the distribution of the Pentagon Papers, the Plumbers assumed that they would need the special services of the Central Intelligence Agency. The deputy director of the CIA, General Robert Cushman, whom Krogh had worked with in developing international narcotics programs, agreed to provide Krogh with financing for "narcotics work," but held that the CIA could not get involved in a domestic investigation of this sort. Krogh did manage, however, to obtain the services of E. Howard Hunt, a former CIA official who reportedly had helped Allen Dulles, the most illustrious of the CIA directors, to write his book *The Craft of Intelligence,* and who officially had been detached from the CIA several months before going to work for Robert R. Mullen and Company, a public-relations firm at times serving as a front for CIA operatives. At the time, Hunt seemed to Krogh to be a logical candidate for the Plumbers and a possible member of the more permanent organization then being planned: Hunt had been in the CIA more than twenty years and had specialized in the distribution of "black," or misleading, information. He also had headed the CIA station in Uruguay and was involved at a high level with the successful CIA coup d'etat in Guatemala and the unsuccessful Bay of Pigs invasion, in Cuba; he therefore could be expected to have wide-ranging contacts with other CIA agents, executives, and independent contractors for various services. Furthermore, he came with the strong recommendation of Charles Colson, the special counsel to the president who specialized in dealing with political "enemies." Hunt saw the possibility of using black information in the Ellsberg case, to denigrate as traitors a whole class of Democratic opponents to the war in Vietnam. While retaining his $25,000-a-year public-relations job at Mullen and Company, and still receiving his $24,000-a-year CIA pension, Hunt was put on the White House payroll as a $130-a-day consultant for special projects.

By the end of July, Hunt proposed a covert psychological assessment/evaluation on Ellsberg which would "destroy his public image and credibility," according to a memorandum which surfaced in the Senate investigation of Watergate. This required special assistance from employees, or former employees, of the CIA. Hunt therefore contacted a number of Cuban exiles who had been involved with him in CIA operations against Castro's Cuba, including Manuel Artimes, a former captain in Castro's army whom the CIA had helped defect from Cuba and had used to train its exile army in Guatemala. Bernard "Macho" Barker, a former CIA infiltrator into the Cuban intelligence apparatus who had been subsequently "exfiltrated" into the United States by the CIA, was also contacted. Hunt explained to Captain Artimes that he had been authorized by the White House to recruit Cuban exiles into "hit teams" which would be used ostensibly to assassinate narcotics dealers. He asked his former comrade in clandestine work to recommend Cubans for these teams. Since Barker had arranged the escape of Artimes from Cuba on the CIA's behalf, he was apparently highly recommended. Hunt already knew Barker from the Bay of Pigs operation, in 1961, and after explaining to him that he was now working for a "higher level structure than either the FBI or CIA," Hunt asked him to assemble a team of Cuban exiles who were burglars and lock-picks.*

---

* Hunt also apparently recruited Frank Sturgis, a self-proclaimed soldier of fortune who was arrested with four others in the burglary of the Democratic headquarters in the Watergate complex, for this new office. Sturgis claims that he undertook several missions for Hunt involving tracking narcotics, and he assumed that this was the nucleus of a new supranational police force that would be expanded after Nixon's reelection.

Meanwhile, Liddy wrote the president a long memorandum analyzing the deficiencies of the FBI and argued that because of these flaws in its organization, it could not be counted on by the White House. The president was impressed with this analysis and remarked to Krogh that it was "the most brilliant memorandum he had received in a long time." Liddy also arranged to funnel money from the dairy cooperatives, which were clients of Hunt's public-relations firm, into the Special Investigative Unit, to pay for the break-ins, wiretaps, and other clandestine activities. By mid-August, Liddy had obtained permission from Krogh and Ehrlichman for a covert operation in which the Plumbers would get access to Ellsberg's psychiatric records, which his psychiatrist, Dr. Lewis Fielding, had steadfastly refused to show to the FBI.

Over that Labor Day weekend Dr. Fielding was not expected to be in his Beverly Hills office. Thus, Liddy, Hunt, Barker, and the two Cuban exiles he recruited for the mission, Eugenio R. Martínez and Felipe de Diego—both of whom claimed to have taken part in CIA clandestine operations against Cuba—flew to Los Angeles to execute what was known in White House circles as Liddy-Hunt Project Number One. According to the plan worked out by Liddy, Martínez and Diego went to Dr. Fielding's office wearing the uniforms of a local delivery service and left a green suitcase addressed to the psychiatrist, containing photographic equipment which the CIA had made available to Hunt. The housekeeper accommodatingly placed the suitcase in Dr. Fielding's office. Later that evening, while Liddy drove a rented car around the office building to be in a position to warn the burglars against any police who might be on the scene, Barker, Martínez, and Diego forced open the door of Dr. Fielding's office, opened the green suitcase they had left there that afternoon, and began photographing Dr. Fielding's confidential files. During the entire operation, Hunt watched Dr. Fielding's home and kept in contact with the other conspirators by walkie-talkie radio. There were, however, no interruptions, and the White House unit returned to Washington, D.C. (When the burglary was discovered the following Monday, a narcotics addict, conveniently arrested for the crime, readily "confessed" to it in return for a suspended sentence; as in other White House crusades, narcotics addicts served as covers for the subterranean activities of White House "investigators.") Liddy-Hunt Project Number One was not a complete success, however, because the records of Ellsberg were not in Dr. Fielding's office and thus could not be photographed. Nevertheless, while Liddy and Krogh worked on plans for a permanent investigative unit which ostensibly would operate against narcotics traffickers, the Plumbers kept busy in room 16, investigating, among other things, the possible leaking of national-security documents to Jack Anderson by the Joint Chiefs of Staff (presumably to undermine Kissinger's détente policies). Finally, in December, 1971, the president ordered Ehrlichman and Krogh to create the permanent White House-controlled investigative unit envisioned in the option paper drawn up by Liddy. The new unit was to be known as the Office of Drug Abuse Law Enforcement.

26

Executive Order

Just before he left for his Christmas vacation in 1971, Attorney General Mitchell turned over to Leo Pellerzi, his assistant attorney general for administration, a White House plan for a new narcotics-enforcement office. He instructed Pellerzi that the White House wanted this office to be administratively incorporated in the Department of Justice, but actually it would operate out of the executive office of the president. When Pellerzi, a careerist in the Department of Justice, read the details of the plan, he became decidedly alarmed. It called for a series of special strike forces to be formed around the country, each staffed with selected agents from the Bureau of Narcotics and Dangerous Drugs, the Bureau of Customs, the Alcohol, Tobacco and Firearms unit, and the Internal Revenue Service, as well as several state police officers. Each strike force would be empowered to use court-authorized wiretaps and no-knock warrants in making arrests of narcotics pushers around the country. Special grand juries would then be convened to indict the arrestees. Both the strike forces and grand juries would be under the direct control of Myles Ambrose, who would operate both from the Justice Department and from the president's executive office and report directly to the president.* What alarmed Pellerzi most about this new organization was that it would employ a group of CIA agents, temporarily detached from the agency, for domestic-intelligence purposes, which in his opinion was clearly illegal. (This was never carried out.) Pellerzi also doubted the propriety of a provision in the plan which gave the new office the authority to assign grants from the Law Enforcement Administration Agency to local police departments that cooperated with the new federal strike forces. Pellerzi read the proposal over several times and then decided to take it to Henry Petersen, who was then the assistant attorney general for the criminal division of the Department of Justice, in which the new office would ostensibly be located.

Petersen, who had worked his way up from a messenger boy to an assistant attorney general, was equally dismayed by this new White House plan. He told Pellerzi that he suspected it was no more than "political crap" designed to help the Nixon administration in the 1972 election, and he suggested that Pellerzi use his special talents in administrative procedures to slow down the implementation of this new office. He also said that he would attempt to select a deputy director for this new office, if it were finally approved, who would resist political pressures. As for the possible illegalities, Petersen assured Pellerzi that he would take them up with Richard Kleindienst, then the deputy attorney general, since Mitchell had left on his Christmas vacation.

Upon hearing the suggestion that this new office would employ CIA liaisons, Kleindienst called Richard Helms and told him what the White House was now proposing. Helms categorically rejected the proposal as a violation of the Central Intelligence Agency's charter, as Kleindienst had assumed he would do, and Kleindienst then suggested that they work together to kill this particularly disturbing part of the proposal. Eventually they succeeded in eliminating CIA agents from the plan. Meanwhile, Pellerzi and Petersen managed to restrict the funds that could be used for special grand juries and to limit the

---

* In fact, the White House staff, which was loosely called the Executive Office of the President and had grown from less than 100 persons when Nixon was vice-president to more than 1,200 by the time he had become president, was housed in a number of buildings, including the old Executive Office Building, the new Executive Office Building, and a row of brownstones, restored by Kennedy, on Jackson Street.

arbitrary use of the new strike forces by adding a layer of red tape which would allow them to maintain at least a modicum of control over expenses for this new agency. But they were unable to reverse the White House plan; even when Petersen objected that the sudden creation of this new office would undermine the BNDD's ongoing programs to suppress drugs, he was overruled by the White House. As Kleindienst explained to him, "The White House wants this office, and nothing is going to stop them." According to specific White House instructions, neither Ingersoll nor Rossides was to be told of this new office.

However, on December 21, Ambrose, then commissioner of customs, stopped by the office of his nominal superior, Rossides, and told him that he was appearing with the president on a national television program that evening and that the president would announce a new narcotics program which Ambrose would head. Although this was supposed to be a secret, Ambrose explained sheepishly to Rossides that he wanted to inform him of the development before he saw it on TV. Rossides, who had become increasingly distrustful of Ehrlichman and Krogh, asked him what the new narcotics program would entail. Ambrose shrugged noncommittally and then said that it was to be a special narcotics task force. He, Ambrose, would be "the new drug czar," replacing Ingersoll. When Rossides expressed some concern that this new task force might interfere with the program of the Department of Treasury which he superintended, Ambrose assured him, Rossides later recalled, that it would not interfere with Treasury's program and that it would only be a temporary expedient to establish a better record in narcotics arrests for the White House. Ambrose denies this and says he told Rossides that the new agency was to be an eighteen-month experimental program designed to improve the nation's narcotics-law-enforcement effort. Rossides decided to watch the television program that evening.

The NBC program "A Day in the Life of the Presidency" meant little to those not privy to the power struggle going on between the White House and the investigative agencies of the government. The hour-long program was mainly a guided tour of the White House, narrated by John Chancellor; however, in the middle of the program the president met with John Ehrlichman, Egil Krogh, and Myles Ambrose to discuss the continuing problem of drug control. While Ehrlichman pretended busily to take notes, President Nixon began by saying:

Now the purpose of this meeting is to get a brief report as to where we are. I don't want any snow job. That is what we have gotten too often. I sat right in this office and we have gotten a snow job, because each department is trying to prove that it is entitled to more people. . . . I am not interested in phony statistics. I mean, the woods are full of those. . . .

The president then turned to Ambrose and asked, "Are we properly organized?" The burly commissioner of customs shook his head authoritatively and replied, "In terms of our being properly organized, right now, quite honestly we are not—not yet." Krogh then elaborated: "What we have talked about is the utilization of federal and state people. . . . We have three hundred fifty thousand police officers in the United States and their resources are not being utilized." The president then pointed to the problem of widespread corruption among local police involved in narcotics control and concluded the meeting by saying, "Law-enforcement officials have got to be like Caesar's wife."

Upon seeing this interchange on national television, Rossides immediately called his superior, Charls R. Walker, deputy secretary of the treasury, and reported that Ambrose was moving to the White House to undertake a new project for the president which, if not closely watched, could undermine the Treasury Department's law-enforcement agency. Specifically, he warned that Ambrose might attempt to requisition IRS agents as liaisons for his new office.

Though Rossides had been warned in advance of the president's television program, Ingersoll had not. He later recalled that he "almost fell out of his chair" when he saw the president meeting with Ambrose and Krogh on NBC. Since narcotics control within the United States was the sole responsibility of his agency, the Bureau of Narcotics and Dangerous Drugs, and not that of either Ambrose or Krogh, he wondered why he had not been asked to attend that meeting. More important, he assumed that the president's references to bureaucratic "snow jobs" and "phony statistics" were a direct attack on the work being done by BNDD. Krogh had been pressing him that month to use the bureau to make mass arrests, which would be useful for advertising the efforts of the Nixon administration in the upcoming election, but Ingersoll had steadfastly refused this White House request. Now, as he heard Krogh and Ambrose discuss being "properly organized" on national television, he realized that a White

House takeover of the drug program was imminent. He immediately called Attorney General Mitchell, who was vacationing in Florida, and asked what this televised "presidential meeting" meant to his agency. Mitchell replied that he had not been told about any White House actions, but Ingersoll was not reassured. (The same evening, at the Playboy Plaza Hotel in Miami, Liddy, who drafted the original presidential option paper for this new office, and Hunt, a consultant on the plan, met with Jack Bauman, a former CIA agent and specialist in surreptitious entries, to discuss other operations that they claimed would function under the aegis of the White House.)

In the next month the White House strategists easily overrode the combined opposition of Assistant Attorneys General Pellerzi and Petersen, Ingersoll, and Rossides. In early January, Krogh told Ingersoll in no uncertain terms that since the BNDD had refused to intensify its efforts to arrest street pushers, the White House was creating another agency to do the job. Moreover, Ingersoll would be ordered to cooperate by turning over the agents, specialists in surveillance, and other unspecified resources required by the new White House agency headed by Ingersoll's rival, Ambrose. Although Mitchell initially told Ingersoll that he would work out a compromise plan with the White House whereby the BNDD would increase the number of street arrests it was making—at least, until the election was over—and, in return, the White House would abandon its plan to create this new investigative agency, he told Ingersoll in mid-January that the White House plans were too far advanced to be changed. At about the same time, Secretary of the Treasury John Connally reported to Rossides that the White House decision on the new agency was irreversible. Ingersoll even offered to increase the mass arrests the White House demanded. He later explained to me, "I was flexible as far as tactics were concerned, and if returning to more street arrests was the only way to save the bureau's programs, I was willing to do it." His last-minute offer was, however, rejected by Krogh as "too little, too late."

On January 28, 1972, less than a month after the director of the BNDD and his counterpart at the Treasury Department learned of the planned agency, ODALE was officially created by an executive order of the president (which, unlike an "executive reorganization order," need not be submitted to Congress for approval). President Nixon simply declared:

Each department and agency of the Federal Government shall, upon request and to the extent permitted by law, assist the Director of the Office for Drug Abuse Law Enforcement in the performance of functions assigned to him or pursuant to this order, and the Director may, in carrying out those functions, utilize the services of any other federal and state agency, as may be available and appropriate.

The president then appointed Ambrose director of ODALE and, simultaneously special consultant to the president on narcotics control.

The next day, taking his furniture and his two secretaries from the Bureau of Customs (Rossides later billed the White House for the removed furniture), Ambrose moved into his new offices—one located in the town-house annex of the White House, on Jackson Street, the other in the Department of Justice. Ambrose, a shrewd and outspoken former politician in New York, fully realized that his new office would be bitterly opposed by the agencies from which it was commandeering agents and money. To some degree, he was "doing their job for them," as he later put it. He thus fully anticipated the opposition from his rivals and was told by Krogh that both Ingersoll and Rossides had fought to abort the creation of his office.

Since there was virtually no precedent for an agency like the Office of Drug Abuse Law Enforcement, Ambrose had to proceed step by step, in assembling his strike forces. The first step was to appoint regional directors who would superintend and select the federal agents and local police on each strike force in each of the thirty-three target cities he selected. Andrew J. Maloney, an assistant U.S. attorney in New York, was put in charge of the East Coast from Maine to New Jersey. Joseph H. Reiter, whom Ambrose knew from his work in the tax division of the Justice Department, was given responsibility for the Mid-Atlantic states. Joseph Martinez, a Miami lawyer with a strong background in narcotics prosecutions, was assigned the Southern states. Fifty other lawyers, many of whom Ambrose knew personally, were deployed in instantly created field offices of the new organization. Four hundred investigators were requisitioned from the Bureau of Narcotics and Dangerous Drugs and the Bureau of Customs, and Ambrose requested more than a hundred liaisons from the Internal Revenue Service, as well as specialists from other agencies of the government. This was all accomplished during the first thirty days of existence of this new office, in what Ambrose himself referred to as a "monumental feat of organization."

However, since the Office of Drug Abuse Law Enforcement was set up without approval of Congress, it had little direct access to Congress-appropriated funds. Though Ambrose succeeded in listing most of the special prosecutors he hired on the payroll of the Department of Justice as "temporary consultants," and managed to requisition funds from various agencies to pay for his clerical and investigative staff, finding money for the operating expenses of his strike forces presented serious difficulties. Finally, Krogh and other White House advisors decided that these strike forces could be temporarily financed through grants from LEAA, although it will be recalled that this fund was specifically established by Congress to finance local rather than federal police activities. As expected, some LEAA officials protested the granting of money to a federal office as a violation of the spirit of the law: "Congress never intended for LEAA grants to be used to bypass the appropriations process," one administrator warned. So, with White House assistance, the new office established a series of local organizations, with such names as "Research Associates," through which grants could be made by LEAA. The money was then channeled back to selected strike forces, with these organizations acting, in effect, as money conduits.

Problems were also encountered appropriating specialists for the new office. Ingersoll resisted supplying the wiretapping technicians requested by the BNDD on the grounds that the strike forces were supposedly set up to pursue street pushers, "which did not require a wiretapping capacity." After Krogh was asked to intervene on the president's behalf, Ingersoll finally was forced to part with a few wiretapping technicians. From Rossides, the new office demanded not only customs agents, who had the unique authority to conduct searches without warrants under certain circumstances, but also IRS agents working on the target-selection program. Rossides provided the strike forces with thirty-five customs inspectors and twenty-five secretaries, but drew the line on reassigning IRS agents. Despite White House pressure, Rossides argued that the strike forces did not need tax examiners to go after street pushers and cautioned that such a transfer of authority could undermine the autonomy of the Internal Revenue Service. Again, the new agency used its connections with the White House. This time, John Connally interceded and persuaded Rossides to allow thirty-five IRS agents to serve as liaisons on the strike forces. Ingersoll and Rossides were understandably confused about the objectives of this office, if only because the new strike forces had little resemblance to more conventional law-enforcement forces. These highly unorthodox units, which were being controlled from the White House through the president's special consultant Myles Ambrose, included not only trained narcotics and customs officers but also Immigration and Naturalization Service officers; Alcohol, Tobacco and Firearms control agents; probation officers; state troopers; and local police officers. From the beginning these strike forces were not simply directed to enforce the narcotics laws but to make arrests by any lawful means possible, even if it meant bypassing the normal channels. For example, the guidelines for the Los Angeles strike force stated:

> What [the Office of Drug Abuse Law Enforcement] is all about is the concept that hitting the heroin traffic in one manner only, particularly a manner which relies eventually on prosecutors or judges to keep heroin dealers out of traffic, must be unsuccessful. . . . In Los Angeles [we] will rely on many approaches, aimed at not only prosecuting heroin dealers, but at harassing and disrupting them by using the many statutes and procedures available to us.

The guidelines then went on to suggest such tactics as using probation officers to revoke the parole of uncooperating suspects, using grand juries to harass suspects, and employing Immigration and Naturalization Service officers to deport targets. It was assumed that very few suspects or uncooperative witnesses could resist the powers of harassment held by this eclectic group of police officers. With the authority of court-authorized no-knock warrants and wiretaps they could strike at will in any of the target cities and against virtually anyone selected as a target. By March, 1972, the strike forces had become operational.

27

Dangerous Liaisons

The White House finally succeeded in 1972 in creating a private police force in the form of the Office of Drug Abuse Law Enforcement. The office reported directly to the president through its head, Myles Ambrose, who simultaneously served as special consultant to the president. ODALE bypassed most of the traditional bureaucratic restraints on its operations; nevertheless, the plan to utilize the intelligence assets of the Central Intelligence Agency was stymied by the opposition of career officials at the Department of Justice and at CIA. This, however, was only a temporary setback. The power struggle at the FBI to succeed J. Edgar Hoover provided the White House strategists with an opportunity to take over at least part of the domestic-intelligence operation at the FBI by playing on the ambitions of its associate director, William C. Sullivan.

During the Johnson administration Sullivan had designed the FBI's counterintelligence program, which among other things harassed Martin Luther King and civil rights organizations and which gave the Nixon White House some leverage over him. In the early years of the Nixon administration he realized that his rise to power in the FBI was being blocked by Cartha "Deke" DeLoach, who was third in command at the FBI. In light of this opposition Sullivan could succeed Hoover only if he was the personal candidate of President Nixon. He thus went to great lengths, according to his associates in the FBI, "to play ball with the White House." He worked with John Dean on drafting the ill-fated Huston Plan, even though Hoover and the FBI executives opposed it. And when the White House wanted to wiretap members of the National Security Council staff and journalists, Sullivan arranged for the FBI to undertake these "national security" tasks for the president. The procedures for the FBI required that such White House requests be routed through the office of Deke DeLoach and Inspector George Quinn, but Sullivan arranged it so that the White House requests would be processed personally by him, and both DeLoach and Quinn would not have direct knowledge of the very unorthodox wiretap operations requested by the White House. DeLoach feared that this arrangement would effectively give the White House control over Sullivan's domestic-intelligence division and demanded that Sullivan return to the more normal procedures of the bureau. Sullivan, who was now working closely with such White House strategists as John Dean, then an assistant to Attorney General Mitchell, and Robert Mardian, the head of the Department of Justice's internal-security division, managed to get Henry Kissinger and Alexander Haig to intervene directly and write memoranda which supported the special arrangement between Sullivan's division and the White House. In the wake of these memoranda Hoover acquiesced and permitted Sullivan to limit the access to the transcripts and authorizations of wiretaps to a few highly placed officials in the domestic-intelligence division, which excluded DeLoach.

In effect, then, Mardian, Dean, and Sullivan controlled a bureau within a bureau which could install "national security" wiretaps for the president. When the White House strategists feared that Hoover might attempt to use the transcripts of these wiretaps to blackmail the White House, Mardian arranged through Sullivan to transfer them from the FBI to John Ehrlichman's safe in the White House. When Hoover found out about this maneuver, he locked Sullivan out of the office (by having his locks changed while he was on vacation). Realizing that his days with the FBI were numbered, and believing that the present administration of the FBI had become inefficient, if not corrupt, Sullivan pressed Dean and Mardian to create another domestic-intelligence unit. Dean fully realized that the White House could use this ambition of Sullivan's for its own purpose. He later explained to the president, "What Bill Sullivan's desire in life is, is to set up a domestic national security intelligence system, a White House program. He says we are deficient. He says we have never been efficient, because Hoover lost his guts several years ago." The problem was simply to find a cover under which such a White House intelligence system could be created for Sullivan. The war on heroin conveniently served this purpose.

The idea of creating a small intelligence unit as part of the White House's narcotics program was first suggested by Egil Krogh in the summer of 1971. Krogh explained to his staff assistants working on the narcotics problem at the Domestic Council that the only organization in the government capable of "tracking the narcotics traffickers" was the CIA, but that agency was reluctant to become involved in a law-enforcement problem. Walter Minnick, a young Harvard Business School graduate who had joined Krogh's staff only two months before, recalled that Krogh complained to him that the CIA was the most "bureaucratically closed" organization in the government, and that in order to cut the "red tape," Krogh instructed him to speak to E. Howard Hunt. (Minnick did not know at that time that Hunt was also working in room 16 as one of the Plumbers in the special-investigations unit.) Krogh's young staff assistant soon found Hunt to be extremely well informed not only about the narcotics trade in Southeast Asia but also about the bureaucratic politics of the CIA. Hunt authoritatively told Minnick that it would be next to impossible "to crank CIA intelligence" into other federal agencies, since CIA employees would be extremely wary about trusting their counterparts at BNDD or at Customs. Instead Hunt recommended establishing a new unit, under tight White House control, which could serve as a liaison between all the law-enforcement agencies involved in suppressing narcotics. He said that he knew key CIA officers who could be temporarily detached from the agency and employed in this new liaison group. Krogh subsequently explained that Hunt had "counseled me in 1971 as to specifically how we should build into the CIA operations narcotics control as an important priority; and he described the priority list which [CIA] station chiefs maintained for their own agent activity. . . ." According to Krogh, Hunt further convinced him that unless he was able "to communicate directly with [CIA] station chiefs and have that backed up at their regional level in the CIA that, while they may say that they are cooperating, in fact [we] would not get much work on the problem at that regional level."

Specifically, Hunt suggested Colonel Lucien Conein, a personal friend of his who had served with the CIA since 1954, as a possible director for the proposed White House intelligence office. It was subsequently decided, however, that Conein would be more useful in the strategic-intelligence office of the BNDD, where he would be in a position to keep an eye on Ingersoll's activities (and there he could supervise the plans approved by the president for clandestine law enforcement abroad, which possibly would include assassination). Since Conein was unavailable to head the new office, Walter Minnick proposed James Ludlum, who had been a CIA official responsible for collecting intelligence on the international heroin trade. Krogh approved this choice because, as he told me years later, "After they had assigned Jim Ludlum to be the liaison in narcotics control, the CIA cooperation increased terrifically ... and he was a very helpful person." The White House, however, had other plans for this new Office of National Narcotics Intelligence (ONNI). To Minnick's dismay, Ehrlichman ordered him to offer the new position to Sullivan, who promptly accepted it. Krogh later explained to Minnick that this was done in return for Sullivan's cooperation in doing "previous favors for the White House." Although the implementation of ONNI was delayed until August, 1972, by the protests of Ingersoll and Kleindienst—and finally had to be located in the Department of Justice rather than in the White House, to at least partly satisfy the strong objections—Sullivan had finally gained control of the domestic-intelligence system, which John Dean presumed to be his "life's desire."

Sullivan immediately chose Russell Asch, a deputy of the National Security Council with contacts in the intelligence community, as his deputy. He also appointed liaisons with the CIA, the FBI, the Defense Intelligence Agency, and a host of the lesser-known intelligence agencies scattered throughout the government. In all, twenty-four liaisons were appointed to assist Sullivan in his intelligence coordination. The CIA agents reassigned to this new office could not entirely resist the temptation of resorting to the sort of fun and games which they practiced in the CIA. For example, one former analyst at the Office of National Narcotics Intelligence recalled that some of these former CIA agents began working on a plan for disrupting the cocaine market in the United States "by poisoning it with methedrene," a domestically manufactured stimulant that could be made to resemble cocaine in color and taste. The bogus cocaine, according to this plan, would cause violent reactions in the cocaine users (if they survived) and thereby turn them against the cocaine dealers. After due consideration, however, the plan for the government to distribute methedrene surreptitiously in key cities in the United States was rejected, and eventually all the plans, analyses, and reports of ONNI dealing with cocaine were shredded and destroyed on White House orders.

The waiting game continued.

28

The Heroin Hotline

After the president designated Myles Ambrose the administration's "drug czar" in 1972, a nationwide program of public appearances and speeches was arranged for him so that he could focus public attention on the administration's war on heroin. "Anyone who isn't aware that President Nixon has been leading the fight against drug abuse hasn't been paying attention," Ambrose said in a typical appearance before the 18th National Republican Women's Conference, at the Bellevue Stratford Hotel, in Philadelphia, on May 20, 1972. "As the president's special consultant on drug abuse, I can assure you that this is true and isn't empty rhetoric. . . . The fight has been all the tougher because, prior to 1969, the government napped for most of the decade while drug abuse ballooned into a national epidemic." Though Ambrose proved to be a "highly dramatic spokesman" for the administration, according to Krogh, the White House also wanted him to undertake a more "media-oriented approach" which could reach tens of millions of potential voters. At one meeting, in March, 1972, Ehrlichman suggested to Krogh that Ambrose should establish "some sort of hotline system" which could be nationally advertised on television throughout the United States. Accordingly, in three weeks of frenetic planning, Ambrose established a national heroin hotline system through which citizens anywhere in the continental United States could call, without charge, a special ODALE "intelligence center" and report suspected heroin sellers in their neighborhood. The intelligence center would then alert a strike force in the area, which would immediately swoop down on the suspect. To make the hotline operational, ODALE took over a communications center located in a mine shaft in Virginia, which was originally planned by the Office of Emergency Preparedness as a nuclear-attack refuge for high White House officials and was already wired for emergency telephone communications. Geoffrey Sheppard, one of Krogh's young assistants on the Domestic Council, later recalled, "When I first heard that Ambrose intended to put all those narcotics agents in a fortified mine shaft in Virginia, I thought he was being overly paranoid about the possibility of having his center attacked by heroin pushers; they later told me that this was the only facility the White House could find on three weeks' notice which had the necessary telephone cables." In order to process the expected flood of telephone calls from informers, ODALE leased twenty wide-area telephone systems (called WATS lines) from the American Telephone and Telegraph Company. Almost the entire staff of the Office of Emergency Preparedness, which had been established in the White House after World War II to plan for nuclear disasters, was requisitioned by Ambrose to man the telephones twenty-four hours a day. Agents who had been transferred to ODALE from the BNDD were reassigned to this mine shaft to evaluate the contents of the tips and, if they were relevant, to pass the information on to the appropriately located strike force. Since the success of the hotline depended on national publicity—the entire citizenry of America had to be made aware of ODALE's toll-free number—Ambrose contracted with Grey Advertising Agency, in New York City, for a nationwide publicity campaign. Television licensees across the country were expected to donate tens of millions of dollars' worth of free time on local television stations for these advertisements from Ambrose's office. Since there was no provision in the budget of any federal agency to pay the Grey Advertising Agency for designing this campaign (which presumably would also help alert the electorate to the Nixon administration's fight against heroin dealers), Krogh arranged to finance Grey's work through grants from the always available Law Enforcement Assistance Administration. In his April 7 statement to the press Ambrose justified this hotline in terms of a new "citizen's crusade." He explained, "To give each citizen the opportunity to join in this battle, the president has today directed that a national heroin hotline be established and manned twenty-four hours a day, seven days a week. Public-spirited citizens having information on heroin traffickers are urged to dial this number [800-368-5363]."

Since the hotline required that a large number of narcotics agents be detached from ongoing investigations of major traffickers in order to process telephone calls, BNDD director John Ingersoll was appalled by what he considered to be nothing more than a "White House publicity stunt." He argued that all analyses of heroin transactions showed that the vast preponderance of addicts acquired their heroin supply from other addicts or from persons with whom they had long-term ties, rather than from strangers who might be likely to turn them in. Therefore, the hotline was not likely to produce many valid tips. An audit of the first three months of telephone calls received over the hotline supported Ingersoll's contention. Of 33,313 calls received and evaluated by narcotics agents, 28,079 were deemed useless—obscene calls, pranks, or simply heavy breathing over the phone. Most of the remaining 5,234 were appraised as sincere, but of no immediate use. For example, agents were told merely that "drugs were bad" or that the caller thought "Nixon was doing a good job." Only 113 calls provided any lead at all for the strike forces, and even these calls produced only four cases of arrests and one seizure—two grams of adulterated heroin, which Ingersoll estimated at "a street value of two dollars." Despite such meager results, and the fact that agents were diverted from more profitable investigations, the hotline messages continued on national television. Playing on popular fears, for example, a typical ODALE commercial designed by Grey Advertising would show a person cringing in his room behind barred windows. The message would state, "The pusher should live behind bars, not you," followed by the hotline telephone number. Indeed, the commercials proved so successful with local television station owners as a means of fulfilling their public-service requirements that they continued broadcasting these messages long after the narcotics agents had deserted the fortified mine shaft in Virginia and relinquished the wide-area telephone system to the American Telephone and Telegraph Company; those who continued to call the hotline (whether to provide valid tips or simply obscene denouncements) received a recorded message asking them to call their local police. Even after the entire concept of a hotline was abandoned, there was simply no way of "gracefully recalling the commercials," Krogh explained.

Ambrose's strike forces proved to be very aggressive: they executed well over one hundred no-knock search warrants in the first six months of their existence, compared to only four such warrants executed by the Bureau of Narcotics and Dangerous Drugs in its entire five-year history. However, they failed to generate as much publicity as had been hoped for, since they were arresting mainly local street pushers. And the night raids on the wrong homes in Collinsville, Illinois, were a source of negative publicity.

Whatever other purposes it may have served, ODALE did not gain the favorable publicity that Haldeman and Ehrlichman desired, even with its hotline.

29

The Philadelphia Story

To finance their 1972 plan to seize power within the federal government, the White House strategists sought control over the Law Enforcement Assistance Administration, which had grown from its inception in 1968 to a nearly $1-billion fund for dispensing grants by 1972. Donald J. Santarelli, the young and very ambitious attorney in the Department of Justice who had already demonstrated his loyalty to the White House group, having worked closely with John Dean and Robert Mardian, was chosen by the president to take over the administration of this agency immediately after the election. The funds of LEAA could be used for financing groups which for one reason or another did not wish to seek congressional appropriations—as they were used to fund, indirectly, the ODALE strike forces. The grants could also be used to reward local politicians and police officials who cooperated with the White House. To be sure, most of these funds were mandated by Congress to go to the states in block grants, over which the White House had little control; but there were still tens of millions of dollars left over for discretionary grants—certainly an amount sufficient to finance the unorthodox projects of the White House. Egil Krogh later explained, "Whatever discretionary money there was ... in many cases would come directly to the

White House, and be addressed there by Mr. Ehrlichman, by my staff, and in some cases the president directly. . . . It is very hard to separate the political interest from the substantive interest; at times this leads you into dangerous waters." When these discretionary grants came before the Domestic Council, Krogh found that the "political dimensions . . . and the substantive issues were impossible to separate." He observed, "In terms of developing [LEAA] programs, my office felt, first, yes, there is something that must be done as a policy proposition, but it is also something that must be done to make a political record in 1972."

As the election approached, the White House demanded that these discretionary grants, originally intended by Congress to help local police departments, be used for political muscle in the campaign. To illustrate how these grants were usurped by the White House for political purposes, Krogh described for me in considerable detail a case study of how $1 million was channeled to Mayor Frank Rizzo in Philadelphia:

> Mayor Rizzo had been making overtures to the president . . . about his interest in supporting Mr. Nixon for reelection in 1972. The president was smitten with the idea of Rizzo supporting him and carrying the state of Pennsylvania. Mr. Ehrlichman instructed me in 1972 to do all that was necessary to get Rizzo's programs on narcotics and law enforcement on the line as soon as possible. I was told to make sure that checks for federal funds were transmitted to his office as fast as possible.

When Krogh asked Rizzo what "services" he could provide, the former police chief and mayor of Philadelphia asked for immediate help in lowering the crime statistics for his city before the election. The newly organized Special Action Office for Drug Abuse Prevention in the White House had just developed a program called Treatment Alternative to Street Crime, or TASC, which arranged for heroin addicts with criminal records to be sent to city-administered treatment programs rather than to jail when arrested for some narcotics violation. If a substantial number of addicts were enrolled in the TASC program in Philadelphia and the local police and courts cooperated in not booking them for narcotics offenses or other minor crimes, there would be an immediate decrease in the crime statistics in Philadelphia (although no decrease in actual crimes). Realizing that such a program could bring some immediate benefits before the election, Rizzo asked Krogh to rush it through. Since Rizzo claimed that his staff had no idea even how to prepare the applications for a grant from LEAA, Krogh dispatched Jeffrey Donfeld, his former staff assistant and now a deputy in the Special Action Office for Drug Abuse Prevention, to Philadelphia to assist Rizzo. Krogh recalled:

> Donfeld was given a seventy-two-hour deadline to prepare the application grant, have it sent to Washington, signed, and transmitted back to Philadelphia. While he was in Philadelphia, I received a call from Mr. Ehrlichman at Camp David, who asked me, prior to the deadline, whether the check—as I recall, for one million dollars—had gone yet. . . . Mr. Ehrlichman said it was the president's decision that the check was to go out by the deadline and that there would be no excuses. Accordingly, the check was transmitted to Rizzo, and he was able to announce very shortly thereafter a greatly expanded mechanism in Philadelphia.

A few weeks later, Krogh paid a personal visit to Rizzo with Jerris Leonard, then the administrator of LEAA. On Ehrlichman's orders, Krogh had told Leonard that "the president felt that supporting Mr. Rizzo was a matter of first importance, that we knew that he had a severe law-enforcement problem, as all cities did have, and that he was to be provided the maximum support that LEAA could provide." Moreover, Leonard was instructed by his immediate superior, John Mitchell, to "provide whatever discretionary funding they could to Rizzo in his hour of need." At a press conference held immediately after the meeting, Krogh was bemused to hear "Leonard and Rizzo proclaiming the new cooperative venture which, at that point, had not been specifically agreed on, but nevertheless structured the relationship for future funding." Rizzo, although a Democrat, publicly supported Richard Nixon for reelection in 1972 (and was himself reelected mayor of Philadelphia).

Though Nixon's predecessors had also used agencies of their administrations to mobilize public support for themselves in reelection campaigns, they were constrained by both congressional oversight and the civil servants in the agencies themselves. However, in the case of LEAA, a newly created fund with virtually no staff except political appointees and with no real congressional control, Nixon had the potential greatly to enhance presidential influence. He was determined to repeat the "Philadelphia Story" in as many cities as possible, realizing that Congress could not easily refuse appropriations for any crime-control measures presented in an election year. The White House strategists thus worked diligently to expand the discretionary grants for this agency and to complete their takeover of its administration.

30

The Consolidation of Power

In March, 1972, the domain of the White House had been effectively extended over all elements of the narcotics program except those in the Treasury Department. The Nixon strategists had succeeded through the creation of new offices in divorcing most of the domestic operations of BNDD agents from the control of Ingersoll, who had been reduced through these maneuvers to little more than a public spokesman for his own bureau. Rossides, however, still remained to be dealt with at the Treasury Department. Ehrlichman and Krogh thus planned, at the March 28 meeting of the Cabinet Committee on International Narcotics Control, to emasculate what remained of Rossides's power by announcing a presidential decision to curtail the overseas operations of customs agents and place them under the direct control of the cabinet committee, of which Krogh was executive director (and which, for all practical purposes, he ran single-handedly). Rossides, however, was not to be so easily defeated: he persuaded Secretary of the Treasury Connally to intervene. The day of the meeting, Connally "pulled an end play," according to Krogh, by walking straight past Ehrlichman into the president's office and then emerging arm in arm with him later. In the few minutes that intervened Connally had persuaded the president to reverse the entire

decision urged on him by Ehrlichman and Krogh. At the opening of
the meeting the president announced that Customs was to be allowed
to send additional agents overseas to investigate narcotics cases, and
that the earlier guidelines restricting Customs were to be eased. Krogh
realized that he had seriously underestimated the determination of
Rossides, but it was only a minor defeat for the Domestic Council and
a Pyrrhic victory for the Treasury Department.

Claiming that the narcotics program was again fragmented among
the Bureau of Customs, the Internal Revenue Service, the Bureau of
Narcotics and Dangerous Drugs, and the new offices, the White
House ordered plans to be drawn up for a new superagency into
which all the competing law-enforcement agencies involved in the
drug program could be merged. In effect, this new agency would be
little more than an expansion of the ODALE concept: the investigative agents of the Bureau of Customs and the Bureau of Narcotics and
Dangerous Drugs would be merged into this new agency along with
prosecutors who handled narcotics cases. The Office of National
Narcotics Intelligence would also be folded into this new agency. In
size, it would resemble a smaller version of the Federal Bureau of
Investigation; it would have both extraordinary search authority
(deriving from that of customs agents) and electronic-surveillance
powers. It would also have liaisons with the target-selection committee of the Internal Revenue Service and the Central Intelligence
Agency. Reorganization Plan Number Two, as the new scheme was
officially called, would also allow the White House to replace all the
top civil servants and careerists with White House loyalists. Not only
would this new agency be free of bureaucratic restraints but it would
be headed by Ambrose, according to some speculation. It was also
assumed by certain members of the White House staff that Sullivan,
Liddy, and Hunt would play important roles in the intelligence-
gathering activities of this new unit.

Rossides foresaw that the creation of this new superagency would
eliminate all the checks and balances that traditionally limited law-
enforcement operations in the field of narcotics, and, although
nominally located in the Department of Justice, it would give the
White House de facto control over strike forces and investigative
agents. In the battle of memoranda that followed, Rossides argued
that ODALE "was ill conceived, alienated local enforcement officials
and was counterproductive," and that "consolidating these vast
powers destroys traditional checks and balances [and] violate[s] the

fundamental American criminal justice concept of separation of the investigating function and the prosecuting function." The White House, however, moved ahead with its consolidation. A three-man hearing board was set up to hear the objections of Rossides, Ingersoll, and others, but since two of its members, Donald Santarelli and Geoffrey Sheppard, were close colleagues of Krogh's and committed to the "reorganization," all objections were easily overridden. (The third member of the panel, Mark Alger, a staff member of the Office of Management and Budget, also approved the consolidation on grounds that it was more "efficient"—which no doubt it was.) To be sure, Congress had the power to veto an executive reorganization plan, but in an election year few Congressmen were willing to oppose a new federal effort to reduce the national heroin epidemic. Without effective resistance the White House would be in control of a major investigative agency soon after the election.

Moreover, the reorganization plan would abolish John Ingersoll's position as director of the Bureau of Narcotics and Dangerous Drugs. Furthermore, Connally, who was resigning as secretary of the treasury to head the Democrats for Nixon committee, reluctantly agreed to replace Rossides as assistant secretary of the treasury for law enforcement with one of Krogh's young staff assistants on the Domestic Council, Edward Morgan. It was also planned that Caulfield, who had helped plan the "private detective agency" for the White House, would be given a controlling position in the Alcohol, Tobacco and Firearms enforcement unit of the Treasury Department. Vernon "Mike" Acree, a former IRS official who had shown a willingness to cooperate with the White House, was chosen to succeed Ambrose as commissioner of customs. A number of other loyalists from the Office of Management and Budget (OMB) were selected for other key positions in the Treasury Department. And the key position of director of the new investigative superagency for "drug enforcement" could be tendered to someone who could be closely counted on by the White House.

On May 2, 1972, J. Edgar Hoover died, and Clyde Tolson, who had been Hoover's right-hand man, offered to resign. The White House immediately saw a possibility of realizing its long-term ambition of controlling that crucial investigative agency and appointed L. Patrick Gray, a former office manager of the Nixon election campaign, as acting director of the FBI. There were still powerful inspectors and executives in that bureau whom the Nixon administration could not count on, but with the help of William Sullivan the White House strategists hoped that after the election campaign was concluded, these men would be replaced by loyalists. Thus, by the spring of 1972, the Nixon administration approached its objective of controlling the investigative agencies of the government, and consolidating power.

PART EIGHT

Unanticipated
Consequences $\star$

We may unwittingly . . . infiltrate a "safe" department and discover that we are dealing with a security agency.

—EDWARD LUTTWAK, *Coup d'Etat*

31

The Revolt of the Bureaucrats

To keep his Minister good, the Prince should be considerate of him, dignifying him, enriching him, binding him to himself. . . . When Prince and Minister are on this footing, they can mutually trust one another; but when the contrary is the case, it will always fare ill with one or the other.

—NICCOLÒ MACHIAVELLI, *The Prince*

The White House timetable for consolidating its power over the investigative agencies of the government was rudely interrupted on June 17, 1972, when Washington, D.C., police arrested five men in the national headquarters of the Democratic party in the Watergate apartment and office complex. Although the arresting officers did not know it at the time, these burglars were actually part of an intelligence-gathering unit working surreptitiously for the Committee to Reelect the President (CREEP). This unit was coordinated by G. Gordon Liddy, who was then working as counsel to the finance committee of CREEP, and by E. Howard Hunt, who still maintained an office in the executive office of the president as a consultant. Under other circumstances the covert relationship between the five burglars, Liddy, Hunt, and the Nixon White House might never have been disclosed; but with Nixon's impending reelection threatening the very independence of the power base of the bureau chiefs of the investigative agencies, there were strong forces within the executive branch of the government which would not only refuse to help cover up the embarrassing connection but would actively work to disclose it.

The most convenient way for the president to assure that the FBI investigation into the Watergate burglary would not uncover any damaging links to the White House, without embarrassing its recently appointed director, L. Patrick Gray, was to ask the Central Intelligence Agency to intrude on the FBI's investigation of the case. Since 1950 the CIA and FBI had a standing arrangement whereby if either agency asked the other to limit its investigation of a case so as not to reveal an intelligence operation or a secret agent, the other agency would acquiesce. When, for example, the Kennedy administration in 1961 wanted to terminate an FBI investigation into a wiretap placed, on the behalf of a Chicago racketeer, in the room of Dan Rowan, the well-known television personality, Attorney General Robert F. Kennedy warned Hoover that the investigation would uncover a CIA operation directed at Fidel Castro. After the CIA supplied the necessary paperwork, Hoover reluctantly called off the investigation.*

In the case of the Watergate break-in, the CIA could also have plausibly claimed that a full-scale FBI investigation into the matter could have disclosed agency operations and secrets. Four of the five burglars arrested in the Democratic headquarters that night had previously worked for the CIA: James McCord had been employed in the highly sensitive position of assistant director for security for the entire Central Intelligence Agency up to a year before the break-in; Eugenio R. Martínez, a Cuban refugee, was still receiving a $100-a-month retainer from the agency and reporting to his case officer in

---

*According to the story supplied to the FBI by the CIA (and Robert Kennedy), the private detectives arrested in Rowan's room for the attempted wiretap were employed by the CIA as a favor to Sam "Mo" Giancana, an organized-crime figure who had been recruited to help in the assassination plots against Fidel Castro by Robert Maheu, a CIA agent (and also a close friend of Larry O'Brien's, who was then Kennedy's chief of staff). Whatever the reasons were for this racketeer's being assisted by the administration, the revelation would have been highly embarrassing.

Miami; Bernard Barker, another refugee, had worked for the CIA both in Cuba and, later, in the preparations for the Bay of Pigs invasion; and Frank Sturgis had also been employed by the CIA in anti-Castro activities. More important, E. Howard Hunt had been a CIA official for more than twenty years, and the CIA's technical-services division had supplied much of the equipment used in previous intelligence operations that Hunt had undertaken for the White House. Indeed, at the time of the Watergate burglary, Hunt was employed by Robert R. Mullen and Company, which was ostensibly a public-relations firm but which handled many sensitive foreign assignments for the CIA and had a case officer assigned to it. President Nixon thus assumed, five days after the burglary, that the CIA would intervene with the FBI to prevent disclosures that would be damaging to his administration. On June 23 the president instructed Bob Haldeman to tell Richard Helms that "Hunt . . . knows too damn much. . . . If it gets out that this is all involved . . . it would make the CIA look bad, it's going to make Hunt look bad and it's likely to blow the whole Bay of Pigs thing which you would think would be very unfortunate—both for the CIA and for the country . . . and for American foreign policy. Just tell [Helms] to lay off." Nixon made it clear to Haldeman that he believed that Helms and the CIA were vulnerable to very damaging information that had been kept secret about the Bay of Pigs invasion for more than ten years, and that the threat of these disclosures would be sufficient to gain CIA cooperation in covering up the Watergate burglary. (Earlier, Ehrlichman had been ordered to ask Richard Helms to submit a report on the secret in-house investigation of the CIA's role in the Bay of Pigs invasion, but Helms resisted the request. After discussing it with Nixon in person, he submitted only an abridged report.)

Richard Helms, however, was not about to provide the cover for Watergate that the president expected. He had been told that Nixon planned to replace him immediately after the election, and he feared, as he told me subsequently, that Nixon also planned "to destroy [his] agency." Nixon, it will be recalled, had already excluded Helms from some meetings of the National Security Council. The director of CIA was also well aware that in the reorganization of the investigative agencies in the narcotics program the White House strategists had twice attempted to detach CIA agents and use them for their own domestic purposes. Krogh had, in fact, demanded and received surreptitious funds from the CIA to pursue his war against heroin.

Although Helms denied that he had specific knowledge of Hunt's activities on the special-investigation unit, he could not have been entirely unaware of the extraordinary nature of the relationship between Hunt and the other Plumbers and the White House. In any case, Helms saw that these White House maneuvers—and the demands being put upon his agency—could jeopardize the integrity of the CIA (and diminish its autonomy within the government). When Haldeman and Ehrlichman approached Helms with the president's suggestion that he inform the FBI that a deeper investigation of the Watergate burglary could uncover CIA activities, he pointedly refused, saying that the burglars arrested in Watergate were not involved with the CIA. The White House was thus deprived of its most expedient way of covering up the burglary.

Not only did the CIA refuse to intervene for the president to limit the FBI investigation, but Robert Foster Bennett, president of Robert R. Mullen and Company, which acted as a coordinator for Hunt in a number of his prior activities, began planting stories in the Washington *Post* which suggested that the Watergate burglary was directly connected to other White House activities. Indeed, Bennett sent a memorandum to his CIA case officer, Martin J. Lukasky—who controlled the covert activities of Mullen and Company—which described how he had established a relationship with Bob Woodward, of the *Post,* and was seeking to direct the attention of the *Post* to Charles Colson's activities and away from those of the CIA. In return for these stories, Bennett said that Woodward was protecting the covert activities of Mullen and Company and the CIA, according to a memorandum written to the CIA on July 10, 1972. As Colson saw material appearing in the *Post* which implied that he was behind Watergate, he began planting detective stories on his own behalf. The "battle of the leaks," as Colson called it, thus began to sink the Nixon administration.

At the Federal Bureau of Investigation there was also an open rebellion. The selection of Gray as acting director after the death of Hoover was resented by FBI executives who were bypassed for the position or who believed that the position should go to an insider at the FBI instead of to a friend of the president. A number of senior agents also believed that Gray was "too liberal" because he allowed agents to wear colored shirts and to grow their hair long, and even considered recruiting women as agents. To demonstrate to the president that Gray could not control the FBI, and therefore would prove a severe embarrassment to the administration, the disgruntled FBI officials leaked to the press the "302" files, which were reports of the interviews FBI agents had with individuals who could supply information about the Watergate affair. Mark W. Feldt, Jr., then deputy associate director of the FBI, also provided off-the-record briefings to journalists that implied that the White House was attempting to conceal its involvement with the Watergate burglars. With these "302" reports circulating around Washington and occasionally surfacing in the newspapers, President Nixon complained to his counsel John Dean, who was then supervising the Watergate cover-up, that "the Bureau is leaking like a sieve." It thus became painfully clear to the president that Gray would not succeed in suppressing the leaks from within.

There were also insurgents in the Treasury Department. Although the White House strategists had succeeded in easing Rossides out of his key position as assistant secretary for law enforcement and operations, and had managed to detach from the Bureau of Customs a large part of its investigative capacity, they had created dangerous enemies for themselves in the Internal Revenue Service and in other branches of the Treasury Department. Early in 1973, officials of the IRS surreptitiously leaked copies of President Nixon's tax returns, which showed that he paid no taxes while he was president, to a Rhode Island newspaper. It subsequently turned out that the tax deduction which allowed the president to forgo taxes during those years proceeded from a document that had been illegally backdated by the Nixon appointee who had replaced Rossides, Edward Morgan. Morgan was forced by the disclosure to resign immediately. The leaks from the Treasury Department thus further undercut the planned reorganization of the Treasury Department's investigative agencies.

Even though the Bureau of Narcotics and Dangerous Drugs was scheduled to lose its independent status as an investigative agency and to be merged into a new superagency in 1973 by Reorganization Plan Number Two (and the position of its director, John Ingersoll, was to be abolished entirely), die-hard officials at BNDD and at other agencies kept fighting the consolidation by leaking damaging information about Myles Ambrose, who was, according to Krogh, being considered by the White House for the job of administrator. For example, it was recalled that Ambrose had been the house guest of a Texas rancher who was later arrested for gun-running, as well as suspected of narcotics-smuggling; and information poured out of

BNDD (and the Bureau of Customs) on the Collinsville raids by the Office of Drug Abuse Law Enforcement. However, Ambrose had no interest in heading the new agency, and he retired to private law practice in 1973.

As late as September 15, 1972, President Nixon believed that despite the leaks he would be able to win control of major investigative agencies through his planned reorganization and then use these agencies to complete his consolidation of power over the rest of the executive branch of the government. He told John Dean, "This is a war. We take a few shots and it will be over...." When Dean replied that he had taken notes on the enemies of the administration, the president further explained:

> I want the most comprehensive notes on all those who tried to do us in.... They were doing this quite deliberately and they're asking for it and they are going to get it. We have not used the power in the first four years as you know. We have never used it. We have not used the Bureau and we have not used the Justice Department but things are going to change now and they [the investigative agencies] are either going to do it right or go.

Dean realized, however, that with each disclosure, the carefully planned reorganization was coming undone, and the domain that Nixon was attempting to gain over the investigative agencies was, in fact, slipping from his grasp.

The new superagency, which was to be called the Drug Enforcement Agency, was still moving ahead; and in this reorganization many of the bureaucrats who had opposed Nixon's will were replaced. The Nixon strategists, however, who were to coordinate the activities of this new investigative agency on Nixon's behalf, were all vulnerable to leaks and disclosures in the Watergate affair. John Ehrlichman and Egil Krogh, who were the powers behind the scene in establishing the new agency, had both supervised the activities of Hunt and Liddy in the special-investigations unit. It was only a matter of time before Hunt and Liddy, who were then indicted as co-conspirators in the Watergate burglary, named Krogh as their immediate superior in other burglaries (and even if they both remained silent, minor officials in the CIA and secretaries in the executive office of the president knew of these activities). Krogh thus was quietly moved from the

Domestic Council to the Department of Transportation. Morgan, Krogh's former staff assistant who replaced Rossides in the Treasury Department, was compromised by the leaks from the IRS on Nixon's tax returns and had to resign. Caulfield, who was to take over the Alcohol, Tobacco and Firearms unit for the White House, had been involved by John Dean in the cover-up, and therefore also had to resign. Santarelli, who had been appointed the new administrator for the Law Enforcement Assistance Administration, had been seriously damaged by a leak from the Department of Justice about candid but embarrassing remarks he had made about President Nixon, which were surreptitiously recorded at a luncheon by FBI agents and disclosed to the press. He was thus forced to resign. In short, all the key loyalists whom the White House strategists had counted on for the takeover of this new investigative agency had been driven from the government either by leaks from the agencies they were planning on reorganizing or by their involvement in the Watergate affair. As Eugene Rossides said to me in 1974, after he returned to his private law practice, "If not for Watergate, can you imagine what they would have done with the Drug Enforcement Agency?" The revolt of the bureaucrats thus succeeded in blocking Nixon's plan to gain control over the investigative agencies of the government in his second term.

32

The Coughing Crisis

I have ordered the Central Intelligence Agency, early in this Administration, to mobilize its full resources to fight the international drug trade.

—PRESIDENT RICHARD M. NIXON, *September 18, 1972 (in remarks before the International Narcotics Control Conference in Washington, D.C.)*

The Turkish poppy flower produced not only the opium base for illicit heroin but also the codeine base for medical preparations. When a State Department official warned the Ad Hoc Committee on Narcotics Control that the White House plan for eradicating the world's poppies might have "dire unforeseen consequences," a White House aide retorted cuttingly, "If we can't foresee the consequences, why presume they will be 'dire.'" He then went on to ridicule "bureaucratic overcautiousness" and demand immediate action. Four years later, the United States faced a massive coughing and pain-killing crisis. The inventories of codeine, which provide more than a half billion doses of cough suppressant and analgesic medicine each year, had fallen so precariously low that the government was forced to release its strategic stockpiles of codeine base. The licensed manufacturers of codeine medicines warned that unless the shortage was soon alleviated, they would have to cut production drastically. They warned that by the end of 1974, they would have less than one month's supply on hand, and the situation would be critical.

The problem was that codeine could be obtained only from the poppy plant, and the Nixon administration, by eradicating the Turkish supply, had inadvertently diminished the world's supply of this crucial base medicine. (India, the only other licit exporter of opium for codeine, doubled the price and reduced exports in 1972.) The antiheroin crusaders in the White House had expected a synthetic substitute for codeine to be developed after ordering the surgeon general and HEW to create such a drug. Despite some frantic efforts, government and industry scientists were unable to produce a synthetic equivalent on demand. With no substitute for codeine even on the horizon, the White House came under increased pressure from the American Medical Association and from drug manufacturers to increase the world's supply of opium. Finally, in 1974, as the coughing crisis loomed larger, the Office of Management and Budget, which was now superintending drug policy for the White House, decided to reverse the policy of annihilating the world's poppy supplies and seek new sources of opium for the drug industry. At the same time, however, political interests dictated that the prohibition on opium-growing in Turkey, which was in the conditioned popular imagination the single greatest victory of the Nixon administration in its war against heroin, be maintained.

To solve this dilemma, OMB directed the State Department to encourage India to increase by 50 percent its production of poppies. The idea was that Indian opium did not have the connotations in the press and with Congress that Turkish opium had, and, because of the relative remoteness of India and the fact that it consumed most of its own opium, an illicit supply might never reach the American market. India, however, was experiencing increased problems with opium-eating and drug addiction, and was reluctant to plant more poppy acreage to please the United States.

At this point OMB more or less designed its own poppy for American production—the *Papaver bracteatum*. This strain of poppy was originally discovered in northern Iran by scientists working for the Department of Agriculture. It had the advantage of producing high-quality thebaine, which can be converted to codeine but not, without difficulty, to heroin. Thebaine, nevertheless, was a white gummy substance similar to opium. Unfortunately, thebaine yielded drugs known as the Bentley compounds, which, although difficult to isolate, are ten thousand times as powerful as heroin. Some government scientists, fearing that the Bentley compounds would replace heroin, suggested growing the *bracteatum* on Air Force bases, surrounded by barbed wire and guarded by dogs. (One White House aide suggested that the Bentley compounds "would kill off half the heroin addicts, but then we might have a real problem with those that survive.") Finally, it was decided to grow the *bracteatum* experimentally at a Department of Agriculture field station in Flagstaff, Arizona (where poppies had already been planted as a "signature" for satellites and U2s). Mallinckrodt Chemical Works, a leading processor of opium, also announced its interest in growing *bracteatum* in Arizona.

The attempt to induce India to increase its opium production and the announced plans to grow poppies in the United States fatally weakened the American position in Turkey. William Handley, the former ambassador to Turkey who had replaced Nelson Gross as senior advisor to the secretary of state for narcotics-related matters, argued that it would prove impossible to maintain the ban in Turkey if "we planted poppies ourselves and encouraged every country but Turkey to go into the opium business." He held that the policy of banning opium in a single country, Turkey, was ultimately untenable. He was unable, however, to garner support from the narcotics agencies for his position. The Drug Enforcement Administration, which succeeded the BNDD in 1973, took the position that Turkish opium would eventually be replaced by other drugs, and that the best way to undermine the profitability of opium would be for America to produce its own poppies. The Special Action Office for Drug Abuse Prevention, which managed the federal methadone and treatment programs, argued that the drug problem could be solved only by reducing demand through treatment, and that therefore the Turkish opium question was irrelevant. Handley took his case to the cabinet committee, presided over by Melvin Laird, and lost. He promptly resigned. Less than six months later, on July 1, 1974, Turkey announced that it was resuming opium production to relieve the world shortage. Angry Congressmen immediately threatened to cut off military aid to Turkey (which grants the United States twenty-five "common defense" bases, mainly monitoring Soviet missiles), and suddenly the eastern flank of the NATO alliance was being thrown into jeopardy by the politics of the poppy.

Eventually, administration officials were able to brief congressional leaders on the fact that Turkey produced only 7 percent of the world's opium, and they claimed now that they had never really believed that the suppression of opium in Turkey would end the supply of heroin to addicts in the United States. As Walter Minnick, the former staff coordinator of the Cabinet Committee on International Narcotics Control, testified before the Senate Judiciary Committee on March 4, 1975:

> The dilemma we now face is that the demand for medicinal opiates around the world continues to skyrocket, inducing ever larger quantities of gum opium to be cultivated, primarily in India. The more opium produced, the larger the stock available for diversion into illicit criminal channels. . . . This will be true whether the opium gum is produced in India, Turkey, the Golden Triangle, or anywhere else.

The Nixon administration's "poppy war" had thus not only contributed to the codeine crisis but had stimulated production in other areas of the world. As Daniel Patrick Moynihan pointed out in a telegram to the State Department in 1973, when he was ambassador to India and the White House was attempting to change the hoary system of Indian poppy cultivation to alleviate the codeine shortage, it was not always possible for the White House to dictate morality with favorable results.

33

The Drugging of America

Power unused is power abused.

—EGIL KROGH, *1972*

While attempting to suppress narcotics, the federal government had inadvertently become a major supplier of narcotics. When the Nixon administration first assumed office, in 1969, it will be recalled, it was discovered that agents in the New York office of what was then the federal Bureau of Narcotics had become the leading dealers in heroin in the United States and were protecting the operations of illicit dealers (who in turn were providing them with their sacrificial "arrests"). Most of these agent-dealers were subsequently indicted, fired, or relocated.

For very different reasons, the Nixon administration also went into the business of distributing an addictive narcotic in the inner cities: methadone. In the belief that methadone was the only practical means they had of lowering crime statistics and overcoming the opposition from both bureaucrats and cabinet officers before the 1972 election, the White House strategists had succeeded in 1973 in funding some 450 methadone programs which distributed more than 7.5 million dosages of this synthetic narcotic annually in the United States. These federally financed treatment centers doled out daily dosages of the drug to over 73,000 persons (and almost any individual over twenty-one who desired to receive the drug could by one means or another enroll in the program). Although a radical change in government policy from narcotics suppression to narcotics distribution had almost been achieved by election time, the White House strategists were unable to persuade President Nixon publicly to identify himself with methadone treatment. Jeffrey Donfeld prepared, he recalled, "dozens of scenarios in which the president would visit a treatment center." But all were peremptorily rejected. In New York, in June, 1972, while the president and his party were flying in a helicopter from the Downtown Heliport to Kennedy Airport, Egil Krogh broached the subject to the president. Pointing downward toward the borough of Queens, the president replied, "The people down there couldn't care less about treatment or education. All they want to do is lock the folks up involved with drugs ... just lock them up." Unlike his young and inexperienced staff assistants, who quested for magic-bullet solutions, Nixon realized, probably instinctively, that pouring out a synthetic drug in the ghettos could produce damaging side effects (with which he did not want to be personally identified before the election).

One such side effect was that the treatment centers rapidly became centers for the illicit distribution of drugs in their communities. Despite the elaborate "blockade" theories which the proponents of methadone advanced, in which methadone was supposed to prevent the use of heroin, patients enrolled in these programs persisted in using illegal drugs. For example, in an extensive month-long examination of a sample of patients drawn from a maintenance program in Philadelphia, Carl D. Chambers and W. J. Russell Taylor found through urinalysis that there was an extensive pattern of cheating. In examining those who had remained in the program for more than six months, Chambers and Taylor found that 77 percent of these long-term patients were still using heroin; 30 percent were using barbiturates; and 25 percent, amphetamines. Nine months later the same sample was again tested for another month-long period. This time 92.3 percent of the methadone patients were found to be using heroin; 43.6 percent, barbiturates; 69.2 percent, amphetamines; and 43.6

percent, cocaine. Moreover, nearly two thirds of the patients tested had evidence of drug abuse half the time they were tested. Chambers and Taylor were thus forced to conclude pessimistically:

> Even after a year on relatively high dosages of methadone, neither a narcotic blockade had occurred nor had drug craving significantly diminished. These findings must also be viewed within the context that neither the patients themselves nor the program within which they were being treated are significantly different from most other methadone programs or patients.

Since a large number of methadone patients continued in their pursuit of illicit drugs (heroin, barbiturates, amphetamines, or cocaine), they not uncommonly sold or traded the weekend methadone dosages for money (or traded them directly for the illicit drugs they preferred). As the BNDD had originally feared, methadone thus leaked into the underworld of drugs; by 1973 it had become the major drug of abuse in the United States. In March, 1974, the New York medical examiner reported that methadone poisoning surpassed heroin as a cause of death from narcotics, and national statistics drawn from emergency rooms and medical examiners around the country confirmed this trend. An April, 1974, report from the statistical and data services division of the newly created Drug Enforcement Agency, entitled "Methadone: A Review of Current Information," stated, "Within the nine months reporting period [in 1973] . . . methadone deaths showed the most rapid rate of increase [of any drug]." It also found that there was "a five to one predominance of methadone to heroin deaths in the last six months," suggesting that "methadone is partially replacing heroin as a drug of abuse." The notion that the methadone addict would be less prone to commit crimes than the heroin addict he replaced was also debunked by this report, which found:

> Methadone addicts are not necessarily rehabilitated heroin addicts. A limited study of heroin and methadone addicts indicates that methadone addicts are equally prone to arrest, are more prone to commit property crimes or crimes of assault, and they are equally unemployed.

Verifying the high leakage from the federally financed methadone programs, the report also discovered that "almost half of those arrested obtained methadone outside of treatment programs" and that "methadone is readily available and heavily abused, contributing substantially to the overall drug problem." In examining police arrest statistics in New York City, the unpublished report further found that "methadone does not necessarily . . . lower the crime rate," and even "where there is an extensive methadone program, there were more methadone addicts arrested for various crimes than heroin addicts." Although this report was never made public, its implications were not lost on the White House, which began rapidly to disassociate itself from the funding of these treatment programs.*

As the methadone problem became more pronounced in urban centers—or at least received more unfavorable publicity—the White House quietly divorced itself from the once-vaunted Special Action Office for Drug Abuse Prevention. This office was moved into the Department of Health, Education, and Welfare, where it was in turn merged into the National Institute for Drug Abuse (NIDA), located in Rockville, Maryland. Dr. Jerome Jaffe, who had been promised direct access to the president, was cut off from the White House staff after the election; in early 1973 his pass to the White House cafeteria was revoked. Fully realizing that the White House strategists had been interested only in election-year public relations rather than the medical rehabilitation of drug addicts, Jaffe resigned in June, 1973.

In the hopes of increasing its election margin the Nixon administra-

---

* Jeffrey Donfeld also found in examining some of the treatment programs in Washington, D.C., that many of the statistical results were extremely dubious, if not entirely fraudulent. For example, in examining one methadone-treatment center in Washington which claimed to have enrolled thousands of addicts but refused to provide the names to the government on the grounds that it would violate its "black militant philosophy," Donfeld found that "the necessary verification and reconciliation of receipts and disbursements could not be accomplished based on the information supplied by the center. The accounting procedures made it impossible to check the application of funds." Of $214,310 in funds made available to this center, $81,579 could not be accounted for in any way; only $55,517 of the money paid to the center was deposited in a checking account, of which $11,000 was used for petty cash (and checks drawn from the account were payable to either the local liquor store or to the mother of the individual who headed the program). Some attempt was made to examine the patients being serviced by this center. The three hundred patients claimed in January dropped to fifty-two patients in September (most of whom were also unavailable for any sort of verification).

tion had willy-nilly brought about the de facto legalization of a narcotic. As Nixon had realized in his dealing with the Veterans Administration earlier, once a problem is turned over to the medical bureaucracy, it becomes difficult and perhaps impossible, in political terms, to phase it out. Thus, even though the heroin "epidemic" by all measures abated and the number of addicts turning up for treatment (or for free methadone) drastically declined after 1973, the methadone programs continued to expand, and the amount of illicit methadone available to addicts increased in direct proportion to the number of treatment programs. The federal government, therefore, again assumed its unwitting role as a major supplier of illicit drugs.

34

Lost Horizons

The proposal for a new narcotics superagency was submitted to Congress on March 28, 1973. Even though the House Committee on Government Operations noted, "The plan was hastily formed. . . . Administration witnesses were able to give the Sub-Committee only a bare outline of the proposed new organization and its functions," Congress refused to block the reorganization plan which purported to heighten the efficiency of the war against heroin. Accordingly, Reorganization Plan Number Two automatically became effective sixty days later, and the Drug Enforcement Agency (DEA) was created on July 1, 1973. The Bureau of Narcotics and Dangerous Drugs, which itself had been created by Reorganization Plan Number One, in 1967, was absorbed into the superagency, along with the Office for Drug Abuse Law Enforcement and the Office of National Narcotics Intelligence. In the process John Ingersoll's position as director of the BNDD was abolished, and the directors of the two other offices—Myles Ambrose and William Sullivan—resigned. Five hundred special agents of the Customs Bureau were transferred to this new agency, which employed, on paper, at least, more than four thousand agents and analysts and resembled the FBI as a domestic law-enforcement agency. John R. Bartels, the son of a federal judge who had been recommended for ODALE by Henry Petersen, was now named acting director of this new conglomerate.

If the Watergate burglars had not been arrested and connected to the White House strategists, the Drug Enforcement Agency might have served as the strong investigative arm for domestic surveillance that President Nixon had long quested after. It had the authority to request wiretaps and no-knock warrants, and to submit targets to the Internal Revenue Service; and, with its contingent of former CIA and counterintelligence agents, it had the talent to enter residences surreptitiously, gather intelligence on the activities of other agencies of the government, and interrogate suspects. Yet, despite these potential powers, the efforts of the White House strategists had been effectively truncated by the Watergate exposures: Ehrlichman and Krogh were directly implicated in the operations of the Plumbers; Sullivan had been involved in the administration's wiretapping program; and Liddy and Hunt were in prison. The grand design could not be realized, and DEA became simply a protean manifestation of the earlier narcotics agencies.

Bartels soon found, however, that it was not an easy matter to turn this superagency into a conventional narcotics police force. For one thing, when the special offices created by executive order were collapsed into the new agency, Bartels inherited some fifty-three former (or detached) CIA agents and a dozen counterintelligence experts from the military or other intelligence agencies—all of whom, under the original game plan, were supposed to work on special projects designated by the White House strategists. These high-level intelligence agents and analysts had a very different approach to narcotics intelligence from that of the traditional narcotics agent, who operated mainly by spreading "buy money" among his contacts in the underworld until someone attempted to sell him a significant quantity of narcotics. James Ludlum, a former CIA official who took over the Office of Strategic Services of the new drug agency, explained to me, "My approach was not to arrest a few traffickers but to build the entire intelligence picture of what was going on in the drug world. . . . I wanted to identify the modus operandi of the major heroin wholesalers, and this meant acquiring a great deal of information which the drug agency did not possess about the patterns of narcotic use." As Ludlum and the other former CIA agents began to demand more definite data on the number of addicts in the United States, their daily consumption habits, the way they routinely contacted dealers, and the names and profiles of the major narcotics traffickers in the world, they soon began stepping on the toes of the traditional narcotics agents. Colonel Thomas Fox, the former chief of counterintelligence for the Defense Intelligence Agency, recalled that "they did not seem to possess any systematic intelligence about narcotics traffic," and the revelation of this dearth of information raised embarrassing questions as to what the narcotics agents had been pursuing over the last ten years—and it also raised tensions between the conventional agents and the newer additions. The older agents fought back: Lucien Conein, for example, who was supposed to head "clandestine law enforcement" activities for the new agency, was given a totally isolated office, without staff, and was named chief of overseas narcotics intelligence. (As a friend and associate of E. Howard Hunt's, Conein was also compromised by the Watergate disclosures.)

The integration of some five hundred agents from the Customs Bureau into DEA also raised serious problems for Bartels. Many of the transferred inspectors had been content working for the Bureau of Customs and resented being treated as pawns in what they perceived to be a political game. They had formerly received a large part of their information about narcotics smuggling from their counterparts in the customs bureaus of other nations, according to Eugene Rossides, and the bureaucratic transfer had deprived them of these valuable sources of information. Also, they tended to be confused by the new reporting procedures of the Drug Enforcement Agency. In order constantly to expand the reported value of DEA seizures, they were instructed to participate in as many foreign narcotics operations as possible, even if it only meant supplying anonymous tips to the foreign police agencies. In practice, this meant that whenever a police agency anywhere in the world announced the seizure of any narcotics, the DEA agent in that country was queried as to whether he participated in that operation; if he answered affirmatively, the seizure's street value in the United States was credited to the total value seized by the DEA. One former customs inspector, who was stationed in Rome, explained to me:

> All they seemed to be interested in was statistics. . . . The three of us sat around the office in Rome all day, looking through the daily newspapers for any news of narcotics busts. . . . If there were any, we simply telexed Washington that we had participated in the bust by supplying anonymous information to the Italian police. Washington

never questioned any of our claims, and just kept sending us more and more buy money which we were supposedly giving to our informants for the anonymous tips. The whole thing was getting crazier and crazier, and finally I asked to be transferred back to the Customs Bureau.

The charges of corruption and "papering the record" by disgruntled employees, and their demands to be transferred back to their former agencies, strained relations within the new agency. These charges also fueled a war of leaks between DEA and rival agencies within the administration, which in turn led to reports widely circulated in the press that DEA was seizing far less narcotics coming into the United States than its predecessors—the Bureau of Customs, the Immigration and Naturalization Service, and the Bureau of Narcotics and Dangerous Drugs.

In reality, the task of intercepting narcotics had been unintentionally complicated by the maneuvers of the White House strategists in 1971. The temporary suppression of the Turkish poppy fields may have succeeded in disrupting the normal channels for distributing heroin, but it also brought many new entrepreneurs into the heroin business, and it thoroughly confused the surveillance procedures of the BNDD (which had formerly focused its attention on a few cities such as Istanbul, Marseilles, and Montreal). Moreover, when Turkey resumed the cultivation of poppies, the distribution channels for heroin had been so dispersed and fragmented that it was impossible to check or even roughly estimate the flow of the narcotic into the United States. Mexico had now become a major supplier of "brown" heroin (a discoloration caused by the laboratory process rather than the quality of the opium), and illicit networks had grown up in Afghanistan, India, Pakistan, and Southeast Asia. DEA could report higher seizures on paper, in terms of the street value of drugs seized in other countries, but this had little effect on the narcotics traffic in the United States.

Furthermore, methadone, the synthetic variant of heroin, was now freely available from hundreds of federally financed clinics around the country. This narcotic was spreading from urban centers to small towns, which traditionally had no narcotics problem or narcotics police. Not only was it harder to police heroin and methadone, but the unfavorable publicity which had emanated from the illegal raids conducted by ODALE raised serious questions in the Department of Justice about how drug agents were to proceed with searches and arrests. Formerly, narcotics agents had acted without much inhibition in breaking into a house or rousing a sleeping informant at four A.M. to question him roughly; now they realized that they might be suspended or indicted for what once had been standard operating procedure.

As the heroin supply became more difficult to intercept, DEA officials focused on heavy users of cocaine and hashish, who for a number of reasons were more easily identified and arrested. Cocaine and hashish, however, had not been connected in the public mind with causing crime or even being highly addictive, and public interest in the activities of the new agency waned—at least as it was measured in the media.

In 1974 dissension within the superagency reached the boiling point. Bartels had been unable to name a deputy director for fear that he would offend the old guard—the agents that had joined the old Federal Bureau of Narcotics and had been subsequently transferred to the Bureau of Narcotics and Dangerous Drugs, then the Office of Drug Abuse Law Enforcement, and finally the Drug Enforcement Agency. When Bartels attempted to introduce some "rationality" into what was largely a "statistics-jimmying operation," according to one of his staff assistants, "the old guard rebelled." A DEA inspector planted a story with Jack Anderson accusing Vincent S. Promuto, a public-relations assistant to Bartels, of associating with dubious characters. Then other stories were leaked to the press charging that Promuto had introduced Bartels to a cocktail waitress in Las Vegas—a charge which had no apparent basis in fact. The press campaign against Bartels and Promuto by the old guard seemed to be little more than what a decade earlier would have been called "guilt by association." But in the Watergate atmosphere that saturated Washington, D.C., in 1974, the failure by Bartels to investigate these charges was escalated into the charge of a cover-up. Senator Henry Jackson then began investigating these charges, and rebellious officials in the Drug Enforcement Agency began feeding him new morsels. When it became abundantly clear to the Ford White House, in May, 1975, that Bartels could not control his agency, he was induced to resign and was replaced by Henry Dogin, a lawyer in the Department of Justice. Six months later, Dogin was replaced by Peter B. Bensinger, a political appointee from Chicago. As one executive in DEA commented, "This was nothing more than a power play—the bureaucrats in the drug agency simply destroy anyone who tries to control them, and they use the press as their messenger boys in the battle." He then added, "The heroin problem remains more or less constant—there are no fewer addicts than there were in 1969—all that changes is the way the information about them is manipulated."

35

Decline and Fall

John Ehrlichman, who had risen in four short years from being the tour director for Nixon's campaign to being the president's principal assistant for domestic affairs, charted the grand design for gaining power over a major investigative agency of the government—the Drug Enforcement Administration—after Nixon's reelection, in 1972. The former real estate lawyer from Seattle had, however, seriously underestimated the countervailing powers within the bureaucracy. In the wake of Watergate he could not escape the flood of leaks from those he had sought previously to control, and his decline was even more swift than his rise to power. After being dismissed by the president (along with H. R. Haldeman) in 1973, he was indicted and convicted for perjury and conspiracy in both the Watergate cover-up case and the Plumbers case. While appealing his sentence, the former chief domestic-affairs advisor to the president resided at an Indian reservation in New Mexico and wrote a racy novel entitled *The Company,* which depicted the power struggle that characterized the Nixon administration. The novel was bought by Paramount for a major film, and currently Ehrlichman is completing a second novel about a domestic-affairs advisor to the president.

Egil Krogh, Jr., Ehrlichman's deputy and protégé from Seattle, had skillfully orchestrated the plans of the White House strategists, but he could not survive the unmasking of the special-investigations unit whose illegal activities he supervised. Although he first attempted to shield the president and Ehrlichman, he quickly saw that there was no way out except a full confession. He therefore pleaded guilty to a charge of violating rights in the Plumbers case and served four months in prison. His complete fall from power became clear to Krogh when he found in prison that the hygienist cleaning his teeth was a former drug trafficker whom he had helped to send to prison. After being released in August, 1974, he visited President Nixon in San Clemente. The president asked him whether he had really known in advance about the break-in at Dr. Ellsberg's psychiatrist's office; Krogh assured the former president that he had not in fact known. For a few weeks Krogh considered writing a book on national security, but was unable to find a foundation to sponsor this enterprise. He did, finally, find a job as an administrative assistant to Paul N. McCloskey, the liberal California Republican in Congress. Later, in 1976, he joined the staff of Swenson's Ice Cream Company, a San Francisco chain.

Krogh's staff on the Domestic Council also disbanded. Edward L. Morgan, who had briefly replaced Rossides at the Treasury Department, was indicted and convicted for his part in backdating the president's tax return; he spent several months in prison. Jeffrey Donfeld, who had been recommended by the president to head the enforcement division of the Interior Department, was denied that position by the Civil Service Commission after Ehrlichman resigned. Discouraged by the turn of events in the American government, Donfeld visited Israel at the time of the Yom Kippur war and then returned to California to practice law at a corporate firm in Century City. Walter Minnick, who had gone from the Domestic Council to the Office of Management and Budget, resigned from the government in 1974, also disillusioned by what he saw. He moved to Boise, Idaho, where he took an executive position in a construction firm. Geoffrey Sheppard, Krogh's young assistant who supervised the law-and-order programs after G. Gordon Liddy left the Domestic Council, moved to the White House as speech writer for the embattled president and stayed there until the bitter end, when Nixon resigned. Sheppard then returned to the state of Washington and joined a law firm.

E. Howard Hunt and G. Gordon Liddy, who advised Krogh on ways to use the war on heroin for other purposes, were both convicted for their part in the Watergate burglary and are still in prison. Both men are reportedly considering writing novels about the political scene in Washington.

Nelson Gross, the former political boss of Bergen County, New Jersey, who directed the international narcotics program under Krogh's tutelage, resigned from the government in 1973 when he was notified that he was about to be indicted for election fraud. He was subsequently tried and convicted for violating the campaign laws. His success in bringing Timothy Leary back from Afghanistan was all but forgotten. The Cabinet Committee on International Narcotics Control, for which in theory Gross worked, was quietly disbanded in 1972 and moved into a two-room suite of offices in the State Department—never to be heard from again.

William C. Sullivan, who cooperated with the White House to replace J. Edgar Hoover as head of the FBI and wound up instead (after being locked out of his office by Hoover) as head of the Office of National Narcotics Intelligence, was recruited by John Dean to write a "Sullivan Report" on the illegal activities of the FBI under other presidents. After Dean defected from the White House in March, 1973, Sullivan was quietly eased out of his office, which was then folded into the new Drug Enforcement Administration. Sullivan returned to New Hampshire, where he suffered a serious heart attack in an automobile accident and was therefore unable to testify before the various committees investigating the excesses of the FBI under Hoover. The White House strategists with whom Sullivan dealt, Robert Mardian and John Dean, were both indicted and convicted in the Watergate cover-up case.

Myles Ambrose, Nixon's first drug czar, opted to retire from the government after the public furor over the Collinsville raids by agents of his Office of Drug Abuse Law Enforcement—and several embarrassing leaks that appeared in the press about his association with a Texas rancher who later ran afoul of the law—even though there was no linkage between these incidents and his retirement from federal service. Ambrose returned to private law practice, although he still occasionally plays basketball in the gymnasium of the drug agency. Caulfield, who had originally proposed the private detective firm planned for the White House in 1971, was forced to resign from the Alcohol, Tobacco and Firearms division of the Treasury Department. Ambrose's office was also consolidated into the Drug Enforcement Administration.

Donald J. Santarelli, the young White House strategist who was appointed head of the Law Enforcement Assistance Administration in 1972, was unable to use its billion-dollar fund to assist any of his former colleagues in the White House (except for Police Chief Jerry Wilson, of Washington, D.C., who received a grant from LEAA to write a book on police). After Santarelli made some unfavorable comments about the Nixon White House, which were duly leaked to the press by FBI agents, he was forced to resign. However, he was retained as a consultant by LEAA to produce a series of television programs about law enforcement.

The bureaucratic enemies of the White House also were forced to resign from the government. John Ingersoll, who resisted the White House strategists until they reorganized his job away, became the security director of the IBM World Trade Corporation and took two of his chief assistants, Richard Callahan and Tony Pohl, with him. Eugene Rossides, although he continued to battle the Drug Enforcement Administration long after he left office in the Treasury Department, eventually found a new cause in Cyprus and became a leading organizer of the movement to deprive Turkey of any United States military aid (he had also attempted this earlier under the aegis of the narcotics-control program). Richard Helms, who had refused to assist in the Watergate cover-up, was appointed ambassador to Iran. And Richard G. Kleindienst, who had assisted Helms in resisting the White House attempts to incorporate CIA agents in the drug program, pleaded guilty to a misdemeanor involving misinformation given to a Senate committee, and then returned to private law practice in Washington.

Dr. Jerome H. Jaffe, who in 1971 had been appointed by the president to head the new Special Action Office for Drug Abuse Prevention, resigned from the government in 1973 after he found that the in-group in the White House showed more interest in public relations than in drug abuse. He was given an appointment at the New York State Psychiatric Institute, and subsequently commented in an article in *Psychiatric News,* a publication of the American Psychiatric Association, on the psychiatric flaws in the Nixon White House. His special-action office was then moved to an annex of the Department of Health, Education, and Welfare in Maryland. The White House annex on Jackson Street that he had shared with Myles Ambrose was ordered vacated in October, 1973, to "make way for the energy crisis." (The first energy czar, John Love, moved into the offices on October 15, 1973.)

John Bartels, Ingersoll's successor, resigned from the Drug Enforcement Administration under pressure in 1975, and is currently working on libel suits against his former subordinates for their leaks and testimony, as well as on a book about the drug agency. Before Bartels had assumed office in 1973, President Nixon declared, "We have turned the corner [in the war against drugs]." As Bartels should have realized at the time, the heroin crusade ended with Watergate.

End Notes

CHAPTER NOTES

Prologue   The Secret Police

I've argued in my book *Between Fact and Fiction* that journalists cannot hope to approach an accurate rendering of an event without revealing their sources. Every source who has supplied a journalist with a part of a story has selected that bit of information, whether it is true or false, for a particular purpose. That purpose may be to advance his own career, to advance the interests of the agency he works for, to discredit an enemy, or simply to assist a reporter in describing a happening. The bits of information thus supplied can be evaluated only in light of the circumstances and context in which the information was given. It is not enough simply to present the assertion of an interested party—even if it can be shown that it is "accurate," in the trivial sense of "accuracy" (which simply means correctly specifying the details touching on the event). One must know who made the disclosure and, ideally, why he made it to that particular individual and at that particular moment in history. Concealing such information from the reader amounts to a deliberate disguising of the event itself, since such a process hides all the interests that selected, shaped, and possibly distorted the disclosures. To be sure, concealing the interests behind the disclosures of sources is in the interest of the journalist, since it assures that his sources will continue to provide him with information for public disclosure. This makes his job much easier, but at the same time it prevents any independent evaluation of his work.

Thus, in describing the efforts of the Nixon administration to organize fear and develop an instrument for political control, I shall identify all my sources in these end notes, and attempt, as far as possible, to give the circumstances and interests behind the disclosures. Since the interviews, documents, and material given to me constitute only a small part of the total amount of information on this subject, I shall also try to specify what I do not know: the individuals I was unable to interview, the documents I was unable to obtain, and the issues I was unable to resolve. And what we do not know is, unfortunately, an important, and perhaps critical, part of the story.

1   Legend of the Living Dead

In March, 1973, as time drew near for the publication of a portion of my book on television news, *News from Nowhere,* in *The New Yorker* magazine, I began looking for a project that would take me to some of the more remote places of the world—if only to avoid confronting some of the television journalists whom I had interviewed between 1969 and 1972 on television talk shows. At that time, the United States' effort to suppress opium production in Turkey appeared to be successful, and as I assumed (at least then) that everyone agreed on the worth of this effort, it seemed a straightforward (and distant) reporting vehicle for *The New Yorker.* Without giving it much thought, I accepted the conventional wisdom that heroin caused crime, and that by reducing the supply of heroin, crime would be reduced. James Q. Wilson, the professor at Harvard under whom I had done my doctoral dissertation in political science, had just been appointed chairman of the National Council on Drug Abuse Prevention, which was supposed to chart the strategy of the war on drugs. In January, 1973, I traveled to Cambridge to discuss how I might report on this "war." Professor Wilson explained to me that the presumed link between heroin and crime had not yet been established by either the government or social science. He said that he himself was reviewing all the studies done on the putative nexus between heroin and crime and suggested that, so far, they were inconclusive.

He added that if I went to his office in Washington—a town house connected to the new Executive Office Building—I could start my study by reading a secret report the White House had commissioned from the Institute for Defense Analysis (IDA), which is a Rand type of think tank. (When the Nixon White House had begun its war on drugs two years earlier, it had discovered that there were no systematic studies of the crime/drug problem.)

I then flew to Washington and read the IDA's report on drug addiction. It found that there was no logical relation between the statistics the government gave to the public and the actual knowledge it had of drug abuse. It concluded that estimates of the number of crimes committed by drug addicts might well be exaggerated by 500 percent or more, and that the number of drug addicts was not known. It indicated, moreover, that most addicts were not addicted to a single drug, such as heroin, but could change their dependency at will from heroin (if the price was too high) to barbiturates or to alcohol. I realized while reading this that if the conclusion were justified, the entire program of curtailing a single drug—heroin—would not necessarily affect the crime problem, since addicts could just as easily switch to narcotics manufactured in the United States, such as barbiturates.

At this point I wanted to know something about the history of drug abuse in America—especially, about the origins of the generally accepted theories about drugs and crime. Wilson's executive assistant in Washington, Roger Degilio, suggested that I might start my research in the library of the Drug Abuse Council, a private foundation located several blocks away. This council was in a state of disorganization when I visited its offices in April, 1973, and while attempting to find the library (which was not yet established), I was introduced to Dr. Jerry Mandel, an offbeat sociologist who had been appointed a fellow at the Drug Abuse Council. When I explained to Dr. Mandel that I was looking for some possible sources of our current thinking about drugs and crime, he immediately told me about Captain Richmond Pearson Hobson. Mandel himself had collected the private papers of Captain Hobson and suggested that I could trace any and all present associations about drug abuse back to Hobson. Subsequently, Mandel recommended me for a Drug Abuse Council fellowship, and in 1974 I received approximately $30,000 to research the subject of drugs for a book.

At about the same time, the National Commission on Marijuana and Drug Abuse was attempting to compile all the systematic studies

of drug abuse, to place the problem in perspective. One member of
the commission, Joan Ganz Cooney, also became interested in my
research, and allowed me to peruse most of the internal reports of the
commission. It became apparent to me that none of the available data
systematically gathered over a period of fifty years conformed to
Captain Hobson's theories about "heroin fiends." By that time I had
reviewed the literature on the subject and knew that a complete
analysis of the way politicians had used and abused the drug problem
would be the subject of my book.

2   Nelson Rockefeller

My account of the ways and means in which the rhetoric of fear was
ingeniously employed by Rockefeller and his staff was heavily based
on the working papers of Rockefeller's staff. These were provided to
me by Rayburne Hesse, who was a member of Rockefeller's Narcotics
Commission and subsequently Rockefeller's lobbyist in Washington
for New York State's drug program. As I read through these speeches,
press releases, and staff memos, it became manifestly clear that the
heroin issue was more or less rolled out at election time to excite the
public and bait the liberal opposition, and was then quietly forgotten
until the next time such rhetoric was necessary. Jerry Mandel, then
my associate at the Drug Abuse Council, provided me with his
analysis of the "vocabulary of fear" which Rockefeller employed.
Finally, I developed the general framework for examining Rockefeller
as a master in psychological warfare by reading through old State
Department files from World War II, when Rockefeller was coordinator of information for Latin America. Originally, research was
undertaken for an article on the Rockefeller family for the *Sunday
Times of London.* Information about Hudson Institute reports and
other private information available through Rockefeller was provided
to me by Mark Moore, whom I met earlier, when he was studying at
Harvard. Later he became a consultant for the Hudson Institute, and
then for the Drug Enforcement Administration, in Washington, D.C.

3   G. Gordon Liddy: The Will to Power

For two years I tried without success to interview G. Gordon Liddy.
Many of those who had worked with him in various illegal enterprises

of the Nixon administration, such as the Fielding or Watergate break-ins, had attributed their participation to Liddy's all-persuasive influence. After discussing Liddy with his employer, Eugene Rossides, and with Charls R. Walker, the deputy secretary of the treasury, I realized that Liddy had taken "the drug menace" to its logical conclusion in terms of law enforcement. If an epidemic was allegedly threatening to destroy the nation, a national police force was necessary. I also spoke to those who worked with Liddy on the working committee of the Ad Hoc Committee on Narcotics Enforcement, including Jim Ludlum, of the CIA, and Arthur Downey, of the National Security Council. Again I was told of Liddy's precise articulation of the drug issue and his powers of persuasion.

Unfortunately, I was not able to interview Liddy. I arranged with Liddy's law partner, Peter Maouroulis, for *Playboy* magazine to pay Liddy for an interview, which I would conduct. In preparing the interview I hoped to answer a number of questions that were still outstanding as to Liddy's articulation of the drug issue. *Playboy* offered Liddy $3,000 for the interview, and his lawyer held out for $5,000. Before the negotiations could be completed, however, Liddy decided to put the matter in the hands of a literary agent, Sterling Lord. Apparently in the hopes of obtaining a much larger contract from a book publisher, Lord then terminated the negotiations with *Playboy*.

Finally, I've quoted from a very impressive letter that Liddy wrote to his wife from prison, and which *Harper's* magazine published in 1974; a television interview with Liddy, which Mike Wallace did on CBS in 1974; and an article that Liddy wrote describing his capture of Timothy Leary.

4   *The Barker of Slippery Gulch*

The definitive biography of Richard Nixon has yet to be written. Although commentators have focused on either his alleged misdeeds or his presumed breakthroughs in foreign policy, no one has explained, at least to my satisfaction, how Nixon rose from being a penniless naval officer in 1946 to vice-president of the United States six years later. Although his meteoric career as congressman, senator, and vice-presidential nominee may be accounted for simply by the Cold War rhetoric against the "enemy within" which he articulated so brilliantly—and viciously—in this period, I do not find this conventional explanation entirely persuasive. His ascendancy might also be related to people and factors that have managed to remain in the background. For example, as a negotiator for the Navy, he dealt with defense manufacturers and received early support from Howard Hughes and other defense suppliers in Southern California. The role these men and their resources played in his rise has not yet been fully clarified.

In discussing Nixon's childhood, I relied very heavily on Theodore H. White's *Breach of Faith*. White, an extraordinary historian in his own right who masquerades in journalist's clothing, has shown how Nixon was shaped by childhood poverty in a way perhaps no other modern president has been, and how one of his main drives in life was to escape that condition.

There have been a plethora of books and reports on Nixon's campaign tactics: I found especially useful Joe McGinniss's *The Selling of the President* and Evert Clark and Nicholas Horrock's book *Contrabandista!* But again, for any serious analysis of the presidential campaigns, one must turn to White's series, *The Making of the President*.

I never had the opportunity to interview Nixon himself, but three of his chief speech writers—Patrick J. Buchanan, Raymond Price, and William Safire—have freely discussed with me some of the considerations that went into major speeches on law and order. Buchanan, who wrote Spiro Agnew's now-famous attack on television, in Des Moines, Iowa, in 1970 (and whom I first interviewed for my book on television news), believed that the president could successfully exploit popular resentment against permissiveness on law-and-order subjects, and often advocated a strident tone. Ray Price, a soft-spoken man who provided me with some of the more trenchant analyses of the Nixon administration, had serious doubts about the practicality of playing with popular fears for political purposes. Safire, who did not involve himself in the disputes over how to present law-and-order issues, argues convincingly that Nixon himself was in firm control of the rhetoric surrounding the various domestic issues and used whichever speech writer best fit his purpose at the moment.

Adumbrations of Nixon's law-and-order issue, especially as it was later to focus on heroin, can be found in Governor Nelson Rockefeller's rhetoric in New York State between 1962 and 1968. The exact extent to which Rockefeller influenced Nixon's heroin crusade, however, is not clear to me. Safire insists that although Nixon admired

Rockefeller's political tactics and skill in New York State, he didn't entirely trust his judgment as a politician. (According to Safire, this antipathy was reflected in Rockefeller's failure to reply to letters that Nixon personally wrote him.) Yet, Buchanan suggests that Nixon modeled much of his rhetoric on Rockefeller's. A comparison of speeches bears this out. Nixon also appointed a number of men who were highly active in the Rockefeller campaign to superintend his narcotics program in 1969. Most of the metaphors used by Nixon, such as "growing cancer," were, in any case, used earlier by Rockefeller.

5   *The Bête-noire Strategy*

I first encountered the "bête-noire strategy" by accident in 1970. William Shawn, the editor of *The New Yorker,* had asked me to investigate the deaths of twenty-eight Black Panthers, allegedly at the hands of police officials. Since at that time I was immersed in my doctoral dissertation at Harvard, I hired one of my students, Gary Rosenthal, as my research assistant, and asked him to collect as much information as he could about each of the twenty-eight cases. Less than a week later he called me and seemed very distressed. He explained that although the number twenty-eight had been repeated in the press for more than a year, even a superficial investigation showed that no more than ten or twelve Panthers had died, and even then the circumstances were fairly ambiguous. We thus wrote a story about reporting rather than about murder. Later Pat Moynihan explained to me that for the better part of a year he had attempted to convince the Justice Department to defend itself against charges of genocide, but that he was turned down because Mitchell "didn't see the dangers in being labeled repressive." In Washington, Moynihan introduced me to Richard Moore, a close advisor to Nixon who had been reassigned to the Department of Justice to assist Mitchell in gaining more favorable public relations. Moore explained to me that his problem was that what was deemed favorable public relations depended on "what public you were trying to relate to." And the public that Nixon and Mitchell were seeking to relate to was the "more conservative [element]." If Attorney General Mitchell appeared to be repressive, in the sense that he was "repressing" criminals, the Nixon speech writers considered it to be favorable public relations. Moore himself disagreed with this bête-noire strategy and tried to reverse it, although there was little hope of succeeding.

Much of the history and analysis that I present on the Justice Department's traditional war on crime is based on the writings of Victor Navasky, who spent three years examining the Justice Department for his book *Kennedy Justice.* The view I present of the Justice Department under Nixon is based on interviews I've had with various members of the department over a three-year period, including former Attorney General Richard Kleindienst; Assistant Attorney General Henry Petersen; Assistant Attorney General for Administration Leo Pellerzi; Donald Santarelli, former director of the Law Enforcement Assistance Administration; John Ingersoll, director of the Bureau of Narcotics and Dangerous Drugs, and his deputy, Richard Callahan; U.S. Attorney Myles Ambrose; U.S. Attorney Thomas O'Malley; William Ryan, a prosecutor in the criminal division; and U.S. Attorney Earl Silbert, who prosecuted the case involving the original Watergate burglary. Even though some of these men were Democrats and opposed the Nixon administration, they all showed an extraordinary amount of respect and affection for John Mitchell. Ingersoll, for example, who was appointed by Ramsey Clark (and rudely dismissed by Nixon in 1973), said that he found Mitchell so "enlightened" when he discussed legal issues that "at times, when John Mitchell was talking about the administration of justice, and I closed my eyes, I thought it was Ramsey Clark talking."

Egil Krogh and Jeffrey Donfeld were also extremely helpful in reviewing memoranda they wrote (see end note for Chapter 6, "The Education of Egil Krogh," for some explanation of their cooperation). Pat Moynihan also provided me with a general overview of what took place in the struggle to fulfill the politics of law and order. When I first presented some of these arguments in *The Public Interest* magazine, James Q. Wilson raised some objections to my characterization of the law-and-order issue. He suggested that it wasn't all "politics" or "image making," but that serious men were sincerely interested in diminishing crime. Though it may be that many of those involved in the war on crime were interested in substantive results, I believe others were less interested in reducing crime than in achieving political objectives.

6   *The Education of Egil Krogh*

When files and information are provided to a journalist, it must be asked why they were made available. Since the meaning of files can be altered by excluding certain documents or including bogus ones, they have historic value only if one can evaluate the circumstances in which they were provided. Is the donor attempting to advance a bureaucratic interest? Is he trying to glorify his own historical role? Or is he attempting to denigrate the reputations of others? Although journalists rarely, if ever, identify their sources, or explain the motives of their sources in providing them with information, such contextual information is vital if anyone is to make a reasonable evaluation of the truthfulness or value of the source.

This chapter is based heavily on files and interviews provided to me by Egil Krogh, Jr. I first attempted to interview Krogh before his role in the break-in of Ellsberg's psychiatrist's office was revealed, but Krogh refused to see me, saying, "I'm writing a book myself." After he was indicted, pleaded guilty, and served six months in prison, I called him again. His fortunes had changed drastically: in less than a year he had gone from being undersecretary of transportation to an unemployed former convict. Any of those whom he had known in government, and who had deferred to his judgment, now shunned him. Although he worked at home, he was desperately trying to get back into public life and agreed to appear on any talk show or give any lecture available. I was then affiliated with the Drug Abuse Council, with whom I discussed the possibility of obtaining a grant or possibly a fellowship for Krogh to write his intended book on drug policies. He said that although he thought it was extremely important to make public his experiences in drug policy, he was too exhausted by his recent experiences to write a book. I then suggested doing a long interview with him for *The Public Interest* magazine in which he could discuss fully his role in formulating the drug policy of the Nixon administration. Since he was flat broke, and had little prospect of earning any money to support himself or his family, I mentioned that perhaps I could arrange a grant from *The Public Interest* for his cooperation in this interview. I spoke to the editor, Irving Kristol, who agreed that it would be a worthwhile project, and said that he could make $2,000 available to Krogh for cooperating in the interview.

Krogh was genuinely elated at the prospect of working with Irving Kristol, whom he greatly admired, as well as at the prospect of earning the money. We thus began meeting for breakfast on a regular basis in the fall of 1974 and prepared the general outlines of the interview. To help familiarize me with his role in the drug program, he gave me ten cases of files, internal documents, notes written for the president's attention, analyses of the drug problem, Domestic Council issue papers, and correspondence. The "Krogh File," as I called it, was not complete. These were only the files that he had brought home to use in working on the book that was never completed, and the files of his assistant, Jeffrey Donfeld, who had sent him material to help in his research. The rest of his files had been seized by the government when he became involved in the Watergate affair and were not available, even to him. I thus worked for several weeks attempting to fill in the files and note the gaps. I cannot be sure, of course, how honest he was in recollecting information that would damage his reputation or that of his associates, though he did not seem to hesitate in providing me with embarrassing documents and insights. In any case, this was supposed to be Krogh's version of the event, and I intended to do a great deal of research on other versions.

The article for *The Public Interest* never turned out to be an interview with Egil Krogh. Irving Kristol's coeditor, Daniel Bell, was concerned that a straight interview might appear to be a defense of the Nixon administration, and we were all concerned about the serious gaps in the Krogh file. I therefore agreed to write an article which would be heavily based on the Krogh interview, but not limited to it. The article, "The Krogh File—The Politics of 'Law and Order,' " finally published in the spring, 1975, issue of *The Public Interest,* understandably disappointed Krogh, since it was my point of view on the issue rather than his.

By basing research on the available files of one person, or even of a group of persons, one naturally tends to focus and perhaps exaggerate that person's role to the neglect of the roles played by others (whose files are not available). Certainly the administration's law-and-order policy did not spring full grown from the head of a small cabal of Nixon strategists; like most other government programs, it gradually emerged from a series of proposals, critiques, counterproposals, and reformulations drafted and redrafted by a multitude of hands representing diverse interests. One level of ideas came from urban-affairs scholars, both inside and outside the administration, who had a serious nonpolitical interest in the substantive problem of controlling crime. Another level of suggestions (and objections) came from the heads of bureaus within the executive branch interested in expanding their activity in the realm of law enforcement. Finally, as might be expected in the wake of any successful presidential campaign, a third layer of ideas came from political advisors to the president interested in maintaining a favorable image of him in the public mind. Krogh, however, became the funnel through which these ideas passed to the Domestic Council and then to the president, and eventually, through his analysis and his choice of staff, Krogh played a heavy role in the formulation of the drug policy.

7 *Operation Intercept*

One interesting way of studying an event, at least one that takes place in the American media, is to study the various press briefings (which are available under the Freedom of Information Act) and the resulting stories. In this case the disparity between the briefings coming from the Departments of Justice and the Treasury (Task Force One) and those from the State Department illuminated the sharp bureaucratic conflict of interest and the resulting battle of the leaks. Further information about the State Department's effort to counterbalance the favorable publicity which Operation Intercept was receiving came from Juan DeOnis, an extremely resourceful New York *Times* reporter whom I met in Ankara, Turkey, while we were both stranded by the war in Cyprus in July, 1974.

Egil Krogh's files were again useful for reviewing Operation Intercept memoranda, one of which I quoted in Chapter 7. Arthur Downey, who was with the National Security Council and worked as a staff person on the ad hoc committee, described the internal conflicts to me after he left government service. We had become friends while he was in Washington in the spring of 1974. Pat Moynihan described the earlier heroin crusades from a different point of view.

In February, 1975, I interviewed a number of the Mexican officials in Mexico City on the diplomatic ramifications of Operation Intercept. They were all grateful to the State Department for reversing the direction of favorable publicity which Task Force One was then providing for Operation Intercept.

8   The War of the Poppies

In June, 1974, I met with Arthur Downey and Ambassador William Handley in the restaurant of the Mayflower Hotel. Four years earlier, Downey had been on the ad hoc working group for suppressing the Turkish opium supply, and Handley was ambassador to Turkey. After the initial victory in the Turkish heroin crusade, Handley was transferred to Washington, where he replaced Nelson Gross (who was on the verge of being indicted for criminal offenses) as senior advisor to the secretary of state on narcotics control. Downey returned to private law practice in Washington. Less than a month before our meeting, Handley had been abruptly fired from his position because he opposed a White House plan to begin the cultivation of poppies in the United States. The White House, under increasing pressure from pharmaceutical manufacturers to provide them with a source of codeine, decided that the most feasible source for future codeine would be American poppies (see Chapter 32, "The Coughing Crisis"). Handley, who had persuaded the Turks to stop growing poppies in their country, believed that the Turks would never stand for Americans' replacing Turkish poppies with American poppies, and would return to cultivating opium themselves. He brought the issue to Melvin Laird, who was then advising President Nixon. Laird decided in favor of the White House decision, and Handley retired from government.

Under these circumstances, Handley was willing to talk about the pressures brought upon him when he was ambassador to Turkey. He understood the Turks better than most of the new potentates on the Potomac (such as Egil Krogh, Gordon Liddy, Eugene Rossides, and others) who were issuing curt and often ridiculous negotiating instructions to his embassy. As Downey was at the time in the White House, he was able to add some details which even Handley didn't know.

After that meeting I decided to go to Turkey, to see how American aid and diplomatic pressure were being put to use. *Esquire* magazine agreed to pay for the trip in return for an article (which it later published under the title "The Incredible War Against the Poppies" [December, 1974]). Soon after I reached Ankara, Handley's prediction came true, and the Turks suspended the ban on opium production. I thus was able to hear the Turkish account of the diplomatic pressure

from various foreign-ministry officials who were anxious to explain
the reasons for the Turkish decision. The new American ambassador,
William Macomber, and the director of the United States Information
Agency bureau in Ankara, Edward Harper, also briefed me on this
situation, and pointed out the strategic importance of American radar
bases in Turkey.

9   The French Connection

Arthur Watson was not a diplomat by profession: his father had
founded the IBM Corporation and was one of its largest stockholders.
Arthur had always sought a public purpose in life. While he was
ambassador to France, unfortunately, he developed a "drinking
problem," which was widely reported after an incident with a
stewardess on a transatlantic flight. The fact that a number of the
leading crusaders in the heroin war were themselves victims of alcohol
(but steadfastly refused to recognize it as a disease or a drug
addiction) intrigued me.

My meeting with Ambassador Watson in June, 1974, was arranged
by Thomas P. Murphy, who still served Watson as aide-de-camp and
friend. The three of us drove from the offices of Watson's investment
company in Connecticut to a roadhouse for lunch. I offered to pay on
my expense account, but Watson answered wryly, "One of the few
ways I have of spending my wealth is buying others lunch." It was a
thoroughly enjoyable meal. Murphy, a clever and amusing journalist,
described many of the adventures that he and the ambassador had
during their drug crusade in France. Watson had then piloted his own
private plane, and together, a curious team, they had flown back and
forth between Marseilles and Paris. Watson recalled one embarrassing
moment, when a French official in Marseilles gave them a packet of
heroin to fly back to police officials in Paris. During the flight
Ambassador Watson realized—and joked about—the predicament that
might arise if the plane crashed on the return flight, and heroin was
discovered on their persons. During this lunch Ambassador Watson
also described with great humor and insight the episode of the
"sniffer" and the descent into the Marseilles sewers.

Two weeks later I went to Paris and visited the "science attaché,"
Edgar Piret, in the United States embassy near the place de la
Concorde. Piret, a former university professor, gave me the usual

briefing that officials give to the press, describing the routes from
Turkey to Marseilles and then to America. When I told him that I was
more interested in the sniffer that he had invented, he looked at me
with horror. "That's highly classified information. . . . Only about
twenty people in the world know about the sniffer." Then he warned
me that if I published information about it, I would destroy the entire
"sniffing operation." I told him that I had heard that the sniffer had
already been dismantled and returned to the United States. He looked
sad for a moment, as if recollecting a deceased pet, then told me that
someday it might be revived, and that it was best not to give out the
modus operandi. He then reached into his desk and produced
photographic albums, with hundreds of nostalgic pictures of himself,
Thomas Murphy, and Ambassador Watson in Marseilles. He had
gone there every weekend with the "team" to chart out the smoke
plumes and the wind directions that various odors might take. He
suggested that designing the sniffer had been "an unusual adventure."

Just as I was leaving, I decided to mention the efforts to detect
heroin in the sewers of Marseilles. The look of horror returned in his
face, and he said, "No one knows about that . . . perhaps only three
people in the world." To reassure him, I told him that Ambassador
Watson had mentioned it to me. As I walked him to his car in the
embassy parking lot, he again tried to swear me to secrecy.

I next saw Paul Knight, the director of the regional office of the
Bureau of Narcotics and Dangerous Drugs in France. He was one of
the few BNDD agents who graduated from Harvard, and I found in
general that those who viewed themselves as part of an "Ivy League
network" were more prone to talk to journalists. When I mentioned
the secret sewers of Marseilles to Knight he described the adventure
as "completely ridiculous." He then offered to allow me to interview
his agents, who, he said, would provide me with "some exciting gang-
buster stories."

10   The Panama Canal

One of the most enjoyable parts of this investigation was interview-
ing American ambassadors in a trip around the world. I spoke to
Moynihan in India, William Cargo in Nepal, William Macomber in
Turkey, Richard Helms in Iran, and, when I returned to the United
States, Ambassadors Arthur Watson, Robert Sayre, William Handley,
and Loy Henderson. These men all gave precise and extremely

perceptive descriptions of the effects of White House narcotics policy on foreign policy. They could not help but be persuasive since they were extremely well briefed on the countries in which they represented the United States, and because they had no political interest at stake. They also seemed to have a healthy detachment from the situations they described. However, the ability of ambassadors to present a skillful case may in itself obscure the fact that they see the world from one particular vantage point, which may tend to diminish the importance of domestic trends and policies.

Consider, for example, the case of Moynihan. When he served in the White House as an assistant to the president for domestic affairs he pressed relentlessly to implement a narcotics-control program in Turkey, and when our ambassador there, William Handley, seemed to be moving too slowly in implementing the president's policy, Moynihan suggested that the White House take a more direct role in the treaty negotiations in Turkey, even if it meant superseding or recalling the ambassador. After Moynihan resigned from the White House in 1971, he was appointed ambassador to India. When, however, the White House pressed him for immediate action in controlling the production of opium in India (in this case they wanted to expand it, not contract it), Moynihan objected to such White House interference, and pointed out in telegrams that the authority of the embassy should not be undermined for purposes of carrying out a domestic policy at home. As one White House staff assistant noted, "What we have here is a case of role reversal." The effect of the location of ambassadors on their perspectives of problems obviously cannot be discounted. Later, as ambassador to the UN, Moynihan espoused an entirely different position.

The description of the episode in Panama is based mainly on interviews with John Ingersoll and Robert Sayre (who was then an inspector general in the State Department). I also relied heavily on Evert Clark and Nicholas Horrock's book *Contrabandista!* and John Finlator's book *The Drugged Nation.* The White House pressures were described for me by Egil Krogh.

11 *The Narcotics Business: John Ingersoll's Version*

One serious problem involved in reporting an event is that participants almost invariably tend to shape their version of it in accordance with their vantage point. This is especially true when dealing with government officials, each of whom tends to reconstruct an event or policy from the perspective of the agency with which he has, or has had, an involvement. Even if one interviews all the actors concerned in a particular drama, their versions of it do not necessarily fit together; nor do the parts equal the whole. It is not a question of who is telling the truth and who is lying; it is a question of what one tends to emphasize or deemphasize in rendering an explanation. John Ingersoll, Eugene Rossides, and Egil Krogh spent considerable time with me attempting an account of the "narcotics business" that was consistent with their particular hierarchy of values. There were no glaring discrepancies or contradictions in the three accounts; nevertheless, each blamed the others for the continuing bureaucratic strife in the early days of the drug program. When I discussed this problem early in my research with James Q. Wilson, he suggested that the only way one could give an honest rendering of the event was to tell in sequence the various stories without attempting to pass judgment. Readers, however, expect some narrative guidance or resolution, and therefore I modified Professor Wilson's suggestion, although the idea behind it still intrigues me.

I had over the course of writing this book fifteen interviews with John Ingersoll, and nine lunches with him. I first met him in the spring of 1973 after he was abruptly and cruelly fired from the Bureau of Narcotics and Dangerous Drugs by President Nixon. We first had lunch at the Italian Pavilion in New York City, and we discussed his ideas for writing a book about his experiences in the "narcotics business." Unlike Egil Krogh, Ingersoll was a discreet man—a professional policeman who knew what to say and what not to say. He was willing to relate his ideas about narcotics and some opinions about the Nixon administration and his tenure in it, but for a long time—our first five lunches—he resisted revealing any specific information to me. After Egil Krogh gave me his memoranda and files, the situation changed with Ingersoll. I now had information he wanted, and as I began revealing it piecemeal, he began to explain the intricacies of the "business" he was involved in for six formative years. When we began our interviews, Ingersoll believed that he had been fired simply because he was not helping the Nixon administration in its efforts in the 1972 election. As I revealed more and more of the Krogh file, and especially how the White House intended to infiltrate and use Ingersoll's BNDD, he began theorizing that there may have been a more sinister motive in his removal—an attempt at setting up a White House investigative agency which would do the bidding of John Ehrlichman and Richard Nixon. He referred to Egil Krogh and his young assistants as the "Boy Scouts," and had little respect for them because they knew almost nothing about narcotics or crime. On the other hand, he respected those in the Department of Justice—especially John Mitchell. After he left Washington, Ingersoll went to work for IBM in New York, in charge of security, and I occasionally met with him in the offices of that corporation. As I would go over documents with him from the Krogh file, he would often break out in laughter—shocked or amused at what the "Boy Scouts" were planning for him. I never believed that Ingersoll gave me the full story. He usually gave me as little information as he could, but it seemed that whatever he told me probably was accurate—at least it was never controverted by other evidence I found.

Most of the books written about the Bureau of Narcotics and Dangerous Drugs, or about its predecessor, the Bureau of Narcotics, tend to be a string of anecdotes of the adventures of gang-busting drug agents. In this genre are the books *The Protectors* and *The Murderers,* by Harry J. Anslinger, written mainly to glorify the work of agents and possibly to build their morale. The only account to date that I am aware of which deals with the inner workings of the drug bureaucracies is John Finlator's book *The Drugged Nation.* For the history of the narcotics program I relied heavily on Dr. David Musto's book *The American Disease.*

12 The Border War: Eugene Rossides's Version

A large portion of the news about law enforcement is authored by agencies within the government, whose agents intentionally leak (or perhaps, more accurately, plant) their stories to newsmen in order to advance an interest of their particular agency or block that of a competing agency. Such news planting may be done in "seminars," in which newsmen are briefed about the exciting exploits of an agency; in news releases, which usually single out one event; or in the private briefing of a newsman. Eugene Rossides was a master in the last of these techniques. Even after he left the government to join former Secretary of State William Rogers in private law practice, he continued his skirmishes on behalf of the Treasury Department. When he briefed me on the narcotics policies of the Nixon administration, I was impressed with his precision and shrewdness. I knew that as a Greek-Cypriot American, and as former public-relations advisor to Prime Minister Makarios, of Cyprus, Rossides had been waging a campaign to penalize Turkey. I, of course, also knew from my interviews with John Ingersoll that Rossides was an "enemy" of Ingersoll and the BNDD. Nevertheless, I was impressed with his arguments for not centralizing the law-enforcement agencies of the government under the Department of Justice, and admired the skills with which he mobilized support in Congress and the press for his position. At one point in early 1974, after I had prepared an article for *The New Yorker* magazine which he (wrongly) assumed was favorable to the Treasury Department, he called me at my office at *The New Yorker* to persuade me to rush the article into publication. He said, "Ed, you're a key man on my team, but I have to call the plays, and we have to get the story out." When I replied that I had no power over the publication schedule of *The New Yorker* (which is certainly true), he suggested that he might himself speak to the editor and warn him of the "impending dangers to civil liberties" that he argued would arise unless the Treasury Department maintained its role in the war on drugs. While I dissuaded him from speaking to the editor, I appreciated his manipulative skills: he knew which levers to press with *The New Yorker*—to wit, endangered civil liberties.

Rossides also arranged for me to see Vernon "Mike" Acree, who replaced Myles Ambrose as commissioner of customs. Acree in turn arranged at Rossides's suggestion for me to interview some former employees of the BNDD who are now working for the Customs Bureau. The former employees, no doubt under instructions from Commissioner Acree, provided me with vivid and dramatic details of the inefficiency of the BNDD (which I listened to but reserved judgment on).

In order to pierce the party line at the Treasury Department, I also interviewed several civil servants who participated in the "border war" with Customs, including Mort Bach and Robert Esterland. Like Rossides, these men did not deviate from the perspective of the Treasury Department.

13 *Conflict of Interests: Egil Krogh's Version*

One serious problem with the technique of interviewing participants in the government process—or in any other event, for that
matter—is that in retrospect they tend to assign rational motives to
their actions. They know what resulted from their deeds, and they
reconstruct the chain of happenings so that all connects logically.
Motives that might be deemed in hindsight to be irrational are often
neglected. Krogh thus reconstructed the struggle against the bureaucracy so that it all seemed to proceed from a logical motive of
putting into effect a more efficient and unified program. Yet, in
reading over Krogh's own file, it appears that there were many
instances of irrationality. Members of the White House staff showed
anger at outsiders and at moments became preoccupied with demonstrating their power—apparently for no other sake than the demonstration. For example, at one point Krogh told a Chicago psychiatrist,
Daniel Freedman, that he would "destroy him" if he stood in the way
of one of his programs. Jeffrey Donfeld threatened to "put away" in
an insane asylum one prominent New York psychiatrist, Dr. Judianne
Densen-Gerber, for advocating drug-free therapy. Such displays of
anger and power are all too human and occur in almost any
administration; they are not the moments, however, that one remem-
bers, or considers relevant, when being interviewed by a journalist.
The young White House staff saw all other members of the
government outside their circle as bureaucrats who usually failed to
respond, or who responded too slowly, to their orders. In such
circumstances many of the actions later attributed by the participants
to a struggle against a recalcitrant bureaucracy might well have been
instances of the exertion of personal power, or even misunderstand-
ings revolving around such exertions of power by men in their late
twenties or early thirties (most of the "bureaucrats" were in their early
fifties). In relating the versions of this struggle rendered by John
Ingersoll, Eugene Rossides, and Egil Krogh, it is important to keep in
mind that each focused on the more logical explanations of his actions
and neglected others. Such a defect in reconstructing an event cannot
be remedied by collating one interview with another, since each
participant is biased in the same direction of "rational explanation."

As far as I know, only one periodical covered this particular war within the Nixon administration, and that was the *National Journal,* which reports on federal-policy-making. In presenting Krogh's version I relied on the series of interviews I did with him in the fall of 1974 (see end note for Chapter 6, "The Education of Egil Krogh"). Similarly, the documents I cite all come from the files given to me by Egil Krogh.

14   The Magic-bullet Solution

In reporting on any medical or scientific controversy, one is confounded by the tendencies of scientists to produce simultaneously both a "hard" and a "soft" explanation for their experiments or programs. In the case of methadone the hard claim was that the drug reduced crime. Doctors operating methadone clinics thus told politicians and journalists that each program was saving the city millions of dollars, since without the programs their patients would be stealing that amount (Dr. Dole actually put the total saved in the billions of dollars). Journalists reported, as in *Look* magazine, that methadone was a "Cinderella drug" that once swallowed by a criminal addict transformed him into a decent, law-abiding citizen. However, when some methadone programs began to show that when addicts substituted methadone for heroin they actually increased the amount of violent crime they committed—since methadone made them more "effective" and gave them more time to pursue their "business" (for example, muggings, robberies, etc.)—methadone doctors redefined their explanations in "soft" terms, which they whispered to federal administrators. The soft claim of methadone treatment was that it brought isolated individuals into a social context. By forcing them to report several times a week for their daily dosages of methadone, to which they were now addicted, it maintained them on a sort of "chemical parole." And once on this chemical parole, they could be counseled, guided, and rehabilitated by doctors and other employees of the treatment centers. In the soft explanation methadone did not have any sort of blockade effect to prevent the addict from using heroin. Rather, since his urine was examined daily, there were strong incentives for him to use the addictive drug provided by the government—methadone—rather than the illicit drug provided by the pushers—heroin. Since heroin addicts were commonly arrested for possession as well as for distribution of the drug, the very fact that they were now using a synthetic narcotic that was legal greatly lessened their criminal activities and their contacts with policemen and courts. In other words, by legalizing the drug-taking behavior of addicts, methadone-maintenance programs could be expected to bring about some statistical decrease in the arrest records of their clients—although this would not necessarily bring about a decrease in crimes such as burglary, muggings, and robberies, which affected other citizens in the community.

When one criticized the hard claim of the methadone doctors by citing the various statistical artifacts used to create the crime-reduction illusion, proponents would rebut with the soft formulation of methadone maintenance: methadone itself did not reduce crime; they never claimed it did, but only that it brought addicts into a "matrix" of treatment and rehabilitation facilities. The defenders of the methadone programs simply said that the hard claims were made in order to win public support or to obtain federal funding for programs, but no sophisticated evaluator of the program ever accepted these claims as the reason for providing this support. The hard claims about the reduction in crime, the blockade against heroin, and the transformation of addicts were thus only for public consumption and for rationalizing a complex program in terms of an immediate public benefit (i.e., the reduction in crime) rather than for a more diffuse social benefit.

I first became involved in the methadone issue in the summer of 1973, at a conference in Aspen, Colorado, where I met Irving Kristol. He suggested that I might want to investigate the rationale behind the methadone programs for his magazine, *The Public Interest*. As I was at work on other aspects of the federal drug program for *The New Yorker* magazine, I agreed to undertake this investigation. The working title was then "The Great White Hope" (we later agreed to change the title when Robert DuPont, who had succeeded Jaffe as head of the special-action office, suggested that this would be taken as a racist article, which it was not). Initially, I analyzed the methods that the methadone doctors used in collecting and evaluating their crime and rehabilitation records. I found that if narcotics offenses (such as possession of heroin, etc.) were factored out of the crime statistics, then the methadone-treatment programs had not really obtained the substantial decreases in crime that their proponents had publicly proclaimed. In other words, they reduced narcotics offenses, but not crimes against persons or property. I also found that when other doctors attempted to replicate the methadone experiments, they found that the great majority of their patients used heroin as well as methadone, and that there was no blockade effect. Finally, it turned out that most of the doctors involved in the methadone program did not themselves believe in the Dole-Nyswander definition of heroin addiction as a "metabolic disease," and the evidence seemed far stronger that addicts returned to heroin not because of any irreversible change in their chemistry but because their environment (poverty, discrimination, etc.) stayed essentially the same when they returned from their treatment program. When the article in *The Public Interest,* now entitled "Methadone: The Forlorn Hope," was finally published in the summer issue in 1974, almost all the serious critics of the article, such as Dr. DuPont, readily admitted that these three findings were correct—i.e., that methadone by itself did not reduce crime, that it did not blockade addicts against heroin, and that heroin addiction was not a "metabolic disease"—but they then resorted to the soft defense. They stated that all the responsible doctors and social scientists involved in the program viewed methadone simply as a lure to entice addicts into treatment programs, where the real "rehabilitation effort" would take place. They also suggested that I had reviewed only the early results of Dole and Nyswander, which they acknowledged were seriously flawed, and argued that the newer programs had better statistical methods of evaluation. In any case, other programs had made their data less vulnerable to investigations by outsiders.

Eventually, the doctors operating methadone programs became far more sophisticated and hired public-relations firms to answer criticisms and to work behind the scenes to prevent the publication of critical analyses. At one point, Dinitia McCarthy, a young NBC television producer who had won an Emmy award, produced a half-hour documentary criticizing methadone clinics in New York for various reasons, pointing to the disparity between their hard claims of crime reduction and the actual crime statistics, which were rising in New York. The public-relations firm representing several methadone clinics hired private investigators to find out about her private life, and wrote intimidating letters to her executive producers at NBC.

The documents I quote from in reviewing how the Nixon administration became involved in methadone all come from Egil Krogh's file. After I obtained this file, which was the year after I had written my original article on methadone, I went to California to interview

Jeffrey Donfeld. At the time of Watergate, Donfeld was the deputy director of the special-action office, and in line for a very high position in the Department of the Interior. After Krogh and Ehrlichman fell from power, however, the Civil Service Commission held up his appointment, and he took a long trip to Israel to "rethink" his service in government. He then resigned from the special-action office and returned to Los Angeles, where he took a job with a law firm in Century City. As we reviewed the documents, which included handwritten notes that he had taken at cabinet-level meetings, he recalled with great enthusiasm his days of power in the White House. For one thing, he had been earning three times as much as he was now earning as a junior lawyer in California. For another, people had deferred to his judgments. Because of his change in station, I think he was a good deal more open in reviewing these documents, and he himself still believed in the efficacy of the methadone program. After our final meeting I arranged with a friend of mine who was a professor at UCLA to have a graduate seminar, with Jeffrey Donfeld, in the political-science department. Upon reflection, I believe that Donfeld had more insights about the real nature of White House politics than most professors.

15   The June Scenario

I found the June, 1971, scenario for the creation of a heroin crusade among the thousands of memoranda that Egil Krogh gave me for preparing an interview with him in *The Public Interest* magazine. The actual scenario was scribbled in pen on legal-size yellow pages by his staff assistant, Jeffrey Donfeld. Donfeld had had a meteoric career. After being president of the student body at UCLA, he went on to law school and then, in 1969, to the Nixon administration as a staff assistant to Egil Krogh. He drew up most of the memoranda concerning drug policy for Krogh and Ehrlichman, became an advocate of the methadone-maintenance program, and was appointed, in 1971, deputy director of the special-action office. When I interviewed him in Los Angeles in 1973, he had returned to the relatively mundane life of a California lawyer. He reflected with great nostalgia about his time in the government and showed considerable interest in reliving momentous decisions by going over with me (and one of my students) a pile of documents that Krogh had given me a few months earlier. Together we reconstructed the administration's plans for launching a heroin crusade.

Some of the most interesting documents in the Krogh file were the various drafts of President Nixon's June 17, 1971, speech, and the comments on it by various staff assistants. The speech writers had tried to specify the number of addicts in America (300,000), the nature of heroin addiction (a fatal, irreversible disease), and the amount of crime which could be attributed to heroin addiction ($10 billion per year). As the war of memos and countermemos proceeded in the drafting of the speech, it became painfully clear that the government had not really established any of these facts. Various estimates had put the number of addicts between 50,000 and 600,000 but without any consensus as to the correct number; there was considerable doubt about the nature of heroin addiction (whether addicts could be detoxified or had to be maintained on heroin for the rest of their lives); and no agency had any firm idea of how much crime was committed by addicts (although $10 billion was an obvious exaggeration). One early draft of the speech claimed that all organized crime in the world was based on the heroin traffic, but that again proved to be a completely unsubstantiated claim which was deleted from the final draft. As nonfacts were winnowed out of the final draft, and as speech writers glossed over the glaring gaps in the state of the knowledge about drugs, it became clear that the crusade was based on very little hard information on drugs.

The strategists at the White House were primarily concerned that the president, and not Congress, receive credit for these "initiatives." In pasting together the vampire metaphors from old speeches of Rockefeller's and Nixon's, the speech writers tried not to make it appear that the "epidemic" began in the Nixon administration. A good deal of rewriting was necessary to collapse periods of time and numbers.

The embarrassment of John Ingersoll, the director of the BNDD, over his inability to pin down statistics for the president was a vital part of this scenario. Ingersoll recalls that his isolation from the White House began after the president publicly humiliated him, at the cabinet meeting televised by ABC, by asking him "hard questions." Donfeld acknowledged that he had briefed the president on these "gaps" in what was known about narcotics addicts. Meanwhile, Krogh had complained to Ehrlichman that Ingersoll was avoiding the "difficult tasks" and not cooperating with the White House.

My main sources for this chapter, other than the Krogh file and Jeffrey Donfeld's elaboration of it, were interviews with Egil Krogh, Donald Santarelli (who told me about the showing of *Triumph of the Will*), and John Ingersoll.

16   Bureau of Assassinations

The assassination bureau was not a subject that any of the former employees of BNDD or the White House desired to discuss. The mention of a "$100 million clandestine law enforcement fund" came quite unexpectedly from the files provided by Egil Krogh. Until then, I doubted the various stories I had heard circulating about assassinations. Krogh, when I called his attention to these documents, was at first abashed, and then explained that most of the activities had taken place in the ungovernable regions of Southeast Asia.

Jeffrey Donfeld, Krogh's deputy, admitted sheepishly, when I pressed him as to what type of law enforcement could possibly be clandestine, that its main purpose was "assassinations." Walter Minnick, who supervised the international activities of the narcotics program for Krogh, said that although the program was then not put into effect, the plan involved assassinations. And Nelson Gross's administrative assistant, Roger Degilio, also confirmed that "clandestine law enforcement" was a euphemism for assassination, but he could add no details of the specific program. Arthur Downey, Kissinger's National Security Council aide assigned to the drug program, said that the "black stuff" had been discussed and even expedited, but he refused to be specific. I then went back to John Ingersoll, who had been extremely cooperative and candid with me, and showed him the outline of the discussion with the president. Ingersoll asserted that his agency had never received $100 million, but he suggested that perhaps it was retained under White House control for their own purposes. Mark Moore, who was director of planning for the drug agency in 1973–74, told me that there had been an appropriation of discretionary money which wasn't "accountable," but he had no idea what it was supposed to be used for.

I was first told about Howard Hunt's attempt to recruit a team of Cuban hit men by Martin Dardis, the assistant state's attorney in Miami. He had an affidavit from Eugenio R. Martínez describing Hunt's request. I was unfortunately not able to identify the Cubans whom Hunt was trying to recruit for this program.

The briefing on the possibility of assassinations which the National Commission on Marijuana and Drug Abuse received on its "heroin trip" was provided to me by Joan Cooney, a member of the commission, who was extremely helpful in providing all the files of the commission for my original study of the link between heroin and crime.

Colonel Conein's dealings in assassination equipment were brought to light by Lowell P. Weicker, Jr., Republican senator from Connecticut, who had been conducting an investigation of CIA involvement with other government agencies, and had obtained a catalogue of the equipment described to Colonel Conein (see the New York *Times,* January 23, 1975).

Missing pieces still remained to be found in the puzzle. Although I attempted to trace the 1972 supplemental appropriation for the assassination fund, it seemed literally to disappear somewhere in the Office of Management and Budget. About $50 million was given to the BNDD, but this supposedly was for recruiting new agents and buying equipment. Since this money was to be "unaccountable," it is possible that a portion of the $50 million was in fact the first payment into the assassination fund.

17   The Screw Worm

The "screw worm" never surfaced in the press and proved an elusive research project. The first hint of biological warfare came from Myles J. Ambrose, the burly former consultant to the president and head of the Office of Drug Abuse Law Enforcement. In the course of our discussing various unorthodox proposals that came up in the ad hoc cabinet committee, he mentioned that at one time it was contemplated that some sort of "bug" might be dropped on Turkey. I next asked Arthur Downey, who recalled some talk of developing a poppy weevil and was familiar with the plan for surveillance from U2s, Phantom reconnaissance planes, and the outer-space satellite. He pointed out to me the tension that existed between the Department of Agriculture and the National Security Council over Henry Kissinger's attempt to achieve détente with China. He suggested that Nelson Gross would be the person most familiar with the poppy-eradication program. Gross, however, had just been convicted of tax evasion and was on the verge of going to prison, and was therefore unavailable for further interviews (he hadn't mentioned the poppy weevil to me in my original interview with him, in 1972). I consulted his executive assistant, Roger Degilio, the former Pentagon analyst who understood bureaucracy in Washington perhaps better than anyone else I had met. Degilio explained to me the Department of Agriculture's role in developing the weevil, but thought I should also speak directly with Dr. Quentin Jones, Agriculture's man in charge of the weevil. I visited Dr. Jones at the Department of Agriculture's vast complex—literally hundreds of buildings identified by number only, in which experiments of an unknown nature go on—who, although he refused to show me pictures of the weevil, told me why the crash program had been rejected by the National Security Council.

When I wrote an article for *Esquire* magazine on the international aspects of the war against the poppies, in July, 1973, I was familiar with the weevil program but had not yet learned of its origins or of Nixon's interest in it. Only when Egil Krogh gave me his files, after he was discharged from prison, in September, 1973, did I find the memo in which Dr. Jaffe suggested the "insect" to President Nixon, and thus the origins of the screw-worm program. This memorandum to the President's File was drafted on July 2 by Jeffrey Donfeld, who attended the June meeting along with H. R. Haldeman; Arnold Weber, from the Office of Management and Budget; John Ehrlichman; Jaffe; and, of course, President Nixon. I later interviewed both Krogh and Donfeld, who also supplied handwritten verbatim notes of the meeting. Donfeld recalled the president's continually using the term "screw worm" and that he was hysterically funny, whether he meant to be or not.

18   The Celebrity File

The "celebrity file" was begun by Jeb Stuart Magruder, who before he went on to engineer the Watergate "intelligence operation" had served as a public-relations advisor to the president. His main accomplishment had been suggesting the idea of a Drug Abuse Prevention Week, which President Nixon proclaimed on April 28, 1970. Jeffrey Donfeld inherited the task of recruiting celebrities, and eventually succeeded in putting together an impressive roster of football players who endorsed President Nixon's stance against drugs. The memoranda on which this chapter is based—the outlines of discussions with the president; the option paper on the creation of a National Drug Foundation; memoranda of the meeting with Sammy Davis, Jr., and the president; the memoranda on Sammy Davis, Jr.'s programming—all come from the files of Egil Krogh. Krogh and Donfeld took great delight in explaining this public-relations side of the drug issue to me.

19   *World War III*

Nelson Gross was responsible for originally interesting me in the "heroin crusade." Soon after Nixon won reelection, in 1972, I was in search of an investigative topic for *The New Yorker*. Hearing about Nelson Gross's adventures on the opium trail, I arranged to interview Gross at his New Jersey estate to see if he would make a suitable profile for *The New Yorker*. Not mentioning his impending indictment, he said that he was about to resign, but would arrange for his secretary and former assistant to provide me with his public papers and statements. I next went to the State Department, where his successors, Harvey Wellington and William Handley, gave me some insight into the disruptive nature of Gross's brief crusade. Later, at the encouragement of Pat Moynihan, I visited a number of embassies around the world, where ambassadors further clarified the unorthodox tactics employed by Gross. The briefing papers I quote from are part of the Egil Krogh file, and they gave me some appreciation of the national-security considerations. Finally, Gross's executive assistant, Roger Degilio, a man I came to admire for his shrewd wit, completed the record of the global war.

20   *The Manipulation of the Media*

The intentions that political actors have at any moment in history cannot be ascertained by journalists and are subject to a form of journalistic indeterminacy: the closer a journalist becomes to a political actor, the more the political actor tends to fashion retrospectively his intent, or motives, to win the approval of the journalist. And since any action can be justified in terms of a public rather than a private interest, most actions tend to be explained in terms of a "justifiable" motive. Jeb Stuart Magruder, Egil Krogh, and Jeffrey

Donfeld thus all explained the staging of these media events in terms of the greater good accomplished in warning American youth of the dangers of drugs; and undoubtedly Richard Nixon would attribute the same motive to his participation in them. Ronald Howard Glass, at the time a student of mine in a political-science course at the University of California, interviewed eleven of the participants at the television conference and found that all but one of them believed that President Nixon, John Ehrlichman, and Jeb Stuart Magruder had no political motive for producing this conference and that their intentions were selfless and sincere. If they believed that there was any motive except absolute altruism on the part of the White House, they would have had to admit to themselves, and to their colleagues, that they were the objects of purposeful—and successful—manipulation. My conclusion that there was definitely a political motive in attempting to propagate fear in the media on the drug issue comes not from interviews with the White House staff but from Krogh's files, especially a hundred pages of scenarios, plans, interoffice notes, and other memoranda providing step-by-step outlines of the conferences and "media hype" with the precision of a military maneuver. Of course, in the search for motives, even such profuse and specific documentation can be discounted. For example, as Jeffrey Donfeld explained to me, "To get anything past Haldeman and Ehrlichman, we had to describe whatever we were doing in the most cynical political terms." According to this rationale, "cynical" documents could be part of the deception used to accomplish altruistic aims. As it is impossible to prove the intent in reporting an event, I can only adopt a tone that seems to me to dovetail with my evaluation of the interviews and the prevailing themes that appear in the documents written contemporaneously with the events. Another researcher, of course, might adopt a different tone—and lead his readers to different conclusions about the intent of the White House.

In reconstructing the manipulation of the media I attempted to match the press releases from the White House or from federal agencies with the stories that appeared in the nation's press. In the vast preponderance of cases, and there were pitifully few exceptions, I found that the news that Americans read—or saw on television—had been manufactured by government officials interested in intensifying fear and concern in the American public. In most instances the press release was printed almost verbatim—or at least in an abridged form.

In this chapter I relied heavily on the files of Krogh and Donfeld, and in their retrospective analyses of the "media hype," as Donfeld called it. I also quoted from Jeb Stuart Magruder's autobiography, *An American Life: One Man's Road to Watergate* (written in collaboration with Patrick Anderson), which provides some perspective on the public-relations operations of the Nixon administration.

21   The Movable Epidemic

Journalists are often themselves responsible for much of the statistical exaggeration and hyperbole produced by federal agencies. John Ingersoll explained to me that it was not only the White House that wanted to manufacture a crisis but also journalists who covered narcotics. Whenever he presented reporters with a "reasonable" estimate of the number of addicts or of the value of seized narcotics, they would invariably press him as to whether a more "dramatic" figure could be given in the press. Ingersoll would accommodate them to assure that his bureau was favorably covered in newspaper accounts. Added to this consideration, congressmen on key appropriations subcommittees always wanted the narcotics problem to be presented on a grand scale, so that they could justify appropriations. Other agencies of the federal government were under similar pressure to produce dramatic numbers.

The fault was not entirely with the government statisticians. In order to make assumptions about the number of addicts in the United States, it was first necessary to establish some definition of what constituted an addict as opposed to an occasional or even moderate user of heroin. If an addict was simply defined as someone who regularly used a drug that was injurious to his health and suffered withdrawal pain if he ceased using that drug, then not only heroin users but cigarette users could be classified as addicts. On the other hand, if addicts were defined as individuals who could not voluntarily stop using a given drug, then only a small percentage of heroin users, even of those classified as addicts by local police departments, would qualify under this definition as addicts. The Bureau of Narcotics and Dangerous Drugs statisticians, lacking any real definition of addiction, simply lumped both categories together in an "addict-user" category. However, the fundamental assumption they used in projecting "unknown addicts" was that once an individual was addicted to heroin, he would continue his addiction for life. While this assumption fit the latter group of addicts, it did not fit the former group, who could be expected to have occasional "runs" on heroin, "mature out" at the age of thirty or so, or simply use heroin when it was in fashion— or easily available. The statistician who applied the "tagged-fish-in-the-pond" formula, Dr. Joseph Greenwood, was not engaged in any sort of statistical flimflam game; he was simply working on assumptions provided to him by others in the BNDD, in answering a problem that was given to him. That his projections of 559,000 addicts were widely reported and used in political speeches by figures in the Nixon administration to increase the atmosphere of fear suggested an inability of journalists reporting the dramatic numbers to analyze the assumptions behind them.

This chapter relies on data provided to me mainly by John Ingersoll on the statistical methods the BNDD used to project estimates. The quoted speeches and briefings of President Nixon and Myles Ambrose were provided to me by Richard Harkness, the press officer of the special-action office.

22   *The Crime Nexus*

One of the most deleterious effects that social science has had on journalism has come from substituting "rational" models of behavior for descriptive reporting of what has been known to happen. Such models tend to focus attention on logical explanations of a phenomenon at the cost of neglecting the irrational factors and downplaying data that are missing or are not fully established. Crime in America is transformed by the application of such models from an irrational complex of lawbreaking into an economically logical means by which addicts pay for the drug they need to maintain their wellbeing. Though such models may provide interesting results when they are based on well-established data (for example, when economists investigate the relation between taxation and inflation), they cannot be applied to areas where the data are problematic at best without creating logical confusions. The crime nexus that was applied to heroin users tended to blur many important distinctions, such as the difference between one who uses heroin and one who has a physical dependence on it. It also imputed causal relationships that might not have existed. To be sure, journalists were not entirely unwilling dupes of this crime-nexus model. If any had pressed government officials on the method they used for estimating the number of addicts in America, or the cost of their daily habit, they would have quickly found out that the government had no way of knowing the number of addicts, had made no distinction between addicts and occasional users of heroin, and had deduced the cost of their daily habit from stories told by ex-addicts—stories which were not necessarily even believable. But since the multibillion-dollar numbers provided dramatic news, and the paucity of statistical data was impossible to write about, journalists usually avoided asking embarrassing questions of their government briefing officer.

I first became interested in the credibility of the crime estimates reported in the press when William Whitworth, an editor at *The New Yorker* magazine, suggested that ex-addicts in treatment centers had a strong incentive to exaggerate the size of their habit, and that the operators of these treatment centers had no incentive to dispute their claims. If an addict claimed that he had to steal $100 or $200 a day before he came in for treatment, society was presumably being saved that amount by paying for the treatment of this addict. Most of the conventional wisdom on drugs was supplied either by ex-addicts or by treatment centers, and as the Domestic Council staff paper quoted in the chapter points out, treatment centers themselves frequently exaggerate, or even quintuple, the amount of reported crime, to justify their expansion. The first question I asked of government officials in drug-abuse programs was, What systematic surveys have been made of the number of addicts or of the relation between addiction and crime? Few such studies existed. Mark Moore, who also studied under James Q. Wilson, developed a typology of heroin users in New York State for the Hudson Institute study on the economics of heroin distribution. Heather L. Ruth also wrote a thesis, "The Street-level Economics of Heroin Addiction in New York City," which explored the modes in which addicts earn their living. The Department of Justice compiled a study correlating drug usage and arrest charges in six metropolitan areas in December, 1971, but this study dealt only with the group of addicts who were arrested by the police. In exploring the types of crimes which addicts did and did not tend to commit, I relied heavily on materials supplied to me by Joseph D. McNamara, who was then a captain in the New York City police department in charge of the analysis of crime records (since then he has become police commissioner of Kansas City, Missouri). The profile that McNamara provided me of the "robbery offender" and "mugger" did not conform to that of the heroin addict (for example, most muggings seem to be the work of teenagers returning home on the subways after they are discharged from school, rather than that of addicts).

The Uniform Crime Reports that I cite present a problem. They are merely compilations of local crime reports, and it is generally presumed that they underestimate the number of crimes, especially in the poorer areas. However, I am using these statistics not to establish any specific amount of crime in America but merely to show that there is a wide discrepancy between the estimates by official government agencies of property stolen by drug addicts and the estimates of all crime committed in America.

The Domestic Council staff papers cited were all given to me by Egil Krogh. The "briefing book" and other press handouts were given to me by Richard Harkness, who was the information coordinator for the drug-abuse program.

23   *Private Knowledge*

The ability of individuals to discount information that contradicts major beliefs or theories they hold cannot be underestimated. When one receives such dissonant information, it is always possible to make an ad hoc assumption that allows that information to be integrated into one's more general beliefs. For example, if a study or an analysis contradicts a theory that one particularly believes in, one can simply assume that the sample was inadequate, that the techniques for evaluating the sample were flawed, or that the evaluator was biased or dishonest. Moreover, since most evidence is incomplete and problematic, it can be interpreted in a number of ways to dovetail with the longer-held, more cherished beliefs. It is therefore very difficult to establish when the White House strategists or the Domestic Council— or President Nixon himself—actually realized that most of the theories they were espousing—and publicly promoting—about drug addiction and crime were extremely dubious. When I discussed the IDA report with Egil Krogh, he said (I believe honestly), "To say that they [Institute for Defense Analysis] could not prove [that there was a connection between drugs and crime] does not mean that there isn't a link." Even though Krogh readily admitted that most of the assumptions were shaken by these studies—that it was impossible to say that most heroin users were heroin addicts (which in turn was the assumption of most projections of "addict-related crime"); that addicts were compelled to steal a given amount of goods every day, or for that matter consume a given amount of heroin (as opposed to other drugs which could be substituted)—he was still able to cling to the belief that drug addiction was a major factor in crime.

Because of this ability to dismiss dissonant evidence, the policy implications of the IDA report were never fully articulated to President Nixon, according to Egil Krogh. If indeed other drugs could be substituted for heroin, then the policy of destroying poppy crops in Turkey and other places in the world made little sense without first confronting the question of which drug was the most socially desirable to have consumed by American drug users. A study of drug enforcement by the New York police actually suggested that "some of the alternate drugs [especially barbiturates and amphetamines] may actually be more socially damaging than heroin, since they induce violent behavior. Moreover, if heroin was not as totally addictive as it had been presumed, then the massive methadone programs, where addicts would be given large dosages of a heroin substitute, would have to be reconsidered or at least rationalized in different terms. Similarly, the expansion of the drug-police agencies would have to be explained in terms other than crime reduction—none of which the White House strategists were interested in doing.

I was given access to the IDA report by James Q. Wilson, who at the time was chairman of the National Advisory Council on Drug Abuse Prevention, a unit of the federal government established by Congress to evaluate the various federal strategies on drug abuse. Professor Wilson was himself perplexed by the fact that the government, after all these years, was still unable to prove that there was a causal relationship between heroin consumption and crime. He was therefore interested in the implications of this report. When I discussed it with several officials in the drug-enforcement field—such as John Ingersoll and Myles Ambrose—they said they had no knowledge of the report, which indicated that it had not been immediately circulated to the bureaus of government.

The ARTC study that I cite was given to me by Professor Irving F. Luckoff, of Columbia University, who was codirector of the evaluation team, and I discussed the implications and reasons for the high crime rate in this project in my article on methadone in *The Public Interest* magazine (Summer, 1974). Richard Wilbur, then an assistant secretary of the Army, provided me with data on the findings of the Department of Defense on drug addiction when I interviewed him in April, 1973, at his office in the Pentagon (he has since become an officer of the American Medical Association in Chicago). The quotes from Krogh all come from interviews I had with him in the fall of 1974; the Domestic Council documents are those which he provided to me.

24　*The Liddy Plan*

In some journalistic investigations the tracks of one project (or plot) tend to cross the roads of another. At that point it becomes unclear whether one is following two separate undertakings that converge by coincidence or a single conspiracy. Thus, while I began by tracking the efforts to develop a "national emergency," I found a new conspiracy developing as the Watergate cover-up unraveled in the spring of 1973. The Administration's much publicized heroin crusade now took on new dimensions. John Caulfield, who had been working as a liaison on drugs, and who had proposed the privately financed White House detective agency, was identified as a White House wiretapper; Egil Krogh, who superintended the drug program, admitted to heading the "special investigative unit," or Plumbers, who broke into a psychiatrist's office on behalf of the White House. Meanwhile, it also turned out that G. Gordon Liddy, the convicted leader of the Watergate break-in, had drawn up the plan which evolved into ODALE; E. Howard Hunt, Liddy's partner in the Watergate crime, turned out to be a consultant to the Domestic Council on the drug program; and Vernon Acree, who replaced Myles Ambrose as commissioner of customs when Ambrose took charge of the new office, had been offered the job as a vice-president of the proposed private detective agency. In short, the same names kept reappearing. While Liddy, Krogh, and Caulfield prepared to take over the drug program, they were also included in covert operations on behalf of the White House. This seemed like possibly more than a simple coincidence. On the other hand, it is not clear to what extent these converging investigative operations were planned with a single objective.

The Watergate investigations have produced documents and materials that otherwise would be unavailable to journalists writing about an event. Almost all of the account I give of the attempt of the Nixon administration to gain some control over the Internal Revenue Service comes from the investigations of the Senate Select Committee on Presidential Campaign Activities (the Ervin Committee). (The balance comes from Victor Navasky's book *Kennedy Justice* and from a research paper by Michael Himmel on the Internal Revenue Service done at UCLA in 1975.) My account of how Caulfield attempted to set up a privately financed detective agency comes mainly from Caulfield's testimony before an executive session of the Senate committee on March 23, 1974, and documents he supplied to the committee. I interviewed Ambrose and Krogh on the subject, but not Caulfield, who at the time was facing indictment. My account of Nixon's long-standing antagonism with the Central Intelligence Agency comes mainly from my conversations with Richard Helms, the former director of the agency, when I visited Iran in 1974. (The balance comes from recent books about the Central Intelligence Agency, such as L. Fletcher Prouty's *The Secret Team,* which I quote in the text.) Finally, my description of the White House strategists' views of recalcitrant "bureaucrats" is derived mainly from interviews I had with Egil Krogh, his staff (Walter Minnick, Geoffrey Sheppard, and Jeffrey Donfeld), Daniel Patrick Moynihan, former speech writers for President Nixon (including William Safire, Patrick Buchanan, and Ray Price), as well as such noted "enemies" as John Ingersoll and Eugene Rossides. I also relied to some extent for this section on two insightful books about the Nixon administration: William Safire's *Before the Fall* (which I quote from), and Theodore H. White's *Breach of Faith.*

25   *The Secret of Room 16*

Though few admit it, journalists do not have the requisite power to uncover crimes in high places (or even in low places). They of course cannot subpoena witnesses or their records. They cannot force individuals to be truthful, or, for that matter, even to grant them an interview. Under such circumstances it would be unreasonable to expect anyone voluntarily to divulge his or her criminal liability to a newsman. When the New York *Times* and CBS News state in headline stories that they are unable to discover any evidence of a conspiracy in an assassination (as they both did in December, 1975, in regard to the assassination of Dr. Martin Luther King), they wrongly imply that a journalistic investigation could produce such evidence. This myth notwithstanding, it is prosecutors who produce evidence of criminal conspiracies, since they have the power to compel testimony, penalize perjury with prison sentences, and offer inducements to reluctant witnesses to testify. The revelations of the operations of the Plumbers and the break-in of Dr. Fielding's office did not come from enterprising newsmen (although this is commonly misstated in the press); they came from John Dean, the counsel to President Nixon, who provided this information to federal prosecutors in 1973 in return for a promise of lenient treatment. The prosecutors provided this information to Attorney General Elliot Richardson, who transmitted it to Judge Matt Byrne, then presiding over the Ellsberg trial, who in turn revealed it to the press.

The account I give of the Plumbers similarly comes from the prosecutors, although I also had extensive interviews with Egil Krogh after he was released from prison, and I incorporate part of his version with that of the prosecutors. The arrest of the narcotics addict for the crime of the White House crew came from Steve Trott, a district attorney in Los Angeles I knew from an earlier reporting assignment.

I have always suspected that there are important gaps in the prosecutors' version of the Plumbers' burglary of Dr. Fielding's office, especially with regard to the cooperation they received from the CIA. For example, it has always seemed possible to me that money which Egil Krogh was receiving for narcotics enforcement from the CIA (which was technically illegal) was being used to finance these Plumbers' operations, but the prosecutors concluded that all the money had been received from the milk cooperatives. Although I discussed this point with prosecutors in the special prosecutor's office, there was no way that I, as a journalist, could develop a theory contrary to theirs (especially since all the witnesses had effectively pleaded guilty and had come to terms with the prosecutors—except for Gordon Liddy, who remained silent). Like so much else in the Watergate story, this version is essentially based on the findings of the prosecutors.

For the backgrounds of E. Howard Hunt and Bernard Barker I relied on Hunt's autobiography, *Undercover,* and Tad Szulc's *Compulsive Spy.* Since Hunt and Liddy are still in prison, I was not able to get interviews with them (although I tried). And, as in preceding chapters,

I relied on the report of the Senate Select Committee on Presidential Campaign Activities (the Ervin Committee).

26   *Executive Order*

In 1973 I had discussed the creation of the Office of Drug Abuse Law Enforcement with John Ingersoll, Eugene Rossides, and Myles Ambrose (Egil Krogh at that time refused to see me). Each had seen the creation of this office from his own bureaucratic perspective, and had described it only in terms of how it injured or advanced his particular agency. I had more or less given up on the possibility of finding an overall perspective on ODALE when by chance I asked Ingersoll if the creation of this office had some sort of code name (like "Clean Sweep") which might be useful in describing it in the article I was then writing for *The New Yorker.* Ingersoll was unable to recall such a code name (which apparently never existed), but he suggested that the only person who would know was Leo Pellerzi, who had just been dismissed as the assistant attorney general for administration in the Department of Justice. When I called Pellerzi to find out the nonexistent code name, he told me that he himself had fought the implementation of this particular White House program—unsuccessfully—and would be glad to describe all the stages through which it evolved. I flew to Washington and had lunch with him at the Ramada Inn, and he described to me the attempts to insert "CIA liaisons" and "granting authorities" in the original plan. Armed with this information, I used the journalistic equivalent of the camel's-nose-under-the-tent technique: I called upon Henry Petersen at the Department of Justice, Richard Kleindienst, and Richard Helms and asked for their comments on this attempt to use the CIA for domestic-intelligence purposes. Since I had already been informed of the development by Pellerzi, all three had reason to comment on what had happened in the establishing of this office. At this time I was also able to speak to Egil Krogh, who had just got out of jail. Krogh then explained that the White House wanted

> to do everything in that final year prior to the election that would support a presidential platform of accomplishment in drug abuse and crime control. The Office of Drug Abuse Law Enforcement [ODALE] was presented in that context, that this could enable us to show some

direct successes and seizures and arrests that otherwise could not be made. This gets into a political dimension as well. . . . There was a great deal of interest that an ODALE program could provide an awareness at the local level of a direct federal activity in narcotics law enforcement.

When I told Krogh that Petersen claimed there was a political motive behind the formation of this office, Krogh replied, "Mr. Petersen's right in saying that there was a political motive behind it, as there is a political motive behind practically everything that was undertaken, in addition to a substantive desire to reduce a problem area." Some of the participants thus agreed that ODALE was not strictly for law enforcement—but each put a different emphasis on the importance of the political motive.

One problem I was not able to resolve was Attorney General John Mitchell's role in the formation of ODALE. Ingersoll had told me that Mitchell did not know of the plan. Walter Minnick, one of Krogh's staff assistants, also said that the White House staff was instructed not to tell either Mitchell or Secretary of the Treasury Connally about the development of this plan, at least in its early stages. Krogh, however, insisted that Mitchell was directly told about the plan by Ehrlichman. Although the information was kept away from Mitchell's staff, and of course from Ingersoll and Rossides, Krogh subsequently explained, "In fact, the Attorney General knew why the president wanted ODALE—and supported his decision." When I told Ingersoll—whom I spoke with over a course of nine months about the development of my study—about what Krogh had said, Ingersoll still doubted that Mitchell ever really realized the extent of the plan. Since I was not able to interview John Mitchell, I was never satisfied with an explanation of exactly what role he was playing in the administration in late 1971. A few months after the Office of Drug Abuse Law Enforcement was created, John Mitchell resigned as attorney general at the president's request in order to take over the Committee to Reelect the President.

27   *Dangerous Liaisons*

Walter Minnick was one of the many young and highly intelligent analysts who were more interested in rational policies than power politics. He had left Harvard in 1969, after his commission as a reserve officer in the Army had been activated, and served in the

Pentagon as a systems analyst in the office of the secretary of defense. His work had brought him in contact with the new "White House Whiz Kids," and he became especially close friends with Geoffrey Sheppard, an assistant to Krogh whom he had known earlier. When Minnick's two-year tour of active duty was completed, in July, 1971, Krogh offered him a position on the Domestic Council, working in the area of international narcotics control. Minnick thus joined Sheppard, Donfeld, Liddy, and three others on the Domestic Council staff. His first assignment was to travel to Southeast Asia with Nelson Gross, the newly appointed State Department coordinator for international narcotics matters. Afterward, he worked briefly with E. Howard Hunt on the creation of the Office of National Narcotics Intelligence, and was then assigned assistant to Krogh for coordinating the Cabinet Committee on International Narcotics Control.

I had known Minnick through mutual friends at Harvard, and when I interviewed him in 1974 on the creation of these new White House offices, he was unusually candid on most issues. For example, when I asked him why the White House had created ODALE, he replied without hesitation, "It was an election-year stunt." When I asked him about ONNI, he explained its origins, as well as the real problem of "coordinating intelligence"—that despite some good intentions, the office had gone astray under the ambitions of William Sullivan. In the months that followed I always found him both accurate and lucid; he seemed much more interested in carefully and rationally explaining the considerations of a decision than in protecting any of the individuals involved in making that decision. In 1972, after Watergate, Minnick was appointed director of a unit in the Office of Management and Budget (OMB) which superintended all the drug policies of the various federal agencies. A year later Minnick resigned and took a job with a construction company in Idaho. The fact that so many young analysts like Minnick were part of the Nixon administration (as well as of preceding administrations, no doubt), made it extremely difficult for the political operators in the administration to accomplish their purposes with complete secrecy.

28   *The Heroin Hotline*

It is always far easier to obtain information from government agencies than it is from private agencies. Though Grey Advertising steadfastly refused to allow me to see the commercials it prepared for the Office of Drug Abuse Law Enforcement, claiming a "privileged relation" between its client and itself, the Government Accounting Office, a congressional agency which monitors the expenditures of the executive branch, provided me with the audits of the heroin hotline. Eugene Abston, who was then working for this agency, was especially helpful in locating this material for my study. Public-relations officers of the Department of Justice, especially Robert Feldtkamp and Con Dougherty, were most accommodating in giving me all the political speeches and briefings of Myles Ambrose. Geoffrey Sheppard, who joined Egil Krogh's staff after graduating from Harvard Law School (and then brought his friend Walter Minnick into the group), gave me a hilarious description of the location of the hotline's intelligence center in the fortified mine shaft in Virginia.

Even though everyone I spoke to who was involved in the heroin hotline—Egil Krogh, John Ingersoll, Richard Callahan (Ingersoll's deputy), Myles Ambrose, John Bartels (Ambrose's deputy and successor), and Walter Minnick—agreed that the heroin hotline yielded few results other than the publicity campaign for the Nixon administration, the press, including the New York *Times,* continued to report about it as if it were a major and successful law-enforcement mechanism. As Egil Krogh pointed out to me, this was further proof that a government briefing officer could create the sort of news his agency desired, no matter what the obvious facts of the situation were. Finally, after three years of reporting its successes, the Associated Press carried the story on September 27, 1975, which noted:

> Posters may still be found here and around the nation urging calls to a toll-free number to turn in a drug pusher. But quietly, the national heroin hotline has turned cold. It went out of service two weeks ago and with it went the $123,000 hotline advertising campaign that started in 1972 in the Nixon Administration's anti-crime drive. There were posters inside buses and subways. Radio and television granted free time to promote it.... Today if a call is made to that number a recording suggests calling another number. At the second number a second recording says that the number is out of service.

The headline of this story, which was buried in an inside page of the New York *Times,* read "National Heroin Hotline Ends as Calls on Pushers Cease."

29   The Philadelphia Story

In discussing the Nixon administration journalists tend to add to the fiction that many of the political actions undertaken by it were an abrupt departure from American politics. Because more documents are available from the Nixon administration than from any other, and in a sense more "defectors" (like John Dean) are willing to dramatize the excesses of this administration (in return for book rights or to keep out of prison), it is easy to create the illusion that the actions of the Nixon administration were not replicated by a previous administration. The journalistic problem, in short, is that there were simply more sources available during this administration, not to mention extraordinary discovery processes, such as the work of the Senate committees and special prosecutors. There is no way of saying that previous administrations could not be similarly indicted for giving federal funds to local politicians to aid with reelection campaigns; the fallout of the Watergate investigations is that it is fairly easy to document dramatic examples, such as the "Philadelphia story" and other actions of the Nixon administration. Only a long-term historic perspective might someday be able to correct the distortions which this bulge of information is inevitably producing about the American political system (and I'm not sure that even historians can compensate for it).

The Philadelphia story was told mainly by Egil Krogh in the tape-recorded interviews I did with him for *The Public Interest*. Jeffrey Donfeld also told me of his part in the story. Donald J. Santarelli gave me a perspective on LEAA after he resigned, in 1974; and Thomas Whitehead, who also worked at LEAA during this period, told me of some of the internal debates when he became a fellow of the Drug Abuse Council.

30   The Consolidation of Power

One of the most important areas of the government which is not covered by journalists is the constant effort of those in power to "reorganize" the bureaucracy, and the equally constant resistance of those in the agencies of the government toward such actions. While this constant struggle generates the embarrassing leaks about individual politicians and bureau heads and provides Jack Anderson's column with much of the grist for its rumor mill, the actual interests which are at stake in these struggles are usually neglected by cooperative journalists (who depend on the leaks for their titillating news stories about the individuals involved). For its part, the administration uses the rhetoric of efficiency—representing any reorganization in terms of concentrating its resources more effectively to accomplish its purpose. On the other hand, the bureaucracy uses the rhetoric of "integrity" in resisting these changes, and depicts each reorganization in terms of abolishing checks and balances or restraints which had previously existed. Whereas the administration represents "fragmentation" as being an unmitigated evil that diffuses responsibility, the bureaucracy represents it as a safeguard that diffuses power. The same reorganization can thus be represented in two different rhetorical manners. At the same time, the real interest that is at stake can be concealed by both forms of rhetoric. In attempting to reconstruct any reorganization in the government by interviewing the participants concerned, the journalist inevitably runs into this dual rhetoric.

Reorganization Plan Number Two was thus depicted to me by Krogh, Minnick, Donfeld, and other members of the Domestic Council as an attempt to achieve efficiency in the narcotics program—and the consolidation of agencies would certainly be more efficient in terms of using the available resources. At the same time, Ingersoll, in the Bureau of Narcotics and Dangerous Drugs, Rossides, in the Treasury Department, and other members of the bureaucracy with interests at stake represented the reorganization as an attempt to set up a "national police force," as Rossides put it—an attack on the integrity or autonomy of individual agencies. With two sets of participants using different vocabularies to describe the same phenomenon there is no simple way to resolve conflicts. One simply has to decide on a standard rhetoric that will be used in interviewing participants. In this case, in the context of my investigation of the entire narcotics program, I decided that the quest for power, and especially the desire of the White House strategists to control an investigative agency, was the dominant purpose (even though a subsidiary purpose may well have been increased efficiency). I therefore chose to represent the struggle to consolidate agencies in the White House in terms of power rather than efficiency. Another observer might have chosen the other approach.

31   *The Revolt of the Bureaucrats*

A novel can often approach a major truth about a subject which journalism, restrained by certain conventions, may miss entirely. John Ehrlichman's book, *The Company,* although it is fictive (and malevolent), is thus capable of illuminating a major part of the so-called Watergate affair that had been almost totally neglected by the press: the power struggle between Nixon and the agencies of his own government. Ehrlichman begins his novel by showing the Machiavellian amorality of presidents: one president (presumably Kennedy) is involved in assassination plots, while another (presumably Lyndon Johnson) assists in the cover-ups and uses the investigative agencies of his government for surveillance in the 1968 convention; and a third president (presumably Nixon) attempts to usurp power within the government.* Ehrlichman then shows that Nixon offended major figures in the established governmental apparatus, which he could not control, and that these figures later worked to destroy him by revealing his illicit operations. In Ehrlichman's view it was not the illegal actions of Nixon—although he recounts these with a vengeance—but his attempt to take power from members of the established agencies which brought about his downfall. While few knowledgeable members of the Washington press corps would doubt that such a power struggle was going on between Nixon and the agency officials in his administration, the Watergate affair was reported in completely moralistic terms. The main questions asked were: Is President Nixon conforming to the letter of the law? Is he telling the truth in his public statements? Is he doing everything within his power to pursue the Watergate burglary to its ultimate conspirators? Most persons who are sophisticated in politics, as are journalists, knew the answers to these questions before they were asked: Nixon was primarily a politician and would exceed the letter of the law when he thought he could get away with it. He was attempting to put the best face possible on the scandal so as not to diminish his lead in the election; he would obviously not want to reveal the role of

---

* Evidence to support these contentions can be found in the testimony of William C. Sullivan, Cartha "Deke" DeLoach, and John Ehrlichman himself before the Ervin Committee, as well as in the interim report on "Alleged Assassination Plots Involving Foreign Leaders" presented on November 20, 1975, by the Church Committee, to study government operations.

his intimate associates, such as John Mitchell, in the Watergate burglary. From the moral point of view, therefore, there were few surprises: journalists simply waited for disclosures to be leaked to them, then waited for Nixon or his press staff to attempt to downplay or negate them, and then pointed to whatever discrepancies they could ingeniously uncover. The alternative of asking why these disclosures were being made by officials of Nixon's government—in other words, what the issue was between Nixon and the executive branch of the government—would have involved questioning the motives of those who were leaking stories to (or, in reality, planting them in) the press. The conventions of journalism, at least those practiced in Washington and by the national press, required that one conceal the identity and interest of the source and make the functional assumption that the source was acting out of complete disinterest rather than in advancing a personal or institutional position in what President Nixon described as a war. It would, of course, have been difficult for journalists not to realize that their sources were not truly disinterested and were giving them information for a very definite purpose. But they also realized that if they attempted to elaborate on this purpose and investigate their sources, they would in a sense expose themselves as conduits of those particular interests.

Consider, for example, the problem of Woodward and Bernstein, of the Washington *Post*. Woodward was receiving information from Robert Foster Bennett, of Robert R. Mullen and Company, that focused the blame for Watergate on Charles Colson. If he had assumed that Bennett was providing him with this information for anything more than a disinterested purpose, he would have had to ask whom Bennett worked for, what the true business of Mullen and Company was, and why Bennett wanted him to steer his investigation away from the CIA and toward Charles Colson. He then would have found that Mullen and Company was a CIA front organization and was aware that Bennett was giving information to Woodward; and that the CIA was trying to divert attention from itself (and succeeding, in the Washington *Post*) because a number of the conspirators involved in the Watergate burglary had also been involved in operations that the CIA had directly supported, such as the Plumbers. Moreover, the very fact that a CIA front group was providing information that was undermining the Nixon administration pointed to a conflict between Nixon and the CIA. Woodward and Bernstein, however, could not have reported these implications and thus could not have depicted the power struggle between the president and the CIA without revealing one of their prime sources. For the same reason, the reporters who received Nixon's tax returns from officials of the Internal Revenue Service could not have revealed this as evidence of a struggle between disgruntled members of the Treasury Department and the president without also revealing that they were no more than messengers for insurgents struggling against the president. By not revealing their sources, they received the Pulitzer Prize. Since the convention of concealing sources is endemic in American journalism, what is systematically covered up by this convention is any struggle within the American government in which the participants use the journalists to embarrass their opponents. Since Ehrlichman was not bound by these conventions in a novel, he revealed what no journalist revealed in covering Watergate.

In terms of sources, this section on the CIA is based mainly on interviews I had with Richard Helms, Egil Krogh, and Charles Colson. I also depended heavily on the book *At That Point in Time,* by Fred D. Thompson, the chief minority counsel of the Senate Watergate Committee, which clarified the "CIA connection" better than any other book I know of on the subject. Ehrlichman's novel, although a vicious and self-serving distortion of the factual data surrounding Watergate, presents an extraordinary perspective on the power struggle. Richard P. Nathan, the assistant director of the Office of Management and Budget from 1969 to 1971, offers a less dramatic and more scholarly version of the same theme in his book *The Plot That Failed: Nixon and the Administrative Presidency.* The section on the FBI is heavily based on interviews with Cartha D. DeLoach, the former associate director of the FBI. Seymour Glanzer and Earl Silbert, of the Department of Justice, also provided me with an overview of the "battle of the leaks." Eugene Rossides and John Ingersoll traced out the leaks between the Department of the Treasury and the Bureau of Narcotics and Dangerous Drugs, respectively. All the quotes from President Nixon are taken from the White House transcripts, as republished by the New York *Times.*

32 *The Coughing Crisis*

Walter Minnick explained in his testimony before the Sub-Committee to Investigate Juvenile Delinquency in March, 1975, that the White House–engineered ban on opium cultivation in Turkey was never intended to be the final solution to the heroin problem in the United States. Furthermore, the White House knew that the Turkish opium would be replaced by opium from other corners of the world. Senator Birch Bayh, who chaired the hearings, replied that he had been misled by the press into believing that the Turkish opium ban, if it had been maintained, would have significantly diminished the drug problem in the United States. He was in fact quite right: the press, in the summer of 1971, had readily reported that most American addicts were supplied with Turkish opium, and that if this supply were suppressed, they would be forced into giving up their addictive habit or undergoing treatment. The press, in turn, had been misled by the White House strategists, who in numerous private briefings had persuaded journalists that the crime problem in America could be greatly alleviated if Turkey took action against its opium growers. For example, Egil Krogh intensively briefed Stewart Alsop, who then wrote three columns in *Newsweek* magazine on this subject. Krogh also spent the better part of a month priming an ABC television crew that was doing a program on international narcotics, stressing the importance of the Turkish connection. Literally scores of reporters were taken along the "trail of heroin," which led from Istanbul to Marseilles to New York, by agents and public-relations men from the BNDD. The White House strategists, in turn, misled themselves by wishful thinking: they realized it was possible to put enough pressure on Turkey to have it at least temporarily suspend opium production. They then hoped that such a concerted effort would have some effect. But the press reports which they generated no doubt reinforced this hope.

This chapter is largely based on interviews with Walter C. Minnick after he had left the government and gone to work with a construction firm in Boise, Idaho. Raymond M. Asher, the general counsel of Mallinckrodt Chemical Works, which manufactures a large amount of the codeine base in America, provided me with a good deal of material on the "opium shortage," its scope, causes, and medical implications. He, of course, was attempting to stimulate interest in the "coughing crisis" so that the government would take action to provide his company with more opium for its products. Ambassador William Macomber provided me with background information on the importance of the surveillance bases in Turkey maintained by the United States (and I subsequently used this information for an article I wrote in the *Wall Street Journal* on this subject on August 29, 1975).

Herman Kirby, the State Department desk officer for Turkey, also provided me with a background briefing. While I was in India, Daniel Patrick Moynihan provided me with some of his more colorful telegrams on the narcotics problem.

33   *The Drugging of America*

There is no practical way in which a journalist can penetrate by himself the mask of statistics which organizations generate to protect their interests. And, as the methadone program proves, if organizations are given enough time, they will sometimes develop statistical systems to produce the results which are acceptable to the federal agencies. For example, a number of programs originally used ex-addicts from their programs as paid counselors to determine whether the patients were also using illicit drugs, such as heroin. These counselors, of course, had an interest in showing that methadone was effective, thereby protecting their jobs. In examining one such reporting system in Philadelphia, Chambers and Taylor analyzed the urine of patients in that program for illicit drugs without telling the counselors. It was found that almost 80 percent of those in the program were taking heroin, although the counselors reported that only 40 percent were using heroin—a discrepancy of 100 percent. Similarly, by setting up definitions in such a way that "education" or "housework" constituted "employment," programs were able to show a high rate of employment. Since doctors administer these programs, they can themselves decide what sort of data should be considered evidence of "cheating" or "antisocial behavior," and what sort of data should be excluded. The computer programs they used for their data reflected these original decisions, and therefore it is not unexpected that the computer print-outs which they sent to their evaluators eventually showed that they were achieving their stated objectives. In a sense, the computer print-out cannot be questioned.

This ability to control statistics through computer print-outs explains the discrepancy between crime statistics on a societal scale and those generated by the treatment centers. Most treatment centers now show that their patients have greatly diminished their criminal activity; yet, the cities in which they are located showed a marked increase in crime between 1972 and 1975. What are generally considered to be addict-related crimes, such as minor burglaries, have increased by more than 40 percent. Since methadone is now available to any addict who wants it at no cost, and since most addicts are presumably enrolled in methadone programs, why has crime increased? One answer obviously is that the only addicts who enroll in programs with serious controls are those who are not interested in committing crimes. Dr. Avram Goldstein, the highly respected director of the Addiction Research Laboratory at Stanford, demonstrated through "double blind" tests that "the dose of methadone is largely irrelevant," and concluded, "Methadone cannot magically prevent heroin use in a patient who wants to use heroin; it can only facilitate a behavioral change in people who have made a conscious decision to change."

This chapter is heavily based on interviews with Dr. Jerome Jaffe, Egil Krogh, Jeffrey Donfeld, and Robert DuPont (who replaced Jaffe as the director of the Special Action Office for Drug Abuse Prevention). The best analysis to date of the effect of methadone treatment on crime and criminal narcotics addicts is the mimeographed report by Irving F. Luckoff and Paula Holzman Kleinman entitled "Methadone Maintenance—Modest Help for a Few" (1975). The Drug Enforcement Agency report that I quote on the extent of leakage of methadone in 1973 was given to me by Con Dougherty, a public-relations officer at that agency. Before it could be released, however, officials of the special-action office protested to the White House that it be suppressed. Paul Perito, a former official of the special-action office, also provided some information for this chapter. The footnote on the methadone-treatment center in Washington, D.C., comes from a memorandum (October 16, 1971) provided to me by Egil Krogh. The National Commission on Marijuana and Drug Abuse has included in the appendixes of its 1973 report the best analysis of why the evaluations done by the various treatment programs have been deficient.

34   Lost Horizons

A number of alternative ways of describing the activities of a government agency are available to a journalist. In the most conventional model of reporting on the government the journalist simply describes the changes in the top executives of the agency, changes in its performance as reported by these executives, or charges of misbehavior on the part of members of this agency. This form of reporting simply involves rewriting press releases from the bureau itself—or possibly from other bureaus in the position to criticize it. Most newspáper reporting of the BNDD and its successors falls into this category.

A second model of government reporting involves chronicling the exploits of a particular agency. In this model the journalist reconstructs a particular operation—the seizure of a large quantity of heroin, the arrest of top figures in a crime ring, or even an adventure story on the part of agents. Journalists who wish to use this form and be critical simply report the excesses of drug agents and the way that they violated the rights of citizens, such as in the Collinsville raid. Public-relations officials at the drug agency would spend considerable time reconstructing the exploits of drug agents for the benefit of reporters interested in publicizing them (the more critical reports usually came from rival agencies interested in discrediting ODALE). Some of the reporting was found in *Time* and *Newsweek,* and in such books as *The Heroin Trail,* an extensive leak by the BNDD and its agents to reporters for *Newsday; Contrabandista!,* a leak to Evert Clark and Nicholas Horrock by inspectors in the Bureau of Customs; *The Secret War Against Dope,* a leak to Andrew Tully, again by the Customs Bureau; and *Heroes and Heroin,* a leak directly provided to ABC News by Egil Krogh and the White House staff. An article on DEA by Frank Browning in *Playboy* magazine, and some excellent reporting in *Rolling Stone* magazine on the world of "narks," provide fine examples of "negative" adventures or exploits in this style of reporting.

A third way of organizing information about a government agency might be called the power-struggle model, and involves the reporter's delineating the various bureaucratic interests which were at stake. This is the model that I use in this book. It assumes that much of the activity of government agencies results from the actions of those in the organization attempting to maintain their position or power. As is necessary in this mode of reporting, I relied heavily on disgruntled officials in the various drug agencies and their rivals in the government. For example, Vernon Acree, then the commissioner of customs, provided me with names of a number of customs agents who had been transferred to DEA and then, because they were dissatisfied, transferred back to the Customs Bureau. Acree knew that these repatriated agents would provide me with negative (though not necessarily inaccurate) anecdotes of how the Drug Enforcement Agency went about hyping statistics—and possibly with accounts of corruption within that agency. The sources also included John Ingersoll, after he was rudely fired from his directorship of the Bureau of Narcotics and Dangerous Drugs; Myles Ambrose; Eugene Rossides; John Bartels; Mark Moore, who became a staff assistant to Bartels and was a former colleague of mine at Harvard; Colonel Thomas Fox; Jim Ludlum; Mort Bach, of the Treasury Department; Richard Callahan, an executive in the Bureau of Narcotics and Dangerous Drugs; Roger Degilio, who was executive director of the National Council on Drug Abuse Prevention; Egil Krogh and his staff at the White House; Bob Esterland, of the Treasury Department; Thomas O'Malley and William Ryan, of the Justice Department's enforcement division; and field agents of DEA in England, France, Turkey, India, Lebanon, and Iran. (The funds to interview these agents abroad came in part from a grant from the Drug Abuse Council, in Washington.)

Other examples of this power-struggle model as applied to the drug agencies can be found in Ron Rosenbaum's article "The Decline and Fall of Nixon's Drug Czar," in *New Times* magazine (September, 1975), and to a lesser extent in John Finlator's book *The Drugged Nation.*

Finally, there is a model of reporting which is more difficult to employ in the time frame available to a journalist and which would attempt to correlate the actions of an agency with the changes in the environment in which it exists. This model might be called the natural-history model. It might be possible, for example, to understand the evolution of what began as the Nutt unit in the Alcohol Tax Division into the Bureau of Narcotics and Dangerous Drugs in the Justice Department, and so on, if one could also chart the psychological and political changes in the population to which the government was reacting. There was, no doubt, heightened anxiety over crime in the 1960s, and this was connected to the fear of drugs promoted by a whole range of public officials, police officials, and politicians. To focus entirely on the bureaucratic power struggle neglects the "environmental changes" that occurred in America. (Conversely, focusing on the natural history of the drug agency in relation to the psychological environment in America might neglect the very real power struggle that took place.) I know of no journalistic work that has attempted to study the natural history of a government agency, but it would add a much-needed dimension to our understanding of political phenomena.

35   *Decline and Fall*

A journalist acts either as a messenger or as a spy in acquiring information. In either case, when reporting on the government, he is almost totally dependent on his sources within the administration. Yet the very fact that his sources have disclosed information to him may be an integral part of the story. In this case, over a four-year period I dealt with a number of high officials in the White House and in the executive branch of the government, including Egil Krogh, John Ingersoll, Eugene Rossides, Walter Minnick, Jeffrey Donfeld, Geoffrey Sheppard, Myles Ambrose, Vernon Acree, Jerome Jaffe, and scores of others (see Personal Sources for a complete listing). In many cases it was obvious to me that these officials were not completely disinterested in the information they gave to me and, to be more specific, were trying to use me as a messenger to deliver a bombshell that would embarrass their opponents. To conceal this would be to conceal the power struggle which is the subject of this book.

One problem in reporting on an event over an extended period of time (and spies everywhere must have the same problem) is that one often accepts the involved individuals as likable human beings. I found Egil Krogh to be intelligent, shrewd, thoughtful, humorous, ironic, and a model family man. I enjoyed the analytic minds of Walter Minnick, Jeff Donfeld, and Geoff Sheppard, and found that many of their skeptical insights about government paralleled my own. I have no doubt that Jerry Jaffe, Nelson Gross, and many others were sincerely motivated in their personal wars against heroin. I also admired Gene Rossides, John Ingersoll, Leo Pellerzi, and Richard Kleindienst for resisting White House pressures. Richard Helms was extremely articulate, insightful, and, I believe, frank in his description of events. I also enjoyed the colorful metaphors Myles Ambrose used in describing the various aspects of his career as a narcotics fighter. John Bartels always seemed to me to be a thoughtful, candid, and thoroughly decent administrator. It is of course difficult not to like those involved in a long-term reportage, if only because they are providing one with the needed information.

The journalist is thus faced with a dilemma: how can likable and presumably decent individuals be coordinated with such disastrous policies? The only answer I can suggest is that many individual characteristics are lost in an organization. When Liddy and Hunt joined together, they had a certain binary effect on each other: both became more daring and more ambitious. To a lesser degree, I suspect that members of the in-group in the White House affected each other in such a way that their actions were not restrained by the reservations of the individuals involved. The defining characteristic of the White House strategists was ambition. When they thought they had power within their grasp, they acted so as to gain it. When I interviewed them after Watergate, when power was no longer within reach, other traits no doubt surfaced. Dr. Jaffe later suggested in his article in *Psychiatric News* that the White House strategists were flawed in other ways:

> Dissent and disloyalty were concepts that were never sufficiently differentiated in their minds. . . . [They] admired people who could be cold and dispassionate in making personal decisions. . . . They deeply distrusted the motives of other people and weren't able to believe that people could rise above selfish motives.

Whether or not this is a fair characterization of the White House strategists, they were young and inexperienced in the ways of either government or private organizations, and seemed to suspect anyone who tried to dilute or diffuse their claim of power. I am not sure, however, that even if one started with a completely different cast of characters (as long as they were of the same general age and inexperience), and if they worked for a president who sought control over an investigative agency of the government in order to plug leaks and control the bureaucracy, that they would have acted very differently. In short, I believe that "personalities" can be overestimated as a factor in explaining policy. In this case the quest for power by the president and his principal advisors simply overwhelmed all those young men serving him—at least, that is the way that I resolved this particular dilemma.

In describing the operations of the Office of National Narcotics Intelligence, I also relied on interviews with Russell Asch, the deputy director, and Sybil Cline, who served as an assistant to William Sullivan in the new agency.

I found Col. Thomas Fox, who put the intelligence operations in perspective, totally by accident. In January, 1976, I was reinvestigating the Kennedy assassination for the *Reader's Digest* and wanted to discuss Oswald's defection to the Soviet Union with someone from the Defense Intelligence Agency. Thomas Fox was recommended to me by John Barron, an editor at the *Digest*. When I finally had lunch with him, he told me, by way of his personal history, of his involvement with the Office of National Narcotics Intelligence. He had no idea that I was writing a book on this subject, and I found his analysis far too perceptive to exclude.

APPENDIX

Operation "Sandwedge," referred to on p. 200, here set forth in detail from the Senate hearings on "Watergate and Related Activities" (Executive Session Hearings before the Select Committee on Presidential Campaign Activities, Ninety-third Congress, Second Session, Washington, D. C., February 8, March 16, 20, and 21, 1974)

SUBJECT: OPERATION "SANDWEDGE"   Tab 31

INTRODUCTION

The 1972 Presidential Campaign strongly suggests a definitive Republican need for the creation of a political intelligence security entity to be located within the private sector. This entity, surfacely disassociated from the Administration by virtue of an established business cover, would have the capability of performing in a highly sophisticated manner designed to ensure that the major offensive intelligence and defensive security requirements of the entire campaign and Republican convention would be professionally structured, programmed and implemented. In the author's judgment, this effort would make a significant and perhaps crucial contribution towards the reelection of Richard Nixon.

Indicated below, therefore, are a series of considerations and suggestions posed in this regard for the review of those requested to endorse the suggested undertaking.

1. OPPOSITION INTELLIGENCE EFFORT

The presence of Lawrence O'Brien as Chairman of the Democratic National Committee unquestionably suggests that the Democratic nominee will have a strong, covert intelligence effort mounted against us in 1972. The 1968 L. A. Times, New York Post, U. S. Marshall team which operated from former U. S. Attorney Morgenthau's office (assertedly without his knowledge) is evidence of O'Brien's modus operandi and indicative of what we can expect this time around.

In this regard, we should be particularly concerned about the new and rapidly growing Intertel organization (See Tab "A"). Should this Kennedy mafia dominated intelligence "gun for hire" be turned against us in '72, we would, indeed, have a dangerous and formidable foe.

Close scrutiny of this organization's activity has been ongoing here. Indicated below are a series of points designed to suggest the political hazards that this group represents:

A) The organization was co-founded by Bill Hundley, former Special Assistant to A. G. Bobby Kennedy and Bob Pelloquin, Kennedy loyalist who functioned as Senior Attorney in Justice's Organized Crime and Racketeering Section, also under Bobby Kennedy.

B) Other Kennedy mafia types, including the so called mysterious David I. Belisle, former Director Investigations for the National Security Agency, are principals in the organization.

C) It has been reliably determined that Stephen Smith, EMK's brother-in-law, has privately visited Intertel's New York office headed by former FBI supervisor Jack O'Connell known by his colleagues to have been a "black bag" specialist while at the Bureau. Smith, unquestionably, would think Intertel should EMK go for the big prize.

D) On Intertel's Board of Directors is Jerome S. Hardy, Executive Vice President of the Dreyfus Corporation which is chaired by Howard Stein. The media reports that Stein will be a heavy contributor to a Democratic-Liberal or Third Party Presidential candidate. Shortly before this media revelation, the aforementioned Jack O'Connell accompanied an electronics specialist to both Stein's and Hardy's offices for sweeping purposes.

E) It has been very reliably determined that some of Intertel's principals possess gambling weaknesses or have been quietly let go from their sensitive federal law enforcement positions because of financial improprieties. One Intertel principal, related to a known Baltimore Cosa Nostra figure and released from federal service because of an established gambling weakness, is now in charge of Hughes' security operation in Las Vegas.

F) The investigative reporter fraternity is taking a closer look at the potential for Intertel to be exposed as a mafia front or a mafia exploitable tool for its Caribbean and Vegas operations. The recent Look article on Howard Hughes alludes to this point. Bill Kolar (former Chief of Intelligence at IRS) and Resorts International's President I. G. (Jack) Davis, recently testified before the New Jersey legislature advocating legalized gambling in that mafia ridden state.

All of the above facts are mentioned to suggest how the weaknesses of Intertel, intertwined with established Democratic Kennedy loyalties make the organization most susceptible to a '72 intelligence gun for hire approach by O'Brien or the Democratic Presidential nominee. The deep concern here is that the assignment could be accepted on a compartmentalized basis and easily hidden from republican James Crosby, Chairman of the Board of Resorts International (assertedly owning 91% of Intertel stock). Jim Golden, formerly with Intertel, has now switched over to the Hughes' Tool Company and is far removed from the day to day intelligence activities of Intertel. Thus the operating headquarters is bereft of any Nixon support or loyalty.

It is recommended that consideration be given to have Intertel neutralized by Justice to preclude such development from taking place or to discourage consideration by O'Brien or Stephen Smith. This can be accomplished by directing Justice (if it has not done so already) to open a case with a view towards determining if the organization has unauthorized access to sensitive government files. It most certainly has.
Among other factors supporting this contention is the consensus in the federal intelligence sector indicating that Intertel, in all likelihood, delivered the details of a reported Justice-IRS skimming investigation of Bob Maheu to Hughes causing Maheu's fall and Hughes' departure from Vegas. The manipulated threat of indictment of Intertel principals would effectively minimize this threat, create a potentially debilitating intelligence weakness for O'Brien's forces and force them to try other, less sophisticated sources. Additionally, "Operation Sandwedge" would be free to operate both offensively and defensively without a dangerous adversary.

PROPOSED "SANDWEDGE" RESPONSIBILITIES

The total offensive intelligence, defensive security requirements for the '72 Presidential Campaign and Republican National Convention will be a large and sensitive undertaking. Operation Sandwedge proposes that it be charged in this regard with the following responsibilities:

OFFENSIVE (New York City based - clandestine operation)

    A) Supervise penetration of nominees entourage and headquarters with undercover personnel.

    B) "Black Bag" capability (discuss privately) including all covert steps necessary to minimize Democratic voting violations in Illinois, Texas, etc.

    C) Surveillance of Democratic primaries, convention, meetings, etc.

    D) Derogatory information investigative capability, world-wide.

    E) Any other offensive requirement deemed advisable.

DEFENSIVE OPERATIONS

    A) Select and supervise the private security force hired in connection with the Republican National Convention. Conduct all political security investigations at Republican Convention.

    B) Establish and supervise nation-wide electronic countermeasures capability in connection with all non-presidential security aspects of '72 campaign.

    C) Supervise all security operations at 1701 Pennsylvania Avenue, RNC. Conduct all security investigations (leaks, personnel, etc.)

    D) Ensure the political security aspects of the travelling campaign staff.

    E) Conduct any Republican Party-Campaign oriented investigation nation-wide.

OPERATION COVER

The consensus dictates that a privately created corporate business entity would be the most effective tool to implement the sensitive responsibilities indicated above. The corporation would posture itself as a newly formed security consulting organization ostensibly selling itself as a group of highly talented investigator-security experts with impeccable Republican credentials who actively seek only Republican Corporations and law firms as clients.

Since the key operating principals (3 or 4 persons) in the corporate entity would be well known Nixon Loyalists in the law enforcement area, the defensive involvement as outlined above, would be plausible and readily acceptable to all friend or foe inquiries.

The offensive involvement outlined above would be supported, supervised and programmed by the principals, but completely disassociated (separate foolproof financing) from the corporate structure and located in New York City in extreme clandestine fashion. My source would be charged with setting up and supervising this operation. In other words, he would not surface. Rather, his responsibilities would be increased and he would be charged with setting up the clandestine operation in exactly the same fashion as he did during his career. You are aware, of course, that his expertise in this area was considered the model for police departments throughout the nation and the results certainly prove it.

"SANDWEDGE" PRINCIPALS

It is suggested that the best method of ensuring the success of Sandwedge is by limiting the principals to an absolute minimum, but to allow for an expansionary backup of consultants on a case by case basis where the need arises. The involvement in <u>defensive</u> campaign activity as indicated above would, under inquiry, be postured as a natural "ad hoc" contribution on the part of the corporation to the '72 Republican effort. The covert or offensive side of the operation, in no way connected to the corporation, would be untraceable to any of the principals or the Administration.

Necessarily then, the principals should be strong Nixon loyalists, possessing the necessary credentials to perform in this highly sensitive area professionally, with the described effective cover. Below are listed the principals who are ready, willing and able to so participate in the manner designated.

JOHN J. CAULFIELD

1. <u>Cover</u> - Because of White House experience and contacts, has decided to create a Washington based security consulting-investigative organization which would seek Republican corporations and law firms as clients.

2. <u>Assignment</u> - Receive and program all activities and assignments, including the New York City operation, set as liaison with selected White House staff before and during campaign for sensitive investigative needs. Liaison with Cabinet when necessary. Liaison with 1701 Pennsylvania Avenue operation on all security-investigative needs. Liaison with Republican National Committee in connection with their investigative needs. . . . Liaison with RNC on the programming of all security at the Republican National Committee.

JOSEPH WOODS

1. <u>Cover</u> - Since only engaged part time as a County Commissioner in Illinois and needing funds to support his large family (true enough!), has

decided to become a principal in a potentially lucrative, Washington based Republican oriented security consulting firm utilizing expertise in law enforcement (FBI - Sheriff Cook County) and political contacts nation-wide. Will seek to build the organization in the mid-west, taking advantage of the large influx of Republican big business into the Chicago area.

2. Assignment - In charge of all private security forces at the Republican National Convention. In charge all covert efforts (discuss) designed to preclude voting frauds in Illinois, Texas, etc. Liaison active and retired FBI agents, nation-wide, for discreet investigative support (Hoover also to Evaluate). Liaison nation-wide with Republican State Chairmen for investigative support. Support New York City covert operation.

NOTE

It is interesting to report that Intertel made a lucrative offer to Joe Woods last week ($30,000 per annum, stock options, etc.) indicating he would be in charge of their new Chicago office. This tack is viewed as an attempt to purchase White House prestige. In the author's judgment, the compartmentalized political hazards, previously indicated, would still constitute a real and present danger.

VERNON (MIKE) ACREE - Deputy Commissioner IRS, Inspection Division

Mike is the highest ranking Republican career official in the Internal Revenue Service. A synopsis of his outstanding career is attached hereto. (TAB "B"). He is a strong Nixon loyalist and has so proved it to me, personally, on a number of occasions. His management and investigative expertise will be invaluable to the undertaking, especially in the financial investigative area - crucial in a campaign of this type.

1. Cover - Mike has decided to retire after 32 years of federal investigative service. He has witnessed the financial success of Intertel and has decided to join a small group of Republican oriented principals who wish to emulate and improve on the Intertel experience dealing only, however, with republican corporations and law firms.

2. Assignment - IRS information input, financial investigations, liaison federal law enforcement establishment nation-wide, preparation of reports, briefings to key Administration campaign figures on results. Support New York City operation.

CONSULTANT PERSONNEL

Under the cover of the corporate entity hiring Republican consultants to assist in meeting the needs of its clients, a medium for the likely required expansion of the covert aspects of the undertaking would be established in compartmentalized fashion, thereby minimizing any threats to exposure inherent in a large covert operation. The consultants would be brought on to perform ad hoc assignments on a case by case basis in any area or undertaking.

CORPORATE STAFF

As suggested, a bright young Nixon loyalist with attorney and business managerial credentials should be brought on board to take complete charge of the corporation's business requirements. He would function as a technician with little or no responsibility or knowledge regarding the covert aspects of the operation.

No candidate will be considered for this assignment until the concept receives a go. Anne Dawson, understandably, would be a key and valuable asset in this undertaking. Trudy Brown (presently in White House Security liaison with FBI) would, if willing and could be spared from her present duties, also be highly valuable. Any other administrative help brought on board would be of the same caliber as Anne and Trudy.

FUNDING

Reviewing the above proposed broad ranged responsibilities of Operation Sandwedge, it is clear that it would be impossible to judge, at this time, what total costs for such an undertaking would be involved. The major initial costs, of course, would relate to principal, management, technical and secretarial salaries, as well as office and equipment in Washington and Chicago. It is expected that substantive additional costs would become evident as the requirements for effective operation come more clearly into focus.

What is obviously needed, therefore, is a funding technique which would enable the corporate cover to raise whatever monies would be required on a legitimate and painless basis. It is suggested that the business cover, indicated above, provides the ideal and proper framework to resolve this problem, as follows:
The overt security consulting services to be offered Republican corporations by the business entity would clearly be a deductible business

expense. There are no IRS requirements dictating the amount, type or quality of service which must be performed for a given consulting fee. This is strictly a matter for negotiation between the client and the entity performing the service.

Thus, it is clear that if the new Corporate Security Consultants International firm were in a position to "negotiate" as many lucrative consulting agreements as required on an expandable, need basis with trustworthy Republican corporate giants, the funding of this effort could go smoothly forward with no direct financial connection to the Administration or Republican National Committee. Further, the sensitive and often traceable area of political contributions would be eliminated as a hazard to this undertaking.

As indicated, funding for the proposed New York City operation would require special measures. There are some very discreet and viable approaches to this matter but, it is suggested that they be discussed on a private basis only.

CONCLUSION

This paper, then, is submitted with a view towards presenting, for review, a highly sophisticated approach to a critical aspect of the 1972 Presidential Campaign. It is suggested that the various subheadings indicated (SEE TAB "C") in the proposal provide a proper agenda after high level review for a meeting between the principals indicated and the officials charged with final decision.

It has been indicated that it is already very late for this proposed undertaking to be in review status - the authors concur. It is respectfully requested, therefore, that the highest priority attention be given this matter. We await your reply.

PERSONAL SOURCES

ABSTON, EUGENE	Government Accounting Office
ACREE, VERNON	Commissioner of Customs
AMBROSE, MYLES	Director, Office of Drug Abuse Law Enforcement
ASCH, RUSSELL	Deputy Director, Office of National Narcotics Intelligence
ASHER, RAYMOND M.	General Counsel, Mallinckrodt Chemical Works
BACH, MORT	Treasury Department
BARTELS, JOHN	Director, Drug Enforcement Administration
BUCHANAN, PATRICK J.	Presidential speech writer
CALLAHAN, RICHARD	Deputy Director, BNDD
CARGO, WILLIAM	Ambassador to Nepal
CLINE, SIBYL	Assistant to William Sullivan, ONNI
COLSON, CHARLES	White House Counsel
COONEY, JOAN GANZ	National Commission on Marijuana and Drug Abuse
CUSACK, JACK	DEA
DARDIS, MARTIN	Assistant State's Attorney, Miami, Fla.

DEGILIO, ROGER	Executive Assistant to Nelson Gross
DELOACH, CARTHA "DEKE"	Assistant Director, FBI
DEONIS, JUAN	Reporter, New York *Times*
DONFELD, JEFFREY	Domestic Council, White House
DOUGHERTY, CON	DEA
DOWNEY, ARTHUR	National Security Council
DUPONT, ROBERT	Director, Special Action Office for Drug Abuse Prevention
ESTERLAND, ROBERT	Treasury Department
FELDTKAMP, ROBERT	DEA
FOX, COL. THOMAS	DEA
GLANZER, SEYMOUR	Justice Department
GROSS, NELSON	Senior Advisor and Coordinator, International Narcotics Matters, Department of State
HANDLEY, WILLIAM	Ambassador to Turkey
HARKNESS, RICHARD	Information Coordinator for Drug Abuse Program
HARPER, EDWARD	USIA, Turkey
HELMS, RICHARD	Director, CIA
HENDERSON, LOY	Ambassador to Iran
HESSE, RAYBURNE	Rockefeller aide for narcotics
INGERSOLL, JOHN	Director, BNDD
JAFFE, JEROME	Director, Special Action Office
JONES, QUENTIN	Department of Agriculture
KIRBY, HERMAN	State Department for Turkey
KLEINDIENST, RICHARD	Attorney General
KNIGHT, PAUL	Regional Director, France, BNDD
KROGH, EGIL	White House deputy to John Ehrlichman
LUCKOFF, IRVING F.	Professor, Columbia University
LUDLUM, JAMES	CIA
MCCARTHY, DINITIA	Producer, NBC Television
MCNAMARA, JOSEPH D.	Police Commissioner, Kansas City, Mo.
MACOMBER, WILLIAM	Ambassador to Turkey
MANDEL, JERRY	Sociologist
MAOUROULIS, PETER	Former Assistant District Attorney, Dutchess County, N.Y.
MINNICK, WALTER	Domestic Council
MOORE, MARK	Consultant, DEA
MOORE, RICHARD	Justice Department

MOYNIHAN, DANIEL PATRICK	Counsel for Urban Affairs
MURPHY, THOMAS P.	Drug Abuse Coordinator, U.S. Embassy, Paris
O'MALLEY, THOMAS	Prosecutor, Justice Department
PELLERZI, LEO	Assistant Attorney General
PERITO, PAUL	Special Action Office
PETERSEN, HENRY	Assistant Attorney General, Criminal Division
PIRET, EDGAR	Science Attaché, U.S. Embassy, Paris
PRICE, RAYMOND	Presidential speech writer
ROSSIDES, EUGENE	Assistant Secretary for Law Enforcement and Operation, Treasury Department
RYAN, WILLIAM	Prosecutor, Criminal Division, Justice Department
SAFIRE, WILLIAM	Presidential speech writer
SANTARELLI, DONALD	Director, Law Enforcement Administration Agency
SAYRE, ROBERT	Ambassador to Panama; Inspector General, State Department
SHEPPARD, GEOFFREY	Domestic Council, White House
SILBERT, EARL	U.S. Attorney
TROTT, STEVE	Assistant District Attorney in Los Angeles
WALKER, CHARLS R.	Undersecretary of the Treasury
WATSON, ARTHUR	Ambassador to France
WELLINGTON, HARVEY	Senior Advisor and Coordinator, International Narcotics Matters, State Department (successor to Nelson Gross)
WHITEHEAD, THOMAS	LEAA
WILBUR, RICHARD	Assistant Secretary of the Army and Public Health
WILSON, JAMES Q.	Professor, Harvard University

BIBLIOGRAPHY

Books

ANSLINGER, HARRY J. (with Gregory, J. Dennis). *The Protectors.* New York: Farrar, Straus & Co., 1964.

———, and OURSLER, WILL. *The Murderers.* New York: Farrar, Straus & Cudahy, 1961.

ASHLEY, RICHARD. *Heroin: The Myths and Facts.* New York: St. Martin's Press, 1972.

BEJEROT, NILS. *Addiction and Society.* Springfield, Ill.: Charles C. Thomas, 1970.

BERNSTEIN, CARL, and WOODWARD, BOB. *All the President's Men.* New York: Simon & Schuster, 1974.

BRECHER, EDWARD M. (and THE EDITORS OF *Consumer Reports*). *Licit and Illicit Drugs.* Boston: Little, Brown & Co., 1972.

CHAMBLISS, WILLIAM J. *Crime and the Legal Process.* New York: McGraw-Hill Book Co., 1967.

CIPES, ROBERT M. *The Crime War.* New York: New American Library, 1968.

CLARK, EVERT, and HORROCK, NICHOLAS. *Contrabandista!* New York: Praeger, 1973.

DAI, BINGHAM. *Opium Addiction in Chicago.* Montclair, N.J.: Patterson Smith, 1970.

EBIN, DAVID, ed. *The Drug Experience.* New York: Grove Press, Inc., 1961.

EHRLICHMAN, JOHN. *The Company.* New York: Simon & Schuster, 1976.

FINLATOR, JOHN. *The Drugged Nation.* New York: Simon & Schuster, 1973.

FIX, JAMES F., gen. ed. *Drugs: The Great Contemporary Issues* (New York *Times* publication). New York: Arno Press, 1971.

HOBSON, RICHMOND PEARSON. *Drug Addiction—A Malignant Racial Cancer.* 1933.

HOFFMAN, WILLIAM. *David: Report on a Rockefeller.* New York: Lyle Stuart, Inc., 1971.

HUNT, E. HOWARD. *Undercover.* New York: G. P. Putnam's Sons, 1975.

KING, RUFUS. *The Drug Hang-up.* New York: W. W. Norton & Co., 1972.

LAMOUR, CATHERINE, and LAMBERTI, MICHEL R. *The International Connection: Opium from Growers to Pushers.* New York: Pantheon Books, 1974.

LINDESMITH, ALFRED R. *The Addict and the Law.* New York: Vintage Books, 1965.

LINGEMAN, RICHARD R. *Drugs from A to Z: A Dictionary.* New York: McGraw-Hill Book Co., 1969.

McCoy, ALFRED W. (with Read, Cathleen B., and Adams, Leonard P., II). *The Politics of Heroin in Southeast Asia.* New York: Harper & Row, 1972.

McGINNISS, JOE. *The Selling of the President, 1968.* New York: Pocket Books, 1969.

MAGRUDER, JEB STUART. *An American Life: One Man's Road to Watergate.* New York: Atheneum, 1974.

MORRIS, JOE ALEX. *Nelson Rockefeller: A Biography.* New York: Harper & Bros., 1960.

MUSTO, DAVID F., M.D. *The American Disease.* New Haven: Yale University Press, 1973.

NATHAN, RICHARD P. *The Plot That Failed.* New York: John Wiley & Sons, 1975.

NAVASKY, VICTOR. *Kennedy Justice.* New York: Atheneum, 1971.

Newsday STAFF AND EDITORS. *The Heroin Trail.* New York: New American Library, 1974.

PROUTY, FLETCHER L. *The Secret Team.* Englewood Cliffs, N.J.: Prentice-Hall, Inc., 1973.

RUBLOWSKY, JOHN. *The Stoned Age.* New York: G. P. Putnam's Sons, 1974.

SAFIRE, WILLIAM. *Before the Fall.* Garden City, N.Y.: Doubleday & Co., 1975.

SZULC, TAD. *Compulsive Spy.* New York: Viking Press, 1974.

THOMPSON, FRED D. *At That Point in Time.* New York: Quadrangle/The New York Times Book Co., 1975.

TULLY, ANDREW. *The Secret War Against Dope.* New York: Coward, McCann & Geoghegan, 1973.

WESTIN, AV, and SHAFFER, STEPHANIE. *Heroes and Heroin.* New York: Pocket Books, 1972.

WHITE, THEODORE. *Breach of Faith: The Fall of Richard Nixon.* New York: Atheneum, 1975.

——. *The Making of the President, 1972.* New York: Atheneum, 1973.

Articles in Books

BADEN, MICHAEL M. "Alcoholism as Related to Drug Addiction—A Medical Examiner's View." In *Drug Abuse,* edited by Wolfram Kreup, M.D. New York: New American Library, 1974.

FREEDMAN, DANIEL X., M.D. "What Is Drug Abuse?" In *Drug Abuse in Industry,* edited by W. W. Stewart. New York: Halos & Assoc., 1970.

Signed Articles

BADEN, MICHAEL M., M.D. "The Changing Role of the Medical Examiner." *Medical Opinion,* March, 1971.

——. "Narcotic Abuse," reprinted from *New York State Journal of Medicine,* April 1, 1972.

BROWNING, FRANK. "An American Gestapo." *Playboy,* February, 1976.

EPSTEIN, EDWARD JAY. "Against the Poppies." *Esquire,* December, 1974.

——. "The Krogh File—The Politics of 'Law and Order.' " *Public Interest,* Spring, 1975.

FREEDMAN, DANIEL X., M.D. "The Cost of Silence Now," reprinted from *Medical Tribune,* February 26, 1970.

HARRIS, DAVID. "Ex-Narks Tell Tales." *Rolling Stone,* December 5, 1974.

HUGHES, PATRICK H., M.D.; SENAY, EDWARD C., M.D.; PARKER, RICHARD, M.A. "The Medical Management of a Heroin Epidemic." *Archives of General Psychiatry,* November, 1972.

LIDDY, G. GORDON. "A Patriot Speaks." *Harper's,* October, 1974.

————. "The Great Dutchess County Dope Raid." *True,* June, 1975.

LIDDY, MRS. G. GORDON, with CHESHIRE, MAXINE. "Watergate Wife." *Ladies' Home Journal,* September, 1973.

MANDEL, JERRY. "Hashish, Assassins, and the Love of God." *Issues in Criminology,* Vol. II, no. 2, 1970.

NIXON, RICHARD. "What Has Happened to America?" *Reader's Digest,* October, 1967.

ROSENBAUM, RON. "The Decline and Fall of Nixon's Drug Czar." *New Times,* September 5, 1975.

SHEPPARD, C. W., and GAYAN, G. B. "The Changing Face of Heroin Addiction in Haight-Ashbury." *International Journal of the Addictions,* Vol. 7, 1972.

WATERS, CRAIG. "The Agony of Egil Krogh." *The Washingtonian,* May, 1974.

Unsigned Articles

"BNDD Trims Customs' Role in Federal War on Drugs." *National Journal,* July 18, 1970.

"Criminal Justice System in Trouble" (including interview with Charles H. Rogovin). *U.S. News & World Report,* October 13, 1969.

"Drug Abuse Now Epidemic—What's Being Done About It?" (interview with Myles J. Ambrose). *U.S. News & World Report,* April 3, 1972.

"Drug Menace: How Serious?" (interview with John E. Ingersoll). *U.S. News & World Report,* May 25, 1970.

"Nixon's Offensive on Drugs Treads on Diverse Interests." *National Journal,* July 2, 1971.

"Victory Soon in Fight Against Drug Traffic?" (interview with Nelson Gross). *U.S. News & World Report,* September 25, 1972.

"White House." *National Journal,* April 11, 1970.

Pamphlets and Dissertations

BADEN, MICHAEL M., M.D. *Homicide, Suicide, and Accidental Death Among Narcotic Addicts.* N.d.

————, and TUROFF, RICHARD S., B.S. *Deaths of Persons Using Methadone in New York City—1971.* Washington, D.C.: National Academies of Sciences, Engineering; and Committee on Problems of Drug Dependence, 1973.

COATES, ROBERT B., and MILLER, ALDEN D. *Precinct Patrolmen and Addicts: A Study of Police Perception and Police-Citizen Interaction Near a Methadone Treatment Center.* July 19, 1973.

GLASS, RONALD HOWARD. *Case Analysis: The April 9, 1970, Drug Abuse Conference in the White House: A Question of Manipulation.* UCLA, 1975.

HAYIM, GILA J. *Changes in the Criminal Behavior of Heroin Addicts: A One-Year Follow-up of Methadone Treatment.* December, 1972.

KLEINMAN, PAULA HOLZMAN, and LUCKOFF, IRVING F. *Methadone Mainte-nance—Modest Help for a Few.* December, 1975.

KOZEL, NICHOLAS J., M.D.; DUPONT, ROBERT L., M.D.; BROWN, BARRY S., PH.D. *Narcotics Involvement in an Offender Population.* Washington, D.C.: Narcotics Treatment Administration, n.d.

LANDAU, RICHARD L., ed. *Regulating New Drugs.* The University of Chicago Center for Policy Study, University of Chicago, 1973.

MALLINCKRODT CHEMICAL WORKS. *Current Statistics and Supply Problems of Opium-Derived Products,* March 12, 1973.

MCNAMARA, JOSEPH D. *An Evaluation of Police Strategies in Drug Enforce-ment.* October, 1972.

MOORE, MARK. *Policy Concerning Drug Abuse in New York State* (Vol. 3: Economics of Heroin Distribution, July 20, 1970). Croton-on-Hudson, N.Y.: Hudson Institute, Inc.

MORALES, OSCAR. *The So-Called International War on Drugs.* UCLA, 1975.

RUTH, HEATHER, L. *The Street-level Economics of Heroin Addiction in New York City: Life-Styles of Active Heroin Users and Implications for Public Policy.* November 1, 1972.

UNGERLEIDER, J. THOMAS, M.D. *Miscellaneous—Notes from the National Marijuana and Drug Abuse Commission's 'Heroin Trip' Through Europe and the Middle East, Sept. 23–Oct. 7, 1972.* N.d.

Conference, Council, and Institute Reports

NATIONAL ASSOCIATION FOR THE PREVENTION OF ADDICTION TO NARCOTICS. *Proceedings: Fifth National Conference of Methadone Treatment, March 17–19, 1973.* New York: Vol. 2, 1973.

NATIONAL INSTITUTE ON DRUG ABUSE. *Quarterly Statistical Brochure.* Rockville, Md.: March, 1975.

NATIONAL INSTITUTE OF MENTAL HEALTH: NARCOTIC ADDICT REHABILITA-TION BRANCH. *Summary Narrative Report: A Training Seminar for Program Development Specialists.* New York: Institute for Social Research, Fordham University, Feb. 5–6, 1973.

THE STRATEGY COUNCIL PURSUANT TO THE DRUG ABUSE OFFICE AND
TREATMENT ACT OF 1972 (prepared for the president). *Federal Strategy for
Drug Abuse and Drug Traffic Prevention.* U.S. Government Printing Office,
1974.

Congressional Committee and Subcommittee Reports

Report to the Congress: Federal Efforts to Combat Drug Abuse. Office of the
Comptroller General of the United States, August 14, 1972.

Report by the Select Committee on Crime: "Drugs in Our Schools." U.S.
Government Printing Office, June 29, 1973.

Staff Report on Drug Abuse in the Military. To: Members of Alcoholism and
Narcotics Subcommittee; From: The Subcommittee Staff, n.d.

*Joint Hearings Before the Subcommittee on Executive Reorganization and
Government Research and the Subcommittee on Intergovernmental Relations
of the Committee on Government Operations, United States Senate.* U.S.
Government Printing Office, 1971.

Uniform Crime Reports for the United States (Advisory: Committee on
Uniform Crime Records International Association of Chiefs of Police. U.S.
Government Printing Office, 1971.

Reports: City of New York

Narcotics: Year–1971. City of N.Y. Police Statistical Report prepared by
Crime Analysis Section, Captain McNamara.

Office of the Chief Medical Examiner, The City of N.Y., Annual Report, 1968.

U.S. Department of Justice Reports

ECKERMAN, WILLIAM C.; BATES, JAMES D.; RACHEL, J. VALLERY; POOLE, W.
KENNETH. *Drug Usage and Arrest Charges.* Bureau of Narcotics and
Dangerous Drugs, Drug Control Division, Office of Scientific Support,
December, 1971.

GREENWOOD, JOSEPH A., PH.D. *Estimating Number of Narcotic Addicts.*
Bureau of Narcotics and Dangerous Drugs, Drug Control Division, Office
of Scientific Support, October, 1971.

Annual Report: January 1–December 31, 1971. Bureau of Narcotics and
Dangerous Drugs, Office of Deputy Director—Operations.

Drug Enforcement Statistical Report. Drug Enforcement Administration, 1973–74.

Efforts to Prevent Dangerous Drugs from Illicitly Reaching the Public. Bureau of Narcotics and Dangerous Drugs (by the Comptroller General of the United States), April 17, 1972.

Efforts to Prevent Heroin from Illicitly Reaching the United States. Bureau of Narcotics and Dangerous Drugs (by the Comptroller General of the United States). October 20, 1972.

The Heroin Hotline. Office for Drug Abuse Law Enforcement, Bureau of Narcotics and Dangerous Drugs (by the Comptroller General of the United States), September 26, 1972.

1969–1971 Appropriations: Testimony of John E. Ingersoll, director, BNDD, Before the House Supplemental Appropriation Bill, 1969. Bureau of Narcotics and Dangerous Drugs, U.S. Government Printing Office, 1969.

1972 Appropriation: Testimony of John E. Ingersoll, director, BNDD, Before the House and Senate Appropriation Subcommittees (given March 18, 1971, and June 25, 1971). Bureau of Narcotics and Dangerous Drugs, U.S. Government Printing Office, 1971.

1973 Appropriation: Testimony of John E. Ingersoll, director, BNDD, Before the House and Senate Appropriation Subcommittees (given March 3, 1972, and March 14, 1972). U.S. Government Printing Office, 1972.

1974 Appropriation and Reorganization Hearings. Drug Enforcement Administration, U.S. Government Printing Office, 1973.

Department of State Bulletins

WELLMAN, HARVEY R. "International Aspects of Drug Abuse Control." Address before 23rd Annual Pharmacy Seminar at University of Georgia Center for Continuing Education, Athens, Ga., on April 16, 1971. Published May 17, 1971.

———. *Drug Abuse: A Challenge to U.S.-Turkish Cooperation in the Seventies.* February 1, 1971.

Television Broadcasts

GOLDIN, MARION, and MANNING, GORDON (producers). "The Man Who Wouldn't Talk . . . Talks." *60 Minutes,* Vol. VII, No. 1, January 5, 1975, 6–7 P.M. CBS Television Network.

SCHULBERG, STUART (producer and director). "December 6, 1971: A Day in the Presidency." With correspondent John Chancellor, December 21, 1971, 7:30 P.M., NBC News.

Drug Abuse Council Publications

(All Copyright © Drug Abuse Council, Washington, D.C.)

BOMBOY, ROBERT P. *Major Newspaper Coverage of Drug Issues.* 1974.

BROWN, GEORGE F., JR., and SILVERMAN, LESTER R. *The Retail Price of Heroin: Estimation and Applications.* Public Research Institute of the Center for Naval Analyses, 1973.

CLINE, SYBIL. "The Federal Drug Abuse Budget for Fiscal Year 1975." In *Governmental Response to Drugs: Fiscal and Organizational.* 1974.

——, and AKINS, CARL. "Federal Policy and Budget for Drug Abuse," and "State Drug Abuse Coordinating Agencies, Varieties and Trends." In *Governmental Response to Drug Abuse: The 1976 Federal Budget Single State Agency Analysis.* 1975.

COHRSSEN, JOHN J. *The Organization of the United Nations to Deal with Drug Abuse.* Controlled Substances Information, Inc., 1973.

FLAHERTY, JOHN E., JR., and DRUG ABUSE COUNCIL. *Army Drug Abuse Program: A Future Model?* 1973.

GOLDBERG, PAUL, and AKINS, CARL. "Issues in Organizing for Drug Abuse Prevention." In *Governmental Response to Drugs: Fiscal and Organizational.* 1974.

HUNT, LEON GIBSON. *Heroin Epidemics: A Quantitative Study of Current Empirical Data.* 1973.

POMEROY, WESLEY A. *Police Chiefs Discuss Drug Abuse.* 1974.

POWELL, DOUGLAS H. *Occasional Heroin Users: A Pilot Study, 1973.* Reprinted from the *Archives of General Psychiatry,* April, 1973.

WARD, HUGH. *Employment and Addiction: Overview of Issues.* June, 1973.

Unsigned Drug Abuse Council Publications

(All copyright © Drug Abuse Council, Washington, D.C.)

A Perspective on "Get Tough" Drug Laws. 1973.

Heroin Maintenance: The Issues. 1973.

Second Report of the National Commission on Marihuana and Drug Abuse: Drug Use in America: Problem in Perspective. March, 1973.

Survey of City/County Drug Abuse Activities, 1972. 1973.

Survey of State Drug Abuse Activities, 1972. 1973.

The Technical Papers of the Second Report of the National Commission on Marihuana and Drug Abuse: Drug Use in America: Problem in Perspective. March, 1973. Appendix: Vol. I, "Patterns and Consequences of Drug Use"; Vol. II, "Social Responses to Drug Use"; Vol. III, "The Legal System and Drug Control"; Vol. IV, "Treatment and Rehabilitation."

Index